The Education of a Black Radical

The Education of a Black Radical

A SOUTHERN CIVIL RIGHTS ACTIVIST'S JOURNEY 1959–1964

D'ARMY BAILEY

with Roger Easson

Foreword by Nikki Giovanni

LOUISIANA STATE UNIVERSITY PRESS

BATON ROUGE

Published by Louisiana State University Press
Copyright © 2009 by Louisiana State University Press
All rights reserved
Manufactured in the United States of America
First printing

DESIGNER: Amanda McDonald Scallan
TYPEFACE: Tribute
PRINTER AND BINDER: Thomson-Shore, Inc.

This book is the author's personal memoir, and all names, dates, and events described herein are true and accurate to the best of the author's recollection. The views and opinions expressed herein are those of the author alone and do not represent views or opinions of Louisiana State University Press.

Library of Congress Cataloging-in-Publication Data
Bailey, D'Army, 1941–
    The education of a Black radical : a Southern civil rights activist's journey, 1959–1964 / D'Army Bailey with Roger Easson ; foreword by Nikki Giovanni.
    p. cm.
Includes index.
    ISBN 978-0-8071-3476-4 (cloth : alk. paper) 1. Bailey, D'Army, 1941– 2. African American civil rights workers—Biography. 3. Radicals—United States—Biography. 4. African Americans—Civil rights—Southern States—History—20th century. 5. Civil rights movements—Southern States—History—20th century. 6. Southern States—Race relations—History—20th century. 7. Southern University and A & M College—Biography. 8. Student movements—Louisiana—Baton Rouge—History—20th century. 9. Northern Student Movement—History. 10. Northeastern States—Race relations—History—20th century. I. Easson, Roger R. II. Title.
    E185.97.B15A3 2009
    323.092—dc22
    [B]

                                                                      2009008301

The paper in this book meets the guidelines for permanence and durability of the Committee on Production Guidelines for Book Longevity of the Council on Library Resources. ∞

To my wife, Adrienne Bailey, and
my sons, Justin and Merritt,
for making me whole

Contents

Illustrations

Foreword

Sometimes you have to wonder about our ancestors. Packed tightly in a cold, damp ship with people they are not sure are human. Those wonderful brave Africans had to find a way to maintain themselves, their dignity, their integrity. They had to find a way to remember. James Baldwin once said, "It's not that so few come out of the Ghetto but that so many do." It had to be the voice, that voice in the back of their heads that kept saying, "Keep your eyes on the prize . . . hold on."

We know they sang a work song in a rhythm to make the work go more smoothly. We know they sang a praise song to let their God know he was not forgotten. They sang a boogie because joy should never be denied. And they confounded their captors by the pride they took in themselves and their work.

> We know they had a dream.
> of freedom
> of a better life for their children
> of a better day coming
> of an education that would make them equal.

We know they did not shirk from the harshness. They never asked the mountain to move; they sought the strength to climb.

And through the generations, black resiliency began to be mistaken for black complacency. The bigots and white supremacists wanted to think blacks were happy with their lot. Then came Emmett Till, Rosa Parks, Martin Luther King Jr., Daisy Bates, the Greensboro sit-ins. And, to quote James Baldwin again, "Our dungeon shook." The students spoke. They had a voice. And this time, compromise was not possible. America had to change.

The Education of a Black Radical by D'Army Bailey gives fresh insight into the young men of the 1960s. We all know their actions, but now we have a voice to enlighten those actions, a strong, uncompromising voice that still dreams of a better America. Judge Bailey has experienced the ugliness of both racism and fear. Yet he has not stepped back. What a wonderful life to share.

Of course, we know that if this were Freddie XX or Rocky 253, there would be a big book auction of the movie rights, star-studied premieres, television and radio coverage everywhere. But this is just the beautiful, loving story of a young man who wanted to right some ancient wrongs. This is a fire to hold in your hands to warm the heart and the soul. It is a book to educate us, another lonely voice from the great era of American history—the civil rights era. This was the best of us, neighbors. This was our shining moment.

Nikki Giovanni

Acknowledgments

It was Dan Siegel, former UC Berkeley student body president and People's Park protest leader, who first put the thought in my mind of doing a book. It was in 1974, when I was preparing to move back to Memphis from Berkeley, California. Dan put me in touch with Cyrilly Abels, who was *Ramparts* editor Bob Scheer's agent.

Though the well-respected agent was unable to generate interest in the project at that time, the book idea stuck with me over the years, and in the late eighties I retained a young writer, Dawn Baldwin, who helped shape the story of an insider's view of history. Publishers found the story compelling. One described the manuscript as a "riveting narrative chock full of rich portraits of little-known participants in this most important period of American History."

Comments like these helped keep my spirits up. Along the way I got positive and helpful feedback from O. T. Wells, Dr. Rachel Emanuel, Connie Curry, Southern University law dean Freddie Pitcher, Francis Goldin, Marie Brown, Phyllis Tickle, Jasmyne Walker, Dr. Maya Angelou, Eddie Tucker, Juanita White, James Williamson, Ellis Chappell, James Duffy, Alli Starr, Van Jones, Walter Bailey, Aimee Allison, Yolanda Hippensteele, and Sterling Lord.

In recent years I have seen an increasing generational disconnect among African American and other underprivileged citizens who fail to combat the demons of fractured race relations, economic inequality, educational underachievement, and deficient self-respect. Seeing this trend inspired me to redouble my efforts to publish this story. The need to spread the story of how young black people of my generation organized and started a revolution and to inspire social conscience and activism in today's youth seems more urgent than ever.

I contacted another writer, professor Roger Easson of Christian Brothers University in Memphis, and requested his assistance on the project. He graciously agreed to help. First Roger retyped the manuscript in digital format so that we could more freely edit it. Then he and I met periodically over coffee at Perkins restaurant on Park Avenue. Roger asked tough questions and sent me back to rewrite parts of the text. He has been a real taskmaster and at times had me feeling I was back on campus. His genius has been a strong part of the final product.

Eventually, LSU Press stepped up to the plate and agreed to publish the book. Freelance copyeditor Susan Murray along with Rand Dotson, Barbara Outland, Judy Collins, George Roupe, and the rest of the LSU Press staff have shown great respect, professionalism, and excitement.

Not to be overlooked, the photographs you see here tell a powerful story themselves. Several friends helped assemble them. Without the help of the following men and women I wouldn't be able to share these pictures: Ed Franks of the University of Memphis Library, Jack Kenner, Terrance Hurt, Tammi Rudge, Rick Jansen, Kelli Engels, Dorothy Stokes, Leigh Russo, Matt Flinn of Clark University, Carolyn McGoldrick, Adolph Reed Jr., John Sykes, Judy Jumonville, Angela Proctor, David Turcotte, Chris Peck, and Rob Sawyer of Law Media Productions gave critical help in reproducing and organizing the pictures. My cousin Luther Hampton sketched the picture based on our collective memories of Bailey's Stand, the small sundries store where I spent many of my youthful hours.

Danny Glover and Morgan Freeman were supportive in their endorsements. My thanks to Esailama Artry-Diouf and Bill Luckett for getting the manuscript to them. Julieanna Richardson of HistoryMakers introduced me to Nikki Giovanni, who wrote the book's foreword. Ms. Giovanni was encouraging and helpful from the start. Her foreword deeply moved me, as I am sure it will you.

During the drafting of this book I have had two fine secretaries: the late Mary Sue Latham and Susan Wilson. To them I say thanks.

And to those four who were my rock, pride, and fountain of nourishment—my mother, Will Ella Bailey; my sons, Justin and Merritt; and my precious wife, Adrienne—I say, you are a blessing.

The Education of a Black Radical

Introduction

THIS BOOK GIVES an insider's view of the first half of the most important decade of black America's fight for civil rights. The FBI under J. Edgar Hoover once labeled me as a "subversive," then changed that description to "black nationalist militant." I and other students engaged in a deliberate campaign to subvert the politically and economically discriminatory order of American life in both the South and the North. We became a mighty force of determined and courageous activists who brought business as usual to a standstill and forced an accounting of the just due of our people.

America systematically fostered a second-class black America that was exploited for generations with consequences from which we are still struggling to recover. Mr. Hoover correctly classified me as "militant," and I remain so in my passion and energy to carry on the fight for racial equality and justice. I plead to the next generation to do their part.

That plea is what this book is all about. I tell the story here of how young blacks arose from the most modest of circumstances and spurred a movement that changed this country and the world. Today's generation of young blacks must again step forward, with courage and selflessness, and bear witness. You must reach across the walls of class and privilege and challenge yourselves to organize for political and social action, to help with tutoring, youth political education, and health initiatives. Like the black kids in Greensboro who launched the first sit-in, black students today must believe in their power to change the world. You can light a spark; you can be an example to other young blacks learning to rechannel our mighty force from the crime, self-hatred, selfishness, and nihilism that today engulfs our black nation.

Obviously, the 1960s were the greatest decade of the twentieth century for black revolution. At the start of that century, we were racially segregated, denied the rights to vote and to receive equal educational and job opportunities. The black community had been cowed, beaten, and murdered into submission. When the century was over, we were still struggling to overcome the aftereffects of brutal and inhuman discrimination. And still we struggle. Yet, in those hundred years, a sea change occurred in blacks' attitudes and strategy: an acceptance of oppression by whites evolved into a determined rejection of any form of discrimination and subjugation.

The courage and unity shown by black Americans in the 1960s in their sustained revolt against racial oppression have proven to be unparalleled in any other period in American history. That decade represented the first time that U.S. blacks set the national agenda and controlled the unfolding debate, changing this country's law and social mores in the process. For the first time, the American electorate was forced to consider the humanity of blacks, to see us as courageous patriots rather than as a submissive and subservient underclass. In some of the most dramatic political action this country has ever seen, not only was the black community awakened to its own oppression, but also the white community was awakened to, and forced to deal with, its role as oppressor. This is a story of revolution and counterrevolution seen up close and personal in the story of my life as a college student caught up in the movement.

There would have been no 1960s civil rights movement without the idealism and courage of the flower of America's black community, especially college students like those depicted here. We were the least compromised by fears of job loss, debt, and retaliation, and by the culture of submission into which we were born. Most of us were the first of our families to go to college. Most of us had watched during the 1950s as one racial outrage after another struck black communities in the South. At the beginning of our decade, we were intelligent, polished, and fueled by a sense of moral and social imperative. Whether it was by our solitary witness at a segregated lunch counter as a handful of us endured being cursed, assaulted, and jailed, or as one of the thousands of students who marched off our campuses to boycott and organize voter-registration drives, we acted. We black students shamed and motivated other blacks and whites to abandon their complacency and complicity.

Many of us young black warriors had come from modest communities that existed below the radar of the white-dominated press, and most have since returned to our communities and have subsequently been forgotten for our roles. Many of us so-called "unsung heroes" are content with the personal fulfillment of having played a part in improving this country and the condition of our people. Although our actions were deserving and worthy, we never became the media darlings of a generation of struggle: we were notoriously absent from the covers of magazines or the front pages of newspapers. Even though the civil rights movement was the frequent focus of the media of the 1960s, we must never forget that, even then, the news we made was used to sell cars, refrigerators, and cleaning powders. Once the ability of our movement to catch the imagination of the general American audience faded, the media largely abandoned it, moving inevitably to the next marketable crisis or fad. Consequently, far from empowering the movement's foot soldiers to broadly disseminate the message of our struggle to future generations, the media sent us careening into the black hole of oblivion once the fight seemed to lose steam.

This book is designed to counter this media neglect by offering a history of the civil rights movement from the intensely personal perspective of one such student foot soldier. It offers a voice from within the black student movement of the 1960s and a narration of events now mostly forgotten and neglected. In the face of the nihilism and the lack of initiative, boldness, and imagination among so many of today's black youth, it is more important than ever for them to know that there are sleeping giants among them. For those whose sense of status is invested in demeaning rap lyrics, in pants sagging below the ass, in gangbanging, or in sucking up to influential whites for personal gain, this book offers a different path to real power and to real change for our communities. Although most of the young foot soldiers of the 1960s civil rights movement had even fewer opportunities and faced more violent and determined obstacles than contemporary youth, we blasted open the doors of political, social, and economic opportunities for ourselves and our communities.

This story follows my own journey through two leading university communities, one black, in the Deep South, and the other white, in the heart of the Northeast. It revisits the drama, conflicts, challenges, courage, and cowardice of students, faculty, administrators, and community leaders engulfed by racial conflict. Where I have rendered words that I heard from others as quotations, most are given as I remember them rather than as verbatim quotations. I have done my best to accurately convey the message and tone of others' comments. In a sense, this is a handbook of what was—and what arguably still is—possible. It is a guide to how to dispel the current apathy and to generate a new energy for social transformation.

The importance of this story was driven home to me when I was searching for photographs to accompany some of the protest events described in this book. I started at Southern University in Baton Rouge, scene of some of the major protests that rocked the South. I was sure the university archives would have preserved written, photographic, and oral histories of the black struggle that had emerged from their campus. Within a month of the 1960 launching of student sit-in protests against the segregated Woolworth lunch counters in Greensboro, North Carolina, Southern University students had quickly followed suit. We made national headlines as we challenged local segregation laws. After a tumultuous two months of protests and harsh suppression of the demonstrations by the school administrators, things remained quiet on the campus for the next two years. Then, between 1961 and 1962, the students revolted again, and this time the university was closed twice, with hundreds—myself included—being expelled or leaving the university, and with scores of students arrested. We were teargassed and set upon with police dogs in downtown Baton Rouge, and some of us avoided criminal convictions only by the intervention of the U.S. Supreme Court.

When I contacted the university's archivist, however, I was astonished to find that not only did the university not have photos of these dramatic events, but the archivist herself was unaware that the 1961 and 1962 protests had even occurred. In the decades since these protests, the school has continued to teach its students American and world history, sociology, economics, philosophy, and political science. And yet, even though what happened on the Southern campus in the 1960s relates to all of these disciplines and is at the center of the very being of the institution, the university's students have been mysteriously shielded from this chapter of their own powerful heritage of struggle and strength.

Let us remember that, in the 1960s, Southern was one of the nation's premier black schools, second only perhaps to Howard in Washington. To protect LSU from being forced to enroll black students, Louisiana leaders had financed it well. It was one of only four black schools in America with its own law school, and it also boasted schools of engineering, education, and physical sciences, an agricultural farm, a campus high school, a student union with bowling alley, and impressive facilities for football, tennis, other athletic activities, and music. Southern and its nearby comfortable ranch-style homes of faculty and administrators provided an oasis for both promising students and secure faculty and administrators.

Louisiana's flagship university, LSU, sits to this day serenely across town from Southern's campus. Interestingly, Southern University is nestled on the banks of the Mississippi River within a stone's throw of the mammoth Standard Oil Refinery, with its plumes of flames burning continuously high into the sky. When I was a student at Southern, this never struck me as an oddity, but my years of visiting other campuses of higher education have made me ponder why Southern was situated so near such a dangerous source of pollution and potential explosion. So close were we to this refinery that one night the explosion of an unloading oil barge on the Mississippi River practically blew me out of my dormitory bed. Apparently, what the right hand gave in financial support, the left took away by situating the future leaders of black America on the doorstep of potential industrial conflagration.

Whereas some black students in the South were heading north to colleges, Southern was, by contrast, a magnet for students from the Midwest, from along the Eastern Seaboard, as well as from other southern states. In some ways, Southern may have appeared to be one of the least likely places for the explosions of student resistance, sacrifice, and turmoil that fueled the racial movements of the 1960s. Perhaps Louisiana's white fathers had invested too well in this idyllic campus. Perhaps Southern's highly capable and dedicated instructors had done too good a job of honing our skills and bolstering our confidence. Perhaps it was the presence of out-of-state students who were less intimidated by, and less compliant with, the segregationist culture of Louisiana. Whatever the cause, Southern's students had been poised to make history.

This newly minted generation of students grew up haunted by pictures of the bloated and disfigured face of Emmett Till, the black kid our own age who was lynched in Money, Mississippi, in 1955. In our time, we learned from the courage of the nine black high school students who walked through hateful mobs to integrate Central High School in Little Rock in 1957. Our youthful hopes had been kindled when the U.S. Supreme Court said, in its1954 *Brown* decision, that segregation was illegal. It was within this explosive context that we were—beneath the surface and in some ways unbeknownst even to ourselves—maturing and acquiring a sober and sensitive awareness that things would have to change. And we soon became painfully aware that, if things were to change, we would have to be the ones to change them.

When it came, the change tore apart the long-held accommodations of both blacks and whites, tearing the fragile sense of community as youthful rebels took action against racism, intransigence, and abusive leadership. My first year on campus began in the traditional way, with academics and student pageantry and partying. It was soon transformed, however, by the harsh, determined, and emotional battles fought first against a monolithic, segregationist white culture and later against our own people in authority who tried to block us. And it proved to be much easier to confront the external foe than our antagonists in the black community who had long been empowered by the very oppressive segregationists we sought to reform.

Once I had been expelled from Southern University, my academic journey continued in the North, a territory alien to me where I would discover that people didn't recognize that they, too, had a problem with civil rights. The white student body at Clark University in Worcester, Massachusetts, had been awakened by our cause and had thrown me a scholarship lifeline to continue my education at their school. The next fall, I stepped onto the welcoming, liberal campus of one thousand students, located in the state's second-largest city. Of Worcester's two hundred thousand people, only three thousand were black.

Through my next two years at Clark, the race wars raged in the South, from the deadly rioting on the Ole Miss campus to the murderous bombing of the Birmingham church that killed four schoolgirls. It would have been easy for me, as a graduate of the southern battlefield, to assimilate into the comfort and security of this privileged environment, with only an occasional ceremonial rant against the racism down south. But that wasn't in me.

Despite the widespread attitude among Massachusetts residents that their state had no race problems, I found no refuge there. When I went into the downtown Worcester department stores and discovered all the professional staff to be white, or when I learned that, of the more than two thousand workers employed at the local factory, only eighteen were black, and all of these were janitors, it became evident to me that Worcester had a problem. An enclave of blacks with modest income lived on the other side of downtown, where the local NAACP chapter provided their only semblance of a support group. And when tested, the leadership of even that group came up short.

For a while I was simply the oddity on campus, a bona fide Negro who had actually been bloodied in the civil rights battles of the bad Old South. But once I saw that Worcester needed a real awakening, I began looking for ways to energize the student body into action. Although in Worcester I didn't have the black student power to wage a civil rights fight, I recruited white fellow students to form the core of our movement. As in Baton Rouge, the university provided a good recruiting base for socially conscious activists willing to risk challenging local authorities. When blacks and other local activists like Abbie Hoffman saw a campus-based civil rights group, they readily came forward to help. Soon we were picketing the largest factory and department store, forcing them to change their personnel policies. And, when the preacher who headed the local NAACP criticized us for picketing the department store, we forced his resignation.

From Worcester, we joined with a northern student group based on the Yale campus. Across the Northeast, we discovered activist leaders who were well organized and well supported by foundations and sympathetic benefactors. When we learned that a key project of our allies at Yale was tutoring black elementary and high school kids in inner-city neighborhoods, we successfully started a similar project in Worcester.

In the summer of 1963, following my first year at Clark, I headed a tutoring project with a staff of a half dozen college students living in a rented house in an inner-city Washington, D.C., neighborhood. We enlisted dozens of student volunteers to help us with our program at Carnegie Junior High. Simultaneously, we launched an ambitious project of picketing and forced one of the city's largest banks to open up job opportunities for blacks. Our small group accomplished more lasting changes in local employment practices that summer than did the much-ballyhooed March on Washington, which assembled more than two hundred thousand that same summer to march for "jobs and freedom," with most participants gone from Washington by sundown.

We crammed a lot of activism into my two years at Clark. We brought such speakers to campus as the great American Socialist leader Norman Thomas and James Meredith, who had integrated Ole Miss eighteen months earlier. I reached out to Malcolm X, who kindly accepted our invitation to speak at Clark. The day he came to Clark I spent a whirlwind seventeen hours shuttling him from radio and newspaper interviews, to dinner with our student-group supporters, to his major speech at Clark, and, finally, to a late-night give-and-take session with interested students and activists. In those days, these leaders weren't looking for major speech fees. Moreover, when they learned that we were independently raising our own funds to bring them and charging modest admission fees, they were very accommodating. Malcolm, for example, charged us only seventy-five dollars!

I tell my story as directly and personally as I know how. It is full of drama and sorrow, of triumph and courage. There are marches and teargassings, as well as real confrontations with the powerbrokers of segregation. Along the way, I crossed paths with many visionary and early activists including the Reverend Will D. Campbell, Malcolm X, Abbie Hoffman, Anne Braden, James Meredith, Tom Hayden, and future congressmen Barney Frank, John Lewis, and Allard Lowenstein. Here is an inside witness to history telling it like it was in the front ranks of protest. It is a story about handsome young people from black America who finally rejected the ugliness of the American apartheid. It is also the story of handsome northern white kids who caught the fever of activism and exposed racism in a northern town that most thought had no racial problems. Few narratives embrace both sides of the struggle—the ugly southern confrontation with overt racists, and the painful confrontation with covert racists in the North. We were so young and so courageous that we hardly thought about what could happen to us, though we knew that we had to fight for what was right and just. It is my hope that you will take from this story a new hope and a new energy that will propel you into leadership opportunities in our communities to bring a new wave of change to America.

~ 1 ~

Growing Up in Memphis

Because of the friendly feeling that I have for Negroes, especially many Negro friends who I hold in esteem and affectionate regard, it is with reluctance that I call attention to weaknesses common in the race. But since these multitudes of Negroes have joined together with others in pressure groups to force on us national programs that would mean calamity to our posterity, there seems to be no honorable choice but to inform the public of what appears to be in store for us if we yield to these pressures. If we can continue to develop a program of friendly cooperation between the races, with separateness in social life, we can go forward in promoting the talents of the white man and the Negro and can contribute to the welfare and happiness of both. Otherwise, tragedy lies ahead for the American people.

— A DECLARATION BY THE SOCIETY FOR THE PRESERVATION OF STATE GOVERNMENT AND RACIAL INTEGRITY, LOUISIANA, 1955

IN LATE SUMMER OF 1959, I was preparing to leave the small world where everything I was—and to some degree much of what I am still— had come into focus. At such times, when we approach the boundaries between the confines of childhood and the larger world of adults, a fog of excitement about what is to come reduces our ability to reflect on what we are leaving behind. It seems to me now that the courage and endurance that was to characterize my experience in the next five years was a potent legacy of the small world of South Memphis where I grew up in the late 1940s and 1950s. In those days, black Memphis was a separate and isolated society. Even though the heavy hand of white oppression was everywhere, I didn't connect the dots and recognize that mine was a small intertwined world in the grip of the larger white-dominated society. In the midst of this slow-burning violence, my family managed to create an insular yet supportive little world off the corner of Mississippi and Walker in South Memphis. I am told that I was born in 1941 in a little shotgun house—about as plain and functional a home as it is possible to imagine—off Mississippi Boulevard, on Wicks Street. It was a quiet and sheltered place to be born, full of hope and gentle wisdom.

My earliest memory of that world is of a rented duplex on Ford Place, significant in my mind later as our next-door neighbor was a girlfriend of the man who was to become the legendary B. B King. He would saunter down the street, guitar under arm, to court one of two sisters. Ford Place was a block of wood-frame shotgun and duplex houses. It was sandwiched between Mississippi Boulevard one block west—the major business and residential thoroughfare in black Memphis—and Porter Street, a block east. Porter Street was the western boundary of the city's largest public housing project, LeMoyne Gardens. Not far away was the kindergarten and grade school where my long encounter with education would begin.

A few years later, we moved to a nicer duplex three houses up, which my grandfather, D. A. Bailey, built for us. D. A. held a prominent place in our small, sequestered community. As a builder and contractor, he was a man strong and intelligent enough to negotiate the thicket of oppression to help create for us this haven of strength. I am named after D. A., whom my brother and I called "Papa." Actually, his name was spelled "Darmy" and pronounced "Dee Army." He went by the initials "D. A." in an apparent effort to simplify a name given to him, as family lore tells it, by a Gypsy midwife in Mississippi. Like Papa, I struggled with the name, so between the eleventh and twelfth grades I added the apostrophe and made the *A* uppercase in the hope that friends would pronounce it correctly rather than call me "Darmie."

The family story goes that Papa was born to Ferry and Mary Jane Bailey in Michigan City, Mississippi, a country area fifty-seven miles away along the Tennessee-Mississippi border. After his father died in 1922, Papa, with his older brother, Uncle Albert, moved to Memphis—often called the largest city in Mississippi—as young men seeking a larger opportunity. Papa's first wife, Georgia Sease Bailey, had died when my father was a one-year-old so that Papa's second wife, Mary, whom we called "Sister," was the only mother he knew and, of course, my grandmother. I remember Papa as an always well-groomed, upright, dark-skinned man with a pleasant face and serious demeanor.

It was Papa who insisted that Walter and I go to the private kindergarten and elementary school our father had attended. He paid the five dollars a week each for us to attend kindergarten at the Rosebud School. Two stately black women, Ms. Jordan and Ms. Williams, ran the school and taught the children. The principal, Ms. Sally Florence Jordan, was in her late fifties, with a slightly wrinkled neck and arms and beautician-curled and demurely coiffed hair. Her assistant, Ms. Bernice Williams, was a strikingly slender younger woman who always wore shoulder-length black hair, had amazing stylized eyebrows, high cheeks, and a classy but businesslike smile. Remarkable for her tailored dresses, she spooled around town in a late-model fish-tailed Cadillac.

As one might expect, a school run by these polished characters was orderly and focused. Somehow Ms. Jordan and Ms. Williams transformed their charges through an admirable balance of learning and playtime. We started each day by singing James Weldon Johnson's "Negro National Anthem." To this day I can still hear our small chorus sing, and I imagine the singing of that song as a formative event in the lives of every child who encountered these two stern and serious educators. Every morning our little voices would carry words destined to give us hope in the midst of soul-breaking frustration. I also remember well how grand our graduations were: we were proud little troopers sporting our short-sleeved white shirts, with tie, short pants, and Oxford shoes, a rosebud pinned to our shirt. When my elder brother, Walter, had gone through his fifth and final year at Rosebud, we both transferred into the Memphis public schools.

Within this little world, Papa lived around the corner from us, on Stephens Place, a short block with no sidewalks that connected our street to the beginning block of the housing project. He and Sister had one-half of a spacious duplex, the other side of which was occupied by Sister's sister, Aunt Azilee, and her husband, Julius. I remember love-filled days visiting at their kitchen table, feeling safe, drinking buttermilk out of heavy, tall-stemmed, rounded glasses as I waited for Sister to put a plate on the table. Our cousin Mae Ella Gholson and her kids lived on the next block over, across from the projects. Here also on Ford Place, next to us in our new duplex, lived Sister's first cousin Miss Onnie, and her husband, Mr. Henry.

On the other side of our house was D. A.'s little sundry store, Bailey's Stand, and next to that was another cousin of Sister's, Miss Verlie, and her husband, Johnnie Edwards. Mr. Johnnie, as we called him, operated an auto and truck mechanic garage just down the street. Two or three men worked with him doing all sorts of repairs to cars, dump trucks, and other heavy vehicles. This small world sat within a three-block radius of the stately grounds of LeMoyne College, a four-year Negro college focused heavily on training teachers. (The school later merged to become LeMoyne-Owen College.) It was a handsome cluster of buildings in a parklike setting that spoke of opportunity and pride. At the opposite intersecting end of Ford was Williams Street, on which sat the black-owned and -staffed Terrell Memorial Hospital. I remember it as a neat, white frame structure on a hill, with a long front porch. When I walked to LaRose Elementary, I passed Terrell Memorial every day, where the nurses in their starched uniforms and crisp nursing caps moving purposefully about the porch and grounds of the hospital gave me to understand that there were many avenues of opportunity open to blacks.

In the same block of Williams, in a second-floor apartment, lived the pop and rhythm-and-blues pioneer Johnny Ace with his wife and children. He was a smooth, romantic crooner in the tradition of Nat King Cole and the later work of Sam Cooke. My father loved collecting records, and as a young teenager at night I would sit on the floor next to one of the speakers of the stereo console listening to Ace and other great musicians. In his late teens, Ace, one of three brothers, supported himself cutting yards in the neighborhood. An old-timer from Ford Place, Cleo Starks, remembered Ace—earlier known as Johnny Alexander—as argumentative and as someone who "would take a chance on anything." Ace's career grew from the Beale Streeters, an influential group that also nurtured B. B. King and Bobby Blue Bland. His life ended tragically at age twenty-five on Christmas Eve 1954, when the burgeoning star shot himself in the head playing Russian roulette backstage in Houston, Texas. Speaking of Ace's death, the longtime Ford Place resident said: "It's a wonder he didn't get killed around here."

Ace's death drew me to the Lewis Funeral Home, and I still remember standing at his casket next to a floral arrangement in the form of a clock, the flowers a reference to one of his biggest hits, "The Clock." Lovers of Johnny Ace transitioned from shock to adoration the next year with the posthumous release of what would be his biggest hit, "Pledging My Love," which rose to the pop top-twenty and spent ten weeks at the top of rhythm-and-blues charts. The jazz great Louis Armstrong had taken a liking to Ace, and the month after his death Armstrong had recorded Ace's "Pledging My Love" as a tribute.

Needless to say, for adolescents our small world had its sexual challenges as well. I remember that, in the ninth and tenth grades, homosexuality—as we later came to call it—was a fact of life in and outside the school. In our little world, we were much easier with gay people than one might expect given the contemporary hysteria over all things gay. There were two or three well-known homosexuals in the school who were popular and very open about their sexual orientation. But there was a predatory side to this even then. There was quiet rumor that one or two of the more handsome and popular high school boys had sex with gays for money. We mostly felt that same-sex relations didn't compromise the manhood of the straight boy so long as it was just a lark. It is a simple reality that gay men have always found a more congenial environment in the South generally, and in the black community particularly. We always knew that gays were among us, and they were relatively welcome, eccentric characters. This all changed rather dramatically, of course, with the advent of AIDS.

Across the street from blues icon W. C. Handy's shotgun Memphis home, and three blocks in the opposite direction from us, lived my maternal grandmother, "Big Mama." Nearby were my Uncle Albert and his family. I remember the momentous event when they became the first family in the neighborhood to have a black-and-white television. As I think now about how we all crowded into their living room to cheer on the black championship boxers like Ezzard Charles, Joe Louis, and Jersey Joe Walcott, I realize that the television was a transformative force in our lives. It gave us electronic community: we black families were as one, cheering around thousands of televisions and radios across America. Somehow, without our understanding how it happened or why, our unbending resolve to fight for equality was nurtured in part in such communal gatherings around the television.

Papa and Sister, my grandparents, eventually moved the half block to Ford Place into an elevated white shotgun house he owned, with brick columns on the front porch that matched those on our duplex. As it happened so often in those halcyon days, houses often served double duty when family needed extra space. Accordingly, built onto the back of Papa's house was Ersula Yarbrough's beauty shop, which we accessed by a side entrance. Mrs. Yarbrough herself lived across the street on Ford, and her husband, Denver, was Sister's first cousin. What Mrs. Yarbrough did for women in our small world, Mr. Yarbrough accomplished for the men: he operated Yarbrough's Barber Shop, which was the main area barber shop, close by at the corner of Mississippi and Walker. I remember Mrs. Yarbrough as friendly, talented, and popular with her customers. I can still hear the steady conversation in her shop just above the quiet hiss of the small gas fires in the cast-iron holders as the pressing and curling irons were heated to accomplish the magic of beautician-coiffed hair.

I have always been amazed that, given his limited education, Papa was able to build a small contracting company, have a handful of men working for him, and to own his own home, as well as the duplex we grew up in. Though he could not read or write, he could build a house according to blueprints, from the deeply rooted concrete foundations through the double-tiered floors, plaster walls, and double-layered roofs. Pacing one foot in front of the other, he would measure the length of a building, and he could tell its height by looking up at it. As teenagers, Walter and I often worked for him, doing the same hard work and being paid the same dollar an hour as his other men. To calculate the payments, Papa made four vertical marks with a fifth mark crossed through. Uncle Albert did the plaster work, including unusual patterns on walls using his trowel and a burlap bag to twist the designs. Papa was also the main repair contractor for Van Court Realty, then one of the largest rental property companies in the city.

My first real encounter with a white person came when Papa did work as the property caretaker and maintenance man for two elderly white women, Mrs. Mattie Ford and her sister, who lived in a large colonial white house on a hill on the corner of Bellevue and McLemore in South Memphis. Occasionally, when I would go over and help Papa, Miss Mattie would drive me home. Although it seems odd now, she would be in the front seat, and I in the back. We chatted as she drove along—a sort of reverse *Driving Miss Daisy.*

Always on the lookout for a way to make an extra dollar or two, Papa convinced the two sisters to let him grow cotton, peanuts, and sweet potatoes on the half block of land behind their house. I will never forget those occasions when Papa would take the cotton he grew on the sisters' land to the cotton gin in Mississippi. Sitting in the cab of the truck in the heat of summer, we drove through the fields of the Delta, watching the teams of pickers with their long bags dragging behind them as they worked the rows. Papa would negotiate the ruts of the dirt road on the way to the huge, barnlike, tin-roofed building containing the cotton gin. As we drove up to the loading dock to get our cotton sacks weighed, I could see into the dark interior where heavy men in overalls tended giant machines with great cog wheels and whirling belts. Mostly I remember the ear-splitting noise the machines made as they chopped up the mounds of raw cotton at one end and spewed out seedless lint from one vent and seeds from another.

In another of his entrepreneurial efforts, Papa and Sister owned and operated a small variety store called "Bailey's Stand" near the center of the block, which drew walk-in business from a three- or four-block radius. The

Stand was a flat-roofed wooden structure with a front door and one large picture window painted with the store's name.

The store was about 30 by 30 feet, with a sink but no bathroom since all the operators lived nearby. In front of the store there was a sloped concrete patio on which sat benches and chairs handmade by Papa and his crew. Because coal oil was a popular heating and cooking source at the time, just next to the entrance of the store was the large, red, steel coal-oil drum, about four feet tall and almost that wide. On top of the drum was an iron hand pump that we used to fill up customers' one- or five-gallon coal-oil containers.

This little store was the epicenter of my small world. On the left, inside the screen door emblazoned with the words "Colonial Bread," was the custom-built L-shaped glass-and-wooden display case and sales counter that showcased the candies and children's goodies that excited us with anticipation as we walked into the store. The wooden cash drawer pulled out to reveal four cupped slots for holding change. On top of the front counter were two one-foot-high plastic see-through Jackson cookie containers with red metal tops that held the freshest and best oatmeal and lemon cookies in memory.

To the right of the entryway were floor-to-ceiling wooden shelves on which canned vegetables, lard, flour, bread, meal, and other goods were shelved. At the center of the back of the store was a waist-high wood-burning stove that was constantly going in the winter as neighbors sat and stood around to talk and share perspectives on sports or the issues of the day. One might hear an adamant voice: "You know, them Brooklyn Dodgers gonna beat the hell out of the Cardinals—that black boy they got, Jackie Robinson, is tough!" Or the center of attention might be a game of checkers, one player emphatically slamming the checker as he moved it for a double or triple jump.

In the midst of all this mostly male fellowship, the one thing I dreaded was the arrival of Mr. Crozier, a one-armed man with a strong garlic smell that would funk up the whole store. He claimed the garlic was for his blood pressure. An accident at the neighborhood icehouse had cost him an arm, so from the elbow down he had what to my youthful eyes appeared a menacing metal clamping arm. Notwithstanding this impediment, Mr. Crozier had a mule he used in plowing and other handiwork that he regularly beat with a plank in front of his house on Ford. Directly across the street from the Stand, the elderly Mr. Johnson sat under a tree in his front yard keeping a particular eye on Walter and me. When he saw Mama returning home, he'd call out, "Lil Bit, I'm going in now."

My sense of community was forged at Bailey's Stand, where, during summers, a half dozen or so neighbors would frequently be found sitting on the armchairs and benches on the store's sloping front patio. A radio outside broadcast the baseball games as we listened to Harry Carey's graphic game commentary. Coal oil–soaked rags burned slowly in five-gallon buckets to generate the smoke needed to ward off mosquitoes, which were a significant plague so close to the Mississippi bottomlands. To provision Bailey's Stand, Papa would drive weekly to the South Memphis docks of the Malone and Hyde grocery warehouse to load up on canned goods and other foods, which we stacked into the jump seat of his black Model-T Ford. White salesmen also came to the store in large trucks to deliver soft drinks, milk, fresh bread, Jackson cookies, and fresh ice cream, which was kept frozen in coolers packed with dry ice. As they made their deliveries during the early and late 1950s, the white salesman rode shotgun in the truck. He took the orders and collected the money in a leather satchel that hung off his hip. Inevitably, the driver would be a black man who loaded the goods off and into the store.

How sharply I remember these encounters. Since these whites were making part of their living off my grandparents, they usually treated them with a modicum of respect. But even then their attitudes reflected the prevailing assumptions of white racial superiority. So there was no "Mr." Bailey, though the salesmen expected courtesy titles in response.

I remember my father early on working with Papa in home repair and construction, as we all did. He was a hard and steady worker. After working a year or so each at three local plants, Daddy landed a job loading mail on and off trains for the Illinois Central Railroad. Then he became a Pullman porter, staying with the company a total of thirty-two years. His supervisor would call the house and say to our mother or one of us, "Shotgun in? Let me speak to Him." "Shotgun, come to work!" he would say to my father. Daddy worked the line from Chicago, through Memphis to New Orleans. He would call Mama to meet him at the Memphis station with clean clothes as he was loading passengers.

My father enjoyed being out in the neighborhood playing checkers or shooting pool with his friends. He considered himself a master checker player, and he and Mama would vacation in various states where he could play in checker tournaments; sometimes women would also play. It was not a very well-kept secret that over the years he had quietly had his girlfriends. Because Daddy worked for the railroad, he was able to travel and sometimes even take us with him. Mama remembered her first trip with Daddy to Chicago to attend a professional baseball game: "I was so dressed up, with my hat and gloves on. I was so embarrassed I eased the gloves off and slipped them in my purse. I never did dress up to go to another ball game."

Walter and I went on a number of trips to professional baseball games on the Illinois Central. We were in the crowd in St. Louis when Jackie Robinson, Roy Campanella, and Don Newcombe first broke the color barrier in professional baseball. Occasionally, we even made pilgrimages to Chicago or Detroit. I never knew until years later how special these train trips were as most blacks in Memphis seldom left town. To see these big, teeming northern cities with all their enormous buildings and milling crowds of every nationality and color was an initiation of sorts. It opened up my young mind to a peculiar kind of mobility that would later be useful as I moved from Scotlandville, Louisiana, to Worcester, Massachusetts, then to Washington, to New Haven, and even to the other side of the continent to San Francisco. Somehow these trips liberated me geographically, taught me how to navigate the nation, and made me a larger man than just another Memphis Negro growing up in the 1950s whose horizons stopped at the city's riverbank.

Where my father opened the world to me, my mother seems, in retrospect, to have given me the kind of structured maturity that has been so necessary to my ability to grow even in adversity. Mama; her mother, Lureana; her two sisters, Bessie and Georgia; and her brother James first came to Memphis when she was three years old. They had been living in Knowlton, Arkansas, about one hundred miles south of Memphis in the Arkansas Delta. They were forced from their home in the Mississippi flood of 1927.

In his book *Rising Tide,* written before Hurricane Katrina, John Barry described the flooding as "the greatest natural disaster this country has ever known. . . . The river inundated the homes of nearly one million people, helped elect Huey Long governor and made Herbert Hoover President, drove hundreds of thousands of blacks north, and transformed American society and politics forever." In Greenville, Mississippi, all blacks were ordered to the levee to handle sandbags and live in a concentration camp that stretched seven miles. For the thousands of blacks, there were too few tents and not enough food. National Guardsmen kept many from leaving as the plantation owners feared they would not return to work the valuable cotton fields. President Coolidge did nothing despite the pleas from overwhelmed governors and mayors, and refused to visit the disaster area.

Mama and her family were among those lucky to escape. Our uncle Johnny Barrow and his family stayed behind to protect his livestock and hundreds of acres of farmland. They were fortunate to have a two-story house where they retreated to live on the second floor. Mama, her mother and her siblings were rescued by a neighbor who picked them up in a row-boat and took them to a levee, where they stayed overnight surrounded by a sea of dark water. The next morning a riverboat steamed its way up to the levee to rescue them, evacuating them to Memphis, where they permanently settled a year later.

The only father Mama ever knew from early childhood was her step-father, Jim Robinson, whom everyone called "Big Daddy." He was a chauf-feur and all-around handyman who stayed during the week at his employer's home on Walnut Grove Road. When Mama was nineteen, that small world came to an abrupt end as the result of a brawl between one of her father's Negro coworkers and his wife. Big Daddy was a man who really disliked vio-lence directed against women, so he tried to defend the wife and was fatally slashed for his trouble.

The story goes that Mama met my father as she was going to and coming from school. She noticed him among a group of young boys who were always standing on the street corner. Their relationship grew as he took to regularly walking her from school; in the course of time, love came.

My mother had very definite ideas about how life should be lived and how children should be raised. She taught us to do things for ourselves around the house from a very young age, to think for ourselves, and to make our own decisions out on the street. She allowed us a great deal of freedom to choose our own friends and go our own way because she trusted we would make good decisions, or at least not go too far wrong. She taught us to "always show respect for other people," saying, "I don't ever want to come home and hear that you did not mind someone, or that you picked on or disrespected someone. But stand up for yourself and don't be afraid to do what's right." I think Mama realized a person's life is his own, even if that person is a child. She was a liberated parent before it was fashionable, one perhaps even Dr. Phil would be proud of. She saw her role as educating and guiding but never controlling or owning the lives of her children. But then this made sense because no one had ever controlled or owned her.

Will Ella Bailey had a mind of her own, and she never hesitated to use it to better herself. In fact, it is largely because of her dedication to her own schooling that Walter and I grew up never doubting we would continue our education past twelfth grade. In our early years, she worked half days at Bailey's Stand so she could be home when we got back from school. She'd then turn operating duties over to Walter and me. For a time she worked as a maid for two supportive white physicians, but then she launched her schooling career, attending night school to prepare for her GED, the only woman among forty-two students taking the test. Afterwards she attended barber school and for five years worked part-time as a barber at Yarbrough's, the barbershop situated between the poolroom and the Four-way Grill. I remember that among her customers was a memorable drunk who regularly lamented, "Nothing holds whiskey better than a bottle." Not content with the prospects at Yarbrough's, she decided to attend a thirteen-month course of evening nursing classes, becoming one of only eighteen to finish the course of study out of an initial group of five hundred students. Two years later, black nurses were allowed to treat white patients. Then, in 1964 or 1965, she became only the third black nurse on the previously white staff of St. Joseph's Hospital.

Mama taught us to have self-respect, and to show that when we were in public. When she took us downtown, she refused to take us into the department stores that required blacks to stand up and eat, often the only service blacks could obtain. As she put it, "I knew I was not a horse, and I was not going to do that."

Perhaps it was because of the rather unconventional way she viewed her own life and position that she gained an appreciation that as kids, we were basically going to do whatever we decided we were going to do, with or without parental blessings. So Mama figured we might as well do it around the house, where we might not get hurt. Consequently, we were never severely chastised about our comings and goings, our friends, or our interests. Instead, we were made to feel generally accepted for who we were—no matter what we were about. This nonjudgmental approach basically eliminated any cause for lying or deceit. There was an accepting, truly loving attitude at the base of our relationship.

Our high school at Booker Washington had a tracking system, though I didn't know it at the time. On entering, I was placed in homeroom 9A, the designation that represented the highest level of academic assessment and expectations for ninth-graders. Our principal, Blair T. Hunt, was a stately, fair-skinned, well-dressed man with a receding hairline. He sought to instill pride and accountability in each student, always telling us in his rich, deep voice, "You are somebody." Hunt ruled the school with a firm hand, always carrying a large bell as he walked through the hallways. If you heard the distant tinkle of that bell, you knew it was time to get to your proper place. Hunt was known on occasion to thrust the bell into a student's back to nudge him to move along. Hunt had guided decades of students, including my parents, and at the same time he pastored one of Memphis's most prominent black churches. Hunt's influence as leader of the city's largest black high school was enhanced by his political association with one of the leading political bosses of the era, E. H. Crump, who built a machine across the state. Hunt was the leading black booster for the Crump machine, similar to the way the great musician W. C. Handy was the machine's leading trumpeter. The halls of Washington were awash with talented black teachers, some new and some having taught there for generations. When you walked off the sidewalk into the school, you knew the teachers and staff were in command and were eager to hone and refine the raw human talent surging through the school's doors. One great teacher of mine was Professor Nat D. Williams. Williams was a short, stocky man, with rich, dark skin, thinning, coarse hair, a broad grin, and eyeglasses as thick as a pop bottle's bottom. He was a favorite among the students as he exhorted us to have multiple skills and to learn how to do the things that would help us get a job. Williams was an intellectual who wrote a weekly syndicated column for black newspapers and was a popular radio host at the city's first black radio station. In front of my Tennessee history class, Williams stood with a broad smile as he summed up his theory of strategic survival: "The Indian fought and died, the Negro grinned and multiplied." In Williams's class, the question wasn't whether you would succeed, but how.

A block and a half from us on Ford, at the corner of Mississippi and Walker, sat Peoples Drug Store. It was only later that I learned that on this very spot was originally the Peoples Grocery. Today a state marker notes the history: "Calvin McDowell, Thomas Moss and Will Stewart, co-owners of Peoples Grocery—were arrested in connection with a disturbance near the store. Rather than being brought to trial, they were lynched on March 9, 1892. Moss's dying words were 'tell my people to go West, there is no justice for them here.' This lynching prompted Ida B. Wells, Editor of Memphis Free Speech, to begin her anti-lynching campaign in this country and abroad."

In my teen years, the Peoples Grocery site was occupied by Peoples Drug Store. This spacious store was owned by one of Memphis's two black pharmacists, Dr. William Pippin, who carried forth the "Peoples" name. Pippin helped nurture me as a store delivery boy. On a heavy, maroon bike with a wire basket in front, I rode the neighborhood delivering ice cream, medicine, and toiletries. I also cleaned the place up at night prior to closing.

The store had a long Formica sundry counter with about eight stools and tubs of ice cream in the freezer behind for service to regulars and the LeMoyne students who piled in after classes in the afternoon. Pippin's wife was one of the teachers at my high school. Working at the drugstore opened a whole new world to me. There was a big, circular wire news rack at the front of the store on which were posted newspapers and magazines covering black affairs around the country. The Memphis black press was in the forefront of reporting civil rights news from Montgomery to Jackson to Little Rock. The racks held black news from the *Pittsburgh Courier, Chicago Defender, Atlanta Daily World,* and *Jet* and *Ebony* magazines, among others. There were also black romance magazines like *Sepia* and *Bronze Thrills,* the latter a bit risqué. I would pass the time when I wasn't busy in the store reading these publications. They propelled me into the midst of the racially motivated lynching of the black youth Emmett Till, Rosa Parks's Montgomery bus boycott, and the violence against black students my age trying to integrate Central High School in Little Rock.

My cousin Ralph Bailey had worked after school as an attendant to the neighborhood's black doctor, James Hose. On finishing school, Ralph turned the job over to me, and I left the drugstore to work with Dr. Hose. Hose was a devout Catholic and operated St. Roch Clinic from a large, converted frame house. Just a half block away lived Dr. J. E. Walker, the city's wealthiest black and owner of Universal Life Insurance Company and Tri-State Bank. Shock waves went through Memphis when a cofounder of the insurance company shot and killed Walker in his office over a long-standing business disagreement.

Dr. Hose kept burning candles and religious statues in the clinic's two waiting rooms and would pray before a religious statue daily. When his long-time nurse, Sis Wilhite, finished work at three in the afternoon, I took over signing in the patients, assisting Dr. Hose with preparations in his treating office and keeping the place clean. Hose, in his fifties, was medium height, slightly stocky, fair-skinned, with straight hair and a reassuring, caring demeanor. He and I both liked ice cream, so Dr. Pippin would occasionally send us a quart of it, which we would share in the back kitchen area. Hose, in his starched white medical coat that buttoned atop the left shoulder, was soft-spoken, attentive, and hardworking. From the time I got there at three in the afternoon until we closed—usually between nine and ten, though sometimes later—both waiting rooms were largely filled. It didn't make me happy when certain patients would come in deliberately late so they wouldn't have to wait long, causing us to work even later. One such patient was patrolman E. C. "Suge" Jones, one of Memphis's first black police officers. When black officers were first hired, they were assigned to the Negro district on Beale Street, had no patrol cars, and could arrest only black people. If they caught a white breaking the law, they would hold the offender and call a white officer to come and take him into custody. Suge Jones had a reputation as one of the roughest black policeman, notorious for "whooping" recalcitrant blacks upside the head with his wooden baton. One black radio jockey framed a lyric around him and the then popular Thunderbird wine: "What's the word? Thunderbird. What's the price? Thirty twice. Who's on? Suge Jones."

When the medical clinic closed, Dr. Hose would drop me off at home four blocks away in his sleek black fish-tailed Cadillac. I remember that car purring like a kitten with its fine carpet and soft leather interior. Many nights before getting to my house, Dr. Hose would stop at one or two houses to make house calls.

My next job was as an orderly at the city's major hospital. Until I got this full-time job at John Gaston, around the age of sixteen, the extent of my interaction with whites was largely a series of passing greetings, instructions, expressions, or glances. The orderly job was different, in both negative and positive aspects. I worked after school from three in the afternoon to eleven at night collecting garbage, running the elevator, and helping in the emergency room. I pushed three garbage cans on a wagon to the outside incinerator and uncovered a large floor opening to empty the cans into the roaring incinerator below. Standing alone on that edge with no protective barriers was the part of the job I dreaded the most. In addition, when a patient died, I would help the ward orderly stuff the openings of the body with cotton to keep fluids from leaking out. Then we would wrap the body in heavy corrugated paper, put it on a stretcher, cover it with a sheet, and take it by elevator to one of the refrigerated morgue compartments in the basement.

One night, on a lark, I climbed up on the empty stretcher as we were coming back from the morgue, and the orderly covered me with the sheet so I looked like a corpse. On entering the elevator, he told the operator the morgue was full, which was my signal to begin moving under the sheet. The resulting pandemonium was gratifying, to say the least. Working at John Gaston was a good job, and I considered myself lucky to have it, especially at the princely wage of about forty dollars a week.

The man who was in charge of hiring was a fat, white homosexual who liked having young black boys around, a preference that I'm sure opened the doors of opportunity for a lot of us. As a result, there were at least a dozen boys from Booker Washington working as orderlies. Usually the work went fairly smoothly. In fact, I hadn't experienced or witnessed any real racial conflict or mistreatment until a friend of mine, Thomas Pigues, got into a fight with a white doctor.

According to Pigues, he was standing in the elevator joking with the elevator operator, an older black man who was an Uncle Tom type, always grinning and shaking his head to the whites with his "yassirs" and "nawsirs" and gladly accepting the hospital's bright lines of racial segregation. By contrast, he often scowled at us and thought we should quickly step aside when a white approached. Pigues had stretched his arm straight up against the wall and leaned against it, inadvertently causing his white uniform jacket to rise above his white pants, exposing his lean six-pack. Then the elevator stopped, and a white doctor and a white woman got on. No one said anything until the two whites started to get off on the second floor to go to the cafeteria. Before the door closed, the doctor said, "Fasten your clothes up, nigger."

Pigues was fuming by the time he got up to the fifth floor where I was working and told me what had happened. "I ought to go down there and kick his white ass," he said, his eyes flashing as he paced back and forth. I said something fairly noncommittal, which was nevertheless enough of an affirmation for Pigues. He took off for the second floor, and I followed him, curious to see what would happen. We waited in the hall for the doctor to come out of the cafeteria, and then Pigues walked up to him. "You shouldn't have said that to me, talking to me like that, calling me a nigger. You didn't have any cause to do that."

The doctor was obviously shocked and angry, and began to puff up into a full-blown, assertive white man. He looked at Pigues squarely and announced, "As a matter of fact, I meant what I said, and if you know what's good for you, you'll keep quiet."

So Pigues hauled back and hit him in the face, sending the doctor's glasses flying.

"You've done it now," the doctor threatened. "You've done it now, nigger."

By that point, Pigues knew he was in trouble and decided that he might as well make the best of it. He hit the doctor two or three more times in the head, knocking him down on the floor, where he kept on fighting him. Even though the doctor wasn't gravely injured, he was beaten up quite badly by the time security arrived and forced Pigues to let him up off the floor. Pigues pulled himself together, went back to the ward where he worked, told his supervisor what had happened, and left the hospital. Of course, they fired him. It may seem strange that Pigues wasn't arrested. The racial climate in Memphis was for the most part carefully balanced and not on edge. My guess is that the doctor and hospital officials preferred to handle this incident quietly rather than suffer the tension and embarrassment of a black teenager beating up a doctor over a racial slur at the hospital.

It wasn't too long after that I, too, was fired. A nursing supervisor complained that my garbage cart was too far out in the hallway, and I spoke up for myself, telling her I was just trying to do my job. Clearly recognizing that I did not know my place, she directed that I be fired. My own white supervisor said he was sympathetic but had no choice in the matter. This was an obvious injustice, so I decided to appeal the matter to the next meeting of the board of directors of the hospital. I sat outside the board room all morning, but they wouldn't hear me. This was no great surprise, but at least I had pushed it as far as I could. In a small way, I had begun my own personal protest, the first in what would become a long line of civil protests.

~ 2 ~
On to Scotlandville

No other issue is as important to you, your family, and your children as the issue of Racial Segregation. Our organization is dedicated solely to maintaining segregation. Our past success . . . fighting integration of schools, keeping Negroes off the televisions and out of our living rooms, preventing the development of Negro subdivisions and fighting integrationist candidates . . . dictates the future. We cannot fail. We are here to stay and so is segregation.
—SOUTHERN GENTLEMEN'S ORGANIZATION, BATON ROUGE CHAPTER, 1956

E VERYTHING IN MY SENIOR year seemed designed to challenge my perspectives, to expose me to a larger world than the small, insulated environment of my childhood on the corner of Mississippi and Walker in South Memphis. I began to come in contact with influential blacks who showed interest in me and treated me with respect as they began my political education. Back then we had three black newspapers in Memphis: the *Tri-State Times,* the *Memphis World,* and the *Tri-State Defender.* Early in high school I took a typing course and enjoyed composing on my new Remington typewriter. I was writing a gossip column for the Booker T. Washington High School paper when I met the editor of the *Tri-State Times,* who invited me to start writing a weekly column of high school student social news for that paper. It was not a whole lot different from my gossip column, but I was being published nonetheless. Eventually, my work at the *Times* led to a weekly column in the *Tri-State Defender,* a leading black newspaper in the South that was very much in tune with civil rights activities. The editor was L. Alex Wilson, a tall, well-dressed, dark-skinned man with alert eyes and a broad forehead. When white mobs descended on Little Rock's Central High School in the fall of 1957 to block the court-ordered enrollment of black students, Wilson was on the scene covering for the *Defender.* When the mob spotted Wilson and three other black journalists, they began threatening and striking them. When Wilson refused to run, he was brutally kicked, knocked almost to the ground, and hit in the head with a brick. Yet, in a show of courage captured by cameras and shown around the world, Wilson bent once to pick his dress hat off the ground, kept his suit jacket buttoned, and walked with dignity back to his car. He never physically recovered from the beating, though he went on a year later to become editor of the *Chicago Daily Defender* and died the next year at age sixty.

In my senior year, I moved from the *Tri-State Defender* to the *Memphis World,* whose editor, Thaddeus Stokes, was educated at Kent State University, initiated as a journalist at the *Cleveland Call & Post,* and moved to the editorial department of the *Atlanta Daily World,* where he covered Dr. Martin Luther King. The black-owned Scott Newspaper Syndicate, which owned the *Atlanta Daily World,* transferred Stokes to the *Memphis World,* which it also owned. Stokes came to work daily in coat and tie: he was a six-foot-tall, light brown–skinned man whose coarse black hair, thick lips, and broad facial features were unusual for a person of his complexion. Stokes was intelligent, dignified, well-spoken, and gutsy. Like the *Defender*'s Wilson, Stokes reported from the scene of the racial rioting at Central High School in Little Rock in 1957. He maintained a quality news standard for the paper, and, though new to town, he quickly gained respect in the community.

I could tell that Stokes saw something in me he liked, and he became my friend and something of a role model. His continual encouragement and insistence that "D'Army, there are great things ahead for you" had a lasting and strengthening impact on me. Stokes came to my graduation, and even came to see about me once when I was confined overnight at juvenile court. That overnight incarceration came about when a high school friend, Melvin Woodruff, was cursing loudly as we waited at a neighborhood bus stop. A white lady coming out of the grocery across the street chastised us for the noise, and my somewhat irreverent friend then began cussing at her. Minutes later we boarded our bus, only to be pulled over by police before the first intersection. The police arrested Melvin and me and took us to juvenile court. A few years later I heard from my friend Stokes while I was home on a break from school in Massachusetts. Stokes said that the FBI had visited him as part of an investigation, telling him that they were doing a security check because President Lyndon Johnson was scheduled to speak in my college town.

At the same time I was writing for the *Memphis World,* I got a lucky break and landed a guest disc jockey position at WLOK, later to be the first black-owned and -operated radio station in Memphis. On Mondays, Wednesdays, and Fridays, I would leave school early and go down to the station on Beale Street and sit at a microphone in one room, while Dick Cane Cole faced me in the control room. Dick Cole was an important black radio personality. He was an interesting character: a man of medium height and stocky build, he had an engaging smile and one leg about three inches shorter than the other, which gave him a peculiar gait. Like other black radio personalities popular in the community, he made frequent guest appearances and could often be seen spinning records at teenage dance parties. Like Stokes, he offered me concern and encouragement. A family friend, he continued to play bid whist—a partnership game somewhat like bridge—with my parents until his death.

On my fifteen-minute show, called *Teenage Roundup,* I would read the high school news and play two or three records. My show warmed teenage hearts with the romantic lyrics of Jerry Butler's song "Your Precious Love," words that still ring in my ears as I think about those days. And few songs received more requests, or better captured the testosterone-charged lives of young men in those days, than the Shirelles' hit "This Is Dedicated to the One I Love."

Not only was my writing being published in important black-owned local newspapers when I was a young teenager, but my voice was also being broadcast across the greater Memphis area by an important black radio station. At the same time, I was campaigning for candidates backed by the Memphis Shelby County Democratic Club, an influential political action organization led by the city's prominent black movers and shakers, several of whom were lawyers. They worked closely with the Memphis NAACP in their effort to support black and pro-integration white candidates. In the 1940s and 1950s, when Memphis was under the control of one of the country's leading political bosses, E. H. Crump, the black vote was organized and delivered by black preachers and leaders for the candidates of the Crump machine. The work of the Democratic Club in the 1950s marked the first significant effort to register blacks and to organize the black vote around the priorities and agenda of the black community. It was a revolutionary thing to do, and we knew it.

My involvement with this new phase of black politics increased my awareness of my leadership abilities and of my value as a human being. It was also key in stimulating my awareness of what blacks in other communities were doing to advance the cause of racial equality. From the Memphis Shelby

County Democratic Club, I learned about the Montgomery bus boycott, the political actions taken in Little Rock, and the implications of the historic *Brown v. Board of Education* decision. Like others in my community, I was appalled at the blatant brutality and fanaticism of the whites who murdered twelve-year-old Emmett Till for allegedly merely whistling at a white woman. I also saw the efforts black leaders in my own city were making to organize our community and advance our political agenda. I observed the insight and intelligence of blacks like Thaddeus Stokes and Blair Hunt, just as I had observed—and, indeed, taken for granted since childhood—the diligence and hard work of the members of my own family.

All of these events and each of these important black role models informed my awakening mind while I simultaneously observed, with my own eyes or through the eyes of reporters, a steady parade of the most ordinary members of the Anglo Saxon race, who never seemed to doubt their presumed superiority. Given the powerful contradictions inherent in the white-dominated world around me, I could not reconcile this presumed superiority with reality.

In my last years of high school, I gained a growing—if as yet undefined—sense that the race issue was coming to a head. The rules of segregated living were pushing blacks too far back into the dimly lit corners and alleyways of society. Even in my self-enclosed and largely self-sufficient community, where I was trained to accept that my life was to be made among my own people, I began to realize that this segregated life was wrong. I knew that white police officers not only came into our community and physically abused us, but also were often casually offensive and rude. Even in this time before the sit-ins, I became acutely aware that whites ran everything, including the government, and that we blacks were at the mercy of their rules and laws. It would be almost a full decade before we would see any way to battle the white system or to force the race issue into the open without losing much more than we would gain.

Finally, the day came when I was to leave that little world of Bailey's Stand, La Rose Elementary, Booker T. Washington High School, WLOK, the *Memphis World,* and the Democratic Club. Leaving Memphis for college at Southern University felt like a natural progression, so I felt little anxiety as the summer came to an end and I began to anticipate my new adventure in Louisiana. Southern University would just be a new world with other young people I had never met, or so I thought. From what I had heard about campus life from my brother and my friend Ricks Mason who had been at Southern for a year on football scholarships, the university offered a very different venue from that of my active community life in Memphis: I thought it would be more confined in a sense and therefore perhaps more intense.

It was nine o'clock on a muggy Memphis night early in September 1959 when my parents took me down to the train station to catch the Lausanne bound for Hammond, Louisiana. Their second son was going off to college, and they were proud, nearly beaming with the special joy that comes when you have made possible for your children what was impossible for yourself.

Tucked into the bank of the Mississippi River, Southern University and Agricultural and Mechanical College in Scotlandville, Louisiana, was the largest black state university in the country. Started in 1880 as one of the first land grant colleges in the South, it was run by an all-black administration and faculty with a reputation for producing capable and productive graduates, assets to the black communities of cities throughout the country. I have always thought it odd—perhaps it was someone's idea of a bad joke—that a major black university would be placed in a town named after Scotland, one of the whitest places on earth. Now, both of Walter and Will Ella Bailey's sons were enrolled there.

"Okay, lift now," Daddy instructed me as we struggled with my trunk. The heat seemed to enclose us like a warm, wet blanket. I noticed beads of perspiration lining Daddy's forehead and felt my own trickling slowly down my chest. "Just three more steps and we got it." We heaved the trunk the rest of the way into the train and slid it behind a nearby seat.

"What? Was that getting too heavy for you?" Daddy teased. "Bill, I don't know if we better let this boy go to college or not. He might not be able to carry his books to class. They might find him passed flat out in the middle of the street." Daddy laughed and put his hand on my shoulder. He glanced sideways at my mother, whom he always called Bill, waiting for a reaction.

"Well, Walter, if that's the case, maybe you ought to go down there and carry them for him," she countered, smooth as ever, smiling at me.

"Daddy, you know I was sweating and struggling on your account." I said, still looking at Mama. "With two boys grown and off at college, I didn't want you feeling like an old man."

"Look at me, D'Army," he said, suddenly serious. "If I am an old man, at least I'm a proud one."

"And that's one thing you'd do well never to forget," Mama added. "You're going to college, and there are no two prouder parents in the world."

I nodded and looked at both of them.

"But of course the way he goes on about it," Mama said under her breath, "you—and the whole city of Memphis along with you—would have to be deaf not to know how he feels."

Mama handed me a big box of fried chicken she had prepared so I wouldn't be tempted to get off the train. "Now, D'Army, you know your father and I don't want you getting off the train at any of these little towns," she warned. "There's no sense looking for trouble. Those depots can be dangerous places, especially if you're traveling alone, you hear? They always put the colored kitchen back in some dark alley or corner where you don't want to be. I know you've heard your father talk about worse than just fights going on down in Mississippi, so, honey, stay on the train. Will you?"

"Yes, Mama, I will."

"It's not that I think you can't take care of yourself, you know."

"I know."

"But there's just no use tempting fate. Don't forget to give Walter my love, now, D'Army. And tell him I said not to forget about his studies," she said as we sat side by side in the car. Daddy nervously paced in the aisle.

"Okay, I will," I assured her, "but I don't know how that'll go over."

"You just tell him I said so and leave it at that." She smiled. "And both of you could write once in a while."

"I don't know, Mama." I said with mock confusion. "This is a lot. I don't know if I can remember all this."

As we kept on talking, chatting about little things, I noticed the car was almost empty except for a woman and her kids up front, and a tall, light-skinned black man sitting near us. It seems an odd thing about the black community that often, even today, the lighter the skin of blacks, the more attractive they are perceived to be and the higher up they often ascend in the class hierarchy of the black community. This may be partly because distant and secret white ancestors have helped pave an easier path for them. And it may also partly derive from blacks' own sense that the more negroid or black our features, the less attractive we were in the eyes of the community. Fairer-skinned blacks seem to be favored in hiring, perhaps because they are presumed to be less threatening, more meticulous, and even more trustworthy. Shortly, the stranger got up and intercepted Daddy in the aisle.

"I'm Oscar Johnson," he said in a clear, northern accent as he extended his hand.

"Walter Bailey." Daddy moved closer to us. "This is my wife, Will Ella, and my son D'Army."

"Well, I'm pleased to meet you," Oscar said as we all shook hands. "It's been getting pretty lonely on this train."

"Where are you coming from?" I asked.

"Philadelphia. And I'm headed down to Louisiana. I'm starting college at Southern."

"No," I said, shaking my head. "No way."

"Yeah, Southern. It's in Scotlandville, I think, outside of Baton Rouge. You ever heard of it?"

"Sure, he's heard of it," Daddy said, unable to contain himself." "That's where he's going too," he said, gesturing at me. "And you better watch out for him 'cause he's gonna be the smartest boy in the school."

Oscar and I stared at each other in disbelief for a few seconds and then burst into laughter. Daddy liked to brag. At that moment, as the three of us stood in the dimly lit train car, I was glad he did. I was glad he was confident enough in himself to take pride in Walter and me and, in his own way, to give some of that confidence to us. There had been other times when his bragging had made me distinctly uncomfortable, times when I thought he enjoyed singing our praises much more than he enjoyed talking to us. When he bragged at those times, it seemed to me almost like he was stealing, taking credit for something underserved. But those times passed. As I grew older, my view of him changed: I began to understand how "his boys" were entering a world he had only dreamed about.

Mama popped open the chicken box, and we all struck up a lively, tension-easing conversation until the conductor hollered, "All aboard!"

"You two boys stick together," Mamma told us. "Look out for each other, you hear?" She hugged me, kissed me on the cheek, and then moved toward the door.

Daddy took me by the shoulders and looked me straight in the eyes. "Now, son, take care of yourself," he said in an uncharacteristically serious tone. It was an admonition he would repeat many times over the coming years. I knew even then it was a sign of his own worries and a reflection of his own experience. In his job with the railroad, he traveled regularly on the Illinois Central through Mississippi and into New Orleans. He knew the route passed through some of the loneliest places in the world for a black man, and my train, the Lausanne, stopped in all of them. There was Yazoo, where a few years later, when I asked to use the restroom at a gas station, a sullen white man had me follow him to the outside back of the building and instructed, "See that hole in the ground, use it right there, and when you get through, take a shovel and cover it up." The Lausanne also chugged on through Mc-Comb and Jackson, both violently segregationist towns.

"Eat your chicken," Daddy said and smiled, his eyes still serious.

"There's nothing in this world better than Mama's chicken," I said, matching his gaze. "Bye, Daddy."

We waved at them through the window as we pulled out of the station. Oscar and I talked on past midnight, both of us speculating about what our new world would bring until the steady shimmying and rocking of the train lulled us to sleep.

I remember at one point looking out the window at my reflection in the inky black night: I saw just another black kid going to college. I was like thousands of other black kids that fall; I wanted more than a job as a truck driver or mechanic. I had been raised to assume I would have more. However, I hadn't considered what fight or sacrifice I might have to make to have it anywhere but inside the black community. Sometimes, I think, we have to enter the battle before we discover just exactly what it is we should be fighting for.

So as the Illinois Central chugged south, carrying me into a future I never imagined would be all that dramatically different from the past, my thoughts were occupied with much more prosaic things. I was wondering who my roommate would be, how the campus would look, and if the women were as beautiful as I had been told. My thoughts at that moment might have been expressed in the words of a traditional black spiritual:

> Lord, hold my hand,
> Lord, guide my feet,
> Lord, answer my prayer
> While I run this race,
> 'Cause I ain't gonna run this race in vain.

~ 3 ~

Protest Comes to Scotlandville

The day is past for us to just encourage each other with words. We know now that this bad dream is not going away; rather it becomes a more frightening nightmare with every action of the federal government and integrationist pressure groups. NOW IS THE TIME FOR US TO UNITE on the level of the moral and the spiritual. Ours is a movement with Biblical authority for the fight it is making for our children and the purity of the races.
—CRUSADERS, INC., BATON ROUGE, 1956

THERE IS NO STRAIGHT train route from Memphis to Scotlandville, which is just outside Baton Rouge, so we got off the train in Hammond stiff and hungry, with a three-hour wait for the commuter bus still ahead of us. Stretching and grumbling, we walked through the depot to the colored café in the kitchen and ordered some breakfast. There was a large opening through which the cook on our side served the food, and through it I watched the white farmers and salesmen arriving for early-morning coffee at the depot's main café out front. Though friendly among themselves, these people would quickly become angry and violent if a black dared to venture into their segregated area. For a while in high school I used to drive for a kindly white shoe salesman to country stores in nearby Arkansas and rural areas around Memphis. The culture of segregation in these small rural towns was a constant reminder to me about my place within white society.

I made the trip to and from Baton Rouge at the beginning and end of the school term and for Christmas breaks. Sometimes, on later stops in Hammond, I would visit a café and pool hall I'd found across the railroad tracks in the shanty-lined black area. Frequently the juke box would be blasting the latest releases; that year Ray Charles was hot with "I've Got a Woman." When I was alone on a nighttime trip, I'd go to the downtown movie house, where

I had to walk down a back alley and climb up to the distant balcony reserved for coloreds. But no matter what diversion I tried, from that first trip on, the three hours I waited for a connection always passed with tortuous slowness and were edged with fear.

When we finally got to Baton Rouge, Walter picked us up at the bus station and drove us the ten miles to Scotlandville, passing the rows of Standard Oil Refinery tanks that turned the skies north of the campus an eerie yellow orange. Scotlandville was an all-black town of twenty thousand whose economy revolved around the university. Railroad tracks formed a barrier between the gutted, unpaved streets of the town and the modern, well-kept campus. In Southern Heights—a sleek, middle-class section of sprawling ranch-style homes that lined the outer edge of Scotlandville—the Southern faculty and administration lived in striking and disquieting contrast to the crumbling shacks and stinking open sewers in the rest of town.

Yet, as we crossed the tracks and began winding toward the admissions building, I quickly forgot these bothersome contradictions. The campus was beautiful, clean, and modern. Louisiana's leaders were generous in offering a well-appointed black university in order to head off court-ordered enrollment of black students at LSU and other white schools. As early as 1947, the state built a law school at Southern in response to a lawsuit filed by a black resident seeking to attend law school at a state institution. My university journey began just five years after the U.S. Supreme Court condemned the inherent inequality of segregated black schools in the 1954 landmark case *Brown v. Board of Education*.

Spanish moss draped the majestic live oaks that dotted the grounds and surrounded silvery Lake Kernan. The dorms, offices, and classrooms were modern and spacious. At night I found the weather warm and pleasant, with crickets and cicadas clamoring in the trees. Turtles wandered up from the banks of the Mississippi River, and every now and then I even spotted an armadillo.

In the first few weeks of school, I met students from all over the country—from the rural towns of Mississippi and Louisiana and from the slick city streets of Chicago and South Philly. Everyone appeared well-dressed and articulate. The Louisiana students probably made up the greatest percentage of the student body. The Louisiana men could be easily distinguished because they cut the heels off their shoes, a style they thought fashionable, but that I found quite strange. Of course, they probably thought my Memphis "tailor-made" pants—with flaps down the seams—were very country and backward. Most of us had taken part of our high school earnings to the white-owned tailor shops on Beale Street and had dress pants and suits custom made, often shopping to pick up shirts and accessories at the same flashy Lansky Brothers Store as Elvis.

On the Southern campus, in addition to the peculiarities of costume, everyone also had their own colloquial pronunciation and slang. Not only were Louisiana students fond of adding a "yeah" to the end of everything they said, but they also had expressions like "you ain't gon' do me nuthin' yeah," which the rest of us mimicked and teased them about. But basically we all got along well. Overshadowing our differences was that most of us were the first in our families to go to college, and this alone seemed to lend a common drive and optimism to the new class of freshmen. We were primed to surge forward, but to where or how? I, for one, did not know. Even so, there was a distinctive momentum about us. We were looking to the future. And on top of all this, I soon discovered the rumors I had heard were true: Louisiana's reputation for beautiful women was well founded.

Less true to life was any notion that the political climate on the Southern campus could be called progressive. The president of Southern was Dr. Felton G. Clark, a fair-complexioned, well-dressed man who unfortunately showed more flair in his selection of attire than in his administration of the university. Like his father, Southern's first president, Dr. Clark ran a respectable and tight ship, selecting faculty who were, for the most part, quite able and, on occasion, exceptional. He espoused academic excellence with his memorable line, "seek you first Alpha Kappa Mu, and all the fraternities will seek after you," and he exposed us as freshmen to mandatory Sunday vesper services, bringing such noted academics and theologians as Morehouse's Dr. Benjamin Mays. But Dr. Clark was, at base, a status quo man. He didn't necessarily seek the exceptional or challenging; he wanted what worked, what sufficed without rocking the boat. He, like the rest of the faculty, was a government employee. Southern was a state-owned institution controlled by the State Board of Education, which was filled with political appointees of the governor. Dr. Clark's job was not his own, and by necessity he walked a very tenuous line.

In the fall of 1959, however, with little evidence of conflict at Southern University, Dr. Clark may not have seen his position as tenuous at all. The white voters of Louisiana had empowered the white governor to empower the white State Board of Education to let Dr. Clark run Southern University. And Dr. Clark fulfilled that charge, running the campus like an efficient and not unpleasant plantation. If he didn't then see the line he was walking in his role as Southern's president, it would soon enough be brought to his attention.

The professors at Southern, as was the case at many state-owned black schools, did not interact a great deal with the students. They did not, for the most part, encourage the students to develop political awareness or to question the existing political structure. Such encouragement was not condoned by the State Board of Education. Moreover, the professors were not about to question the white power structure that paid for their houses in Southern Heights. They were happy with their jobs and their houses; anything that jeopardized that security, even if it was good for the student's growth and advancement, simply wasn't worth the risk to most of them. So they did their jobs, period. If the narrowness of their happiness did not appear to bother them, perhaps this was because for a long time they, like Dr. Clark, were not forced to face the awkwardness of their contradictory lives or to foresee a time when they would be. When I arrived at Southern, there was no prior history of students coming together to question the political or economic status of blacks or to force recognition of the need for change. In fact, there was essentially no *political* climate at all. Eventually, though, that would change; the entire Southern administration and faculty would be tested, and many would fail.

Of course, when Walter and Oscar and I drove onto campus that September afternoon, I had no knowledge of these things, and I wouldn't for quite a while. My decision, in the coming weeks, to run for freshman class president was strictly egocentric. The thought of holding a little power among the students and of standing out among the crowd appealed to me, even more so because I thought I could win. During those first weeks, Walter, Oscar, and I pooled our skills and organized a highly visible campaign, combing the dormitory lounges and holding uproarious political rallies that made us instant favorites among the women. On election day, we were confident we had a sweep.

Soon my attention turned to more serious matters. It was early March 1960. I was on my way to a student assembly, where all 1,500 freshmen were congregating in the old gymnasium, when I stopped by the student union to pick up a newspaper. Glaring at me from the front page were horrible pictures of unarmed, slaughtered black men, women, and children. The Sharpeville Massacre in South Africa was one of the most shocking news stories since the Little Rock Central High school riots, when Governor Faubus counseled defiance of federal orders for integration, and black youngsters were ushered to school by federal troops through mobs of screaming, vicious white adults. Except this time there were no screaming jeers and taunts, only guns. I read with horror of the evils of apartheid and the inevitable destruction that is the by-product of separation and hate. As I walked into the women's gym, already packed and noisy, I was still reeling with helpless anguish, my mind spinning with questions, and my body tense with anger. Sixty-nine unarmed black protestors killed, many shot in the back as they fled for safety, shot for no other reason than because they were black.

At the assembly we talked about improving scholastic, athletic, and social programs and about involving more students in campus government. In my remarks, I spoke of the need for campus reform, but as the newspaper photographs flashed in my mind, I resolved, almost before I realized what I was doing, to devote part of my statement to the massacre.

"What is it about us as a people that enables us to promote and endure this most barbarous and inhumane treatment of others?" My voice was thick with emotion as I continued:

Yesterday, there was a massacre. It happened in Sharpeville, South Africa. Several thousands of that oppressed majority of black Africans marched peacefully into the center of Sharpeville. They came from throughout the countryside. Men, women, children—many of whom had walked many miles—hoped to stage a peaceful and silent protest of government apartheid. They were met in the center of town by heavily armed South African troops. Without a word being spoken, the troops opened fire. When the shooting was over, scores of black Africans lay dead in the streets of Sharpeville. As yet there has not been one word of effective protest from the celebrated capitals of the Western world. Not even a whimper. What was their crime in Sharpeville? Their crime was that they had the audacity to pull themselves out of the oppressive squalor of their isolated encampments and go to demand some human compassion and decency from their South African overlords. For this they were brutally murdered. How long will we sit silently in the face of such genocide? In times like these, the routine business of student government is of little importance. We should call upon everyone connected with this university to scream out in protest of this ugly, dastardly and criminal slaughter.

Hundreds in the auditorium jumped to their feet, applauding wildly. I stepped back from the mike, inwardly trembling with the emotion of the speech and simultaneously charged by the enthusiasm with which my words were received.

My concerns as freshman class president, in light of the change that occurred within me after the speech, seemed almost inconsequential. The position had made me a little bit bigger on campus, allowing me to relate to some of the administrators more directly than I could have otherwise and permitting me to organize good class activities and dances and to bring in the bands I wanted. I could travel to out-of-town games with the class queen and the band and football teams. We had a memorable trip by train to Tennessee. The school chartered the whole train. The band, in uniform and with instruments blaring, marched from the campus to the train track at Scotlandville depot, where we boarded. The train rocked all the way into Nashville, where the band then led another high-stepping march onto the Tennessee State University campus. Another one of my duties was the class homecoming dance. When I was in high school, a group of us used to rent a local nightclub and have dances where we charged admission and heard one of the two local rhythm-and-blues bands, Ben Branch and Gene "Bowlegs" Miller. So for our homecoming at Southern, I brought Bowlegs to campus. Southern students had never seen such a rollicking good time as this Memphis crew showed them.

Before my remarks about the Sharpeville Massacre, I had not envisioned my leadership in a political context. When I delivered that speech, my leadership became political. In my passionate condemnation of injustice, I had demonstrated a power of which I had been previously unaware: the power of the spoken word. Although I had been doing all the ordinary student things—playing ping-pong or nickel, dime, and quarter tonk, chasing women, or enjoying the petty privileges of student class president, as well as reading and following the details of antisegregation protest in the South— something changed inside me when I became aware of my own passion, and felt the power that lay within it. The administration saw that passion, and they remembered it. Though I was careful to remain low-key, I think they marked me then as a potential troublemaker. Soon, however, they would have much more immediate and pressing troubles.

~ 4 ~
Klieg Lights and Microphones

Throughout the years, Louisiana State University has advocated a policy of segregation of the races. To my knowledge, no one at LSU has communistic leanings.

—TROY H. MIDDLETON, PRESIDENT, LOUISIANA STATE UNIVERSITY, 1958

ON FEBRUARY 1, 1960, four black college students sat down at the whites-only lunch counter of the Woolworth's store on Elm Street in Greensboro, North Carolina. They refused to leave after they were denied service. This set off a wave of similar protests among black college students around the South. Louisiana had not yet been touched by protest. Blacks in New Orleans and Baton Rouge sat watchful and wary, waiting for a spark, waiting for a sign of change.

There was a group of us who seemed more interested in these events than did the campus at large, and, for some reason, we became centered in a political science class taught by Professor Adolph Reed. Reed was one of those rare teachers who forced students to analyze and question their world. He challenged us and pushed us and in so doing took risks for us. He'd pace in front of the class, chain-smoking while he worked up a drenching sweat in the warm Louisiana weather and lectured incisively on the Cold War, Eisenhower, the Supreme Court, or the vast economic gap between the haves and the have-nots. His eyes captured everything beneath his dark, heavy brow, and when he suddenly stopped, turned, and leaned back on his heels to question you, there was no escaping him.

Reed's class drew some of the brightest minds on Southern's campus, though not necessarily the students who made the best grades. Reed had a reputation as a heretic of sorts, and the students who signed up for his class were aware of this. They tended to be more political and perhaps off-center in their perception of things, and therefore open to Reed's often scathing analysis of the world. Indeed, Reed's commanding intelligence and incisive wit on all current topics and on black/white issues formed the focus of the class. "Why do black folks go around singing in their spirituals, 'Take all the world and give me Jesus,' as if that hasn't happened yet? Look around you—he's all you've got," Reed would quip with jarring irreverence. Other Southern professors weren't exactly talking that way. He was a gadfly, and he knew it. We eagerly absorbed his words. Though there was interplay between Reed and the class, most of us took his class not so much to discuss our views as to discover Reed's.

We were a mixed group from different areas of the country and with different personalities and beliefs. Most of us eventually would become involved in and committed to the protests that would rock Southern's campus. Charles Peabody from East St. Louis, Illinois, was a well-informed and articulate if somewhat free-spirited man who walked tall beneath a thin-brimmed hat and ran a rap, or slick talk, a mile a minute. He, Walter, and I often went drinking together Saturday afternoons at the Triangle Lounge, a dark hole of a bar in Scotlandville. Mack Jones, from Minden, Louisiana, a reserved, intense married man, was also in the class, along with James Thomas, an actor from New York City with a carefree, "kiss-my-ass" attitude and long curly hair. Then there was Major Johns, a twenty-eight-year-old reverend whose conversation was a steady mixture of scripture and politics and who never hesitated to call on the ladies in the name of the Lord. My brother, Walter, was also in the class. He was going through a period when he began to rethink a career in sports and to look instead at careers addressing social, political, and legal issues.

Although Reed's class provided our most open forum for discussion of race-oriented topics, the classroom talk of protest seemed largely remote, like peripheral reverberations of struggles elsewhere. Even so, just a stone's throw away on Capitol Hill, the Louisiana legislature in special session was passing a record thirty-five bills and four proposed constitutional amendments, spurred mainly by the impending integration of the Orleans Parish schools. I remember falling asleep in my dorm room at night as I listened to radio broadcasts of the legislative sessions, with fiery attacks on the "Fed'rl Guvment" and "integrationist judges."

At Southern, interest in the protests occurring in other cities seemed scattered at best. I assumed that Southern students didn't want to get involved. For the most part, they seemed like other college kids: they were more interested in having fun, going to dances, and even studying—as unlikely as that may sound—than in what was going on in Greyhound stations and dime stores throughout the South. Given what I presumed to be general apathy, I imagined that protest at Southern would be a lost cause. I would later discover that my assumptions couldn't have been more wrong.

Though I had not at that time heard of him, Shelby Jackson was in his third term as the powerful elected state superintendent of public education. A cagey politician with openly segregationist views, the sturdy-built, pleasant-faced man counted on blacks in Scotlandville and elsewhere for political support. As superintendent, Jackson served as an ex officio member of the Louisiana State Board of Education, which controlled all levels of state education, including Southern, with the notable exception of LSU. From Jackson's office suite on Capitol Hill overlooking Southern in the distance, he kept watchful eye on things at Southern.

Since January, Dr. Clark had reportedly been passing along certain unpleasant rumors that unnamed "organizers" were in the state working with students at Dillard, Xavier, Grambling, and Southern. As a result, by March 1960, Jackson and other board members were fairly well riled up.

On March 15, the State Board of Education issued a warning that any student participating in a sit-in would be "dealt with in a degree of discipline gauged according to the spirit of the violation of a law." When Dr. Clark called Jackson to ask him what that statement meant, Jackson replied, "The board means expulsion."

Following the board's pronouncement, Dr. Clark called a meeting of student leaders rumored to be planning demonstration activity, soliciting financial support within the community, or holding unauthorized student assemblies. He warned that the consequences of such a demonstration would be immediate and irrevocable separation from the university. Consequently, academic and administrative personnel began holding one-on-one conferences with suspect students in an effort to head off a demonstration. In addition, Dr. Clark invited community leaders to speak on campus about the inappropriateness of students demonstrating in the Baton Rouge community. The student leaders responded to this tactic by calling impromptu assemblies after university-sponsored movies and dances to permit pro-sit-in guest speakers equal time. And while student government president Marvin Robinson was severely and repeatedly chastised for his actions, he explained to an exasperated Dr. Clark that though he realized the board's orders should lawfully be observed, should he decide to go through with the demonstration activities, he would "individually accept the consequences, knowing I have achieved personal satisfaction." On March 25, in the midst of all this ruckus, Dr. Clark left for Washington, D.C., to attend an Eisenhower White House conference as one of the nation's top Negro educators.

Remarkable as it may seem, on the quiet afternoon of March 28, as I walked across campus to the student government offices in the student union building, I had no idea that all of this had been going on. Although I knew of the Board of Education's directive, had attended a couple of the student gatherings, and certainly considered myself knowledgeable about current events, the immediacy of these issues had no impact on me. Blame it on my unwillingness—conscious or unconscious—to jeopardize my education that first year and really get involved; blame it on my preoccupation with being a class president; or blame it on Dr. Clark, who had included only seven student leaders in his discussions with the local ministers, businessmen, and "organizers." It is difficult to understand how he imagined that including only seven out of five thousand students in these crucial discussions might be an effective strategy. In retrospect, it is a mystery why I didn't know what I should have known.

More to the point, it is an utter mystery how those seven kept to themselves their planning for what was to come. All I remember is that Monday afternoon I was deeply jarred, as if I had been violently shaken from head to toe. And I remember I wasn't alone in feeling I had been blindsided. When I arrived at the union, I found Oscar, my friend from the Lausanne train, and Peabody, from Reed's class, in one of the rooms. They were staring at each other, totally bewildered by the news that had just come over from the president's office. Seven Southern students, two women, and five men, had just been arrested in downtown Baton Rouge for sitting at the whites-only Kress lunch counter. We gaped at each other in disbelief, not sure whether this was cause for elation or for real fear, and then we hurried down to the student union director's office to await more news. As word of the arrests spread quickly throughout the campus, hundreds of students began gathering. Soon we learned that Marvin Robinson, the student body president, and Donald Moss, a second-year law student, were among the group. Slowly, as more news came in, the impact of what was happening began to dawn on us. The battle had come home at long last. And each of us knew there was no way we would not be swept up within it as well.

"Did you have any idea this was going to happen? Did you know they were going to do this?" I asked Peabody incredulously.

"No, man, this is news to me. I can't believe it. Why would they throw themselves into jail when they had to know they couldn't make any money off it?"

I laughed. "Is making money all you East St. Louis boys can think about?"

"No, man, but seriously, what did they think they were going to gain from this thing? I mean, bail is $1,500 per student. Who has that kind of money?"

"We've got to talk to Major Johns. I know he's involved in this thing. I'm willing to bet he knows what's going on, man. And he was right there in class with us while all this planning was going on. He never told us a thing," Peabody continued. "That man is a reverend, too. Can you believe that?"

Mrs. Hudson, the sympathetic union director, joined us. "I'm about ready to say I'll believe anything," she added, obviously worried. "What could Marvin be thinking? He has a wife and a young daughter. And Donald . . . with all that schooling? He just doesn't seem the type at all. What do they hope to gain from this?" Her anguished words echoed our own thoughts; we just didn't know. What was worse, we couldn't even imagine.

"Where is Johns?" I asked Peabody. "We've got to talk to somebody who can tell us something. C'mon, let's go."

Peabody shook his head very slowly. "Suit yourself, but I ain't moving from this spot. Any news that's news comes through the student union first. All we can do is wait." He pulled out a chair. "Have a seat."

"Okay, so we'll wait."

We waited. We wandered around the student union building through the poolroom and the snack bar, past the barber and the beauty shop. We sat out in the lobby. We sat in our office. We felt at once very much a part of what was happening—we certainly knew we would be affected by the outcome— and at the same time we were in the dark, left out in the cold. We knew we were very much at the mercy of many unfair segregation laws we had grown up with, laws we hated but that we knew were beyond our ability to either control or change. All we could do was wait and hope that somehow, someone would finally include us.

Eventually, word came that Major Johns was holding a meeting in University Stadium for the purpose of raising the student protestors' bail.

When we arrived at the stadium, we realized that the sit-in had indeed been planned and that several local black ministers and lawyers—many of them wealthy and influential—were backing the protestors. Suddenly it became clear that this was larger than just the campus community.

Major Johns spoke briefly but firmly, calling for whatever donation we could give to support the cause. "When the Board of Education spoke earlier this month, it became a challenge to all of us," he said. "Those seven students could not ignore it. And, we cannot ignore it, either. He then introduced several of the ministers who had offered their financial support, among them Reverend T. J. Jemison, a wealthy and influential black minister, who promised that the students would be released before sundown. Reverend Jemison was pastor of the largest middle-class black church in Baton Rouge, a church that, ironically, had among its congregation many of Southern's administration and faculty, including Dr. Clark. Jemison was not a reserved man and minced no words concerning his belief in civil rights and the value of protest. Most of us knew that he had led a bus boycott in Baton Rouge that was reported to have served as the model for the boycott in Montgomery, Alabama, and also that during this time he had had a close working relationship with Dr. King and his people. While Jemison had been quiet in the years preceding the Southern sit-ins, he had not been apathetic. In a time of crisis like this, he became a dynamo who easily could rally local black ministers, businessmen, and lawyers to join the cause. These formidable black community leaders formed the support base for the students who protested that day and over the next couple of years.

Throughout that late March afternoon, an electric, if naïve, excitement passed from student to student as initial word of the arrests and the "promised" release spread. After Major Johns had instructed us to rally at the student union at seven o'clock that evening, most of us spent the rest of the afternoon milling around the area talking and waiting. Besides our excitement, we felt a palpable sense of dread that things were spinning out of control. By sundown an artificial, strained quiet filled the building and the surrounding lawn as a cool breeze blew eastward from the Mississippi and the setting sun turned the sky from gold to red. Soon the media arrived, setting up their cumbersome cameras and huge lights on the steps outside the student center.

As darkness fell across the green lawns of the campus, our near-silent reverie was suddenly interrupted when the crowd of students spotted two long, black Cadillacs pulling onto the campus. Blinding TV klieg lights switched on as the two sleek, shiny cars worked their way into the center of the crowd, which parted before them like the Red Sea for Moses. Reverend Jemison climbed out of the lead car, beaming proudly for the cameras, his diamond stickpin glittering in the light. Reverend R. H. Tucker, Reverend W. T. Handy Jr., and attorney Johnny Jones followed him into the lights. But when the student protestors climbed out of those beautiful black cars, the crowd really erupted into cheers and applause. The delegation moved through the crowd and climbed onto a large platform truck that had been driven into the crowd earlier.

Student government president Marvin Robinson was the first to speak as he gestured broadly for calm. His strong, resonant voice echoed across campus and seemed to be carried into the night by the swirling muddy river at the edge of the campus. He began calmly, trying to reassure those of us who were wrestling to understand the events of that day: "Our act today was not a reckless or hostile act. We are not agitators. Our means are peaceful; our goals are simple. We are standing up for what we believe. . . . Segregation is wrong . . . and we believe the government of the State of Louisiana must recognize it."

I was riveted where I stood, filled at once with overwhelming surprise and bright admiration. This man, who was student government president and seemed to have everything going for him, a man we all respected, would stand on a truck and cast it all into the wind to challenge both the administration and the State of Louisiana in its own capital city. He was unquestionably making a sacrifice that was all the more meaningful because its proportions were unknown. From that night on, I had a deep and abiding respect for those whose convictions were so strong that they were willing to sacrifice and take risks in the face of overwhelming authority and legislative power. I had never before encountered such commitment—or such a man, for that matter. Here was a new kind of black man, it seemed to me, and that made all the difference. My first experience with civil disobedience—looking at the hard, determined faces of the students under the glare of the inescapable klieg lights and realizing what they had done—stayed with me, changed me, and no doubt changed the way I handled the rest of my stay at Southern, if not the rest of my life.

Then the defiant and determined student leader Major Johns spoke to us. He gave us an inspiring line that Victor Hugo had written about the French experience with revolution, a line that would become our slogan: "Our movement is a force stronger than the might of any army. It is an idea whose time has come."

Suddenly the humdrum, almost apathetic air of the campus exploded into a dynamic, intense, and emotional wind of change. We could believe that anything was not only possible but was probable. This wasn't just a prideful or assertive gesture we were witnessing; it was part of history. Marvin Robinson, Donald Moss, John Johnson, Kenneth Johnson, JoAnn Morris, Felton Valdry, and Janette Houston had lit a fire that would burn away irrevocably whatever was left of our idyllic, plantationlike university on the shores of the mighty Mississippi in this deeply southern state of Louisiana. We knew that conflagration would not be contained on our campus but that it would ignite the imagination of other black people across the state. We had no idea what was going to happen the next day. The university had to respond, but the question was how. Would the administration merely require an apology or retraction, or would they would follow through on their threat and expel the students from school? We felt as if we were behind the barricades waiting for the French troops to respond to our act of rebellion. We didn't know what our leaders had planned, or even if the protest could continue. And we didn't really know what our role was or what we could do to help. The only certainty among us who gathered that night was that we admired these seven protestors and that their cause was now our cause. We would be swept into it, and soundly buffeted by it, as surely as if the Mississippi itself had swept across the campus. While swept along, we all, in our own ways, would find ourselves challenged as never before.

> Which side are you on, boy?
> Which side are you on, my Lordy?
> Which side are you on, boy?
> Which side are you on?
> Oh, brother can you hear me?
> Tell me if you can.
> Will you be an Uncle Tom?
> Or will you be a man?
> —Lyrics adapted by civil rights activists
>   from a song by Florence Reese,
>   "Which Side Are You On?"

~ 5 ~
How to Kill a Protest

Ordinarily, a person leaving a courtroom with a conviction behind him would wear a somber face. But I left with a smile. I knew that I was a convicted criminal, but I was proud of my crime.
—MARTIN LUTHER KING JR., MARCH 22, 1956

THE NEXT DAY, John Garner and Vernon Jordan were apprehended by the Baton Rouge police for sitting at the whites-only lunch counter of Sitman's Drug Store. At about the same time, Larry Nichols, Conrad Jones, Eddie C. Brown, Lawrence Hurst, Charles L. Peabody, Sandra Jones, and Mary Briscoe were arrested at the Greyhound bus station for sitting at the whites-only terminal coffee shop. Charles Peabody—my whisky-drinking, high-living buddy who just twenty-four hours earlier had told me he couldn't see the point in such protest—was among the group, along with Conrad Jones, the reserved, married lawyer-to-be from Reed's class.

I couldn't believe it, but there it was. The spark had caught fire, and the fire was spreading. At this point, my involvement at the core of the protest was limited; I was carrying messages from the student leadership to the various dorm meetings and fund-raising rallies. I was still holding back, more an observer than an active participant. Had the protestors asked me to sit in with them at that point, I am not even sure I would have. I was not yet ready to take action or risk, not yet an initiator. I believed in the rightness of what the students were doing; but it simply never occurred to me to become more intimately involved. It was, I suppose, my year to just be eighteen, to watch and learn. But the seeds of change were firmly planted within my mind, just as they were in Scotlandville and Baton Rouge.

Later in the afternoon of March 29, Ulysses Jones, dean of men, sent out a notice that Dr. Clark had been called back to campus by Superintendent

Jackson. As the afternoon passed, state police arrived—also in response to Jackson's directive—and took up strategic positions throughout the campus, including along the only two roads leading onto the campus with the Mississippi River at its back. The police presence added significantly to the already extreme tension we were all feeling and transformed the pleasant cocoonlike atmosphere of Southern to that of an armed camp or prison. But who was being protected from whom? Did Jackson and Clark perceive us as potentially volatile, even dangerous? Did they feel physically threatened? That they perceived a need for state troops was not only insulting but foreboding. We could only guess what retaliation against the protestors they had in mind.

Dr. Clark arrived back on campus very early Wednesday morning and called an emergency universitywide convocation for 9:00 a.m. But the student leadership, following the advice of Reverend Jemison and his citizens' group, had already planned to call for a class boycott and a march to the State Capitol, so they moved the march up to 8:00 a.m. Boycotting was unanimous. Nearly three thousand students marched to the State Capitol, where they held an hour-long prayer meeting. I boycotted classes, but I didn't march. Later Oscar told me that Major Johns had spoken, and that all in all the protest had been surprisingly peaceful. No harsh words, no tear gas, no violence. It was a classic nonviolent expression of civil disobedience.

That afternoon, Clark met with Dean Jones and Martin Harvey, dean of students, and prepared orders for the expulsion of the sixteen students who had participated in the sit-ins and Major Johns. This action suddenly shifted the focus of the protest from the lunch counters to the university administration. Robinson, Johns, and Moss held another rally in front of a house on Swan Street, across the railroad tracks from the campus, and called for a continuing boycott until the seventeen students—nine of whom were still in jail—were reinstated. Speaking from a second-floor balcony, Robinson asked: "Which is more important—human dignity or the university? We feel it is human dignity."

The next morning, classrooms were empty, and Governor Earl K. Long, horrified at this turn of events, called Dr. Clark to the Capitol for still more protracted meetings. Meanwhile, Major Johns was delivering a spine-tingling speech from the balcony on Swan Street calling for Southern students to withdraw, "five thousand strong." It was a move designed to bring the university administration to heel. Without students there could be no university. It was a powerful strategy that could not go unanswered.

It was just after 8:00 a.m. on March 31 when Johns stood on that balcony, holding one arm straight up in the air above him, and compared the position of the expelled students to that of Martin Luther when the church called upon him to recant. It was a powerful analogy, evoking an action that had cast Europe into three hundred years of tumult. "I shall not, I cannot recant," he paraphrased Luther. "Here I stand."

"It is our desire, the desire of your brothers and sisters who have been expelled and who are now in jail, that you withdraw from school, all of you, five thousand strong. We do not want you to return to class until Marvin tells you to. We must all stand together in this—all of us."

Then Robinson spoke: "There are certain people in the United States today who are living in legalized slavery. Do you know who you are? We can't do this; we can't do that; we can't do the other. We are calling upon you to awaken the moral conscience of our fellow citizens through the use of 100 percent passive, nonviolent resistance to this slavery."

The crowd cheered; this was language they could understand and relate to.

"Negroes who claim to be satisfied with the present situation fall into one of three categories. One, they are either too scared or they haven't got enough sense; or two, they're making more profit from segregation than they would from integration, and they like living in a luscious jail; or three, they're lying to themselves and everyone around them." Robinson commended the police for their cooperation during the march and encouraged the students to attend an organ recital Thursday night. "We need all the culture we can get," he said simply.

That afternoon, some two thousand students lined up at the registrar's office and began filling out pink slips, sending shock waves went through the administration building. The university was being dismantled. Later that afternoon, for reasons we were never quite sure of, the organ recital was canceled.

As the boycott entered its fourth day, Dr. Clark returned from another meeting with Governor Long and Superintendent Jackson and informed the deans, faculty, and community supporters that the future of Southern University, his university—or, more succinctly, *his* future *at* the university—was in jeopardy. State legislators were pressing for a complete change in administration, cuts in the flow of state funds to the school, and direct supervision by state authorities of a new "get-tough" policy at the school. Dr. Clark then mapped out a strategy designed to bring maximum pressure upon the university community, the students, and the alumni to support and repair the damage already done to the university. The now desperate administrators began calling on community leaders who had supported the protest and Southern alumni in scattered areas of the state. Days later, this new group of black business and academic leaders met with Clark to plan a new strategy for restoring order at the now chaotic campus. After a short morning conference, they emerged and issued an urgent plea for the protest leaders to meet with them that afternoon. When Johns, Robinson, and Moss agreed, the meeting was scheduled to start at 5:00 p.m. at the guest house, which sits adjacent to the student union in the center of campus.

As the time approached, hundreds of students began gathering on the vast green lawn in front of the guest house. Alumni leaders, local attorneys, administration officers, and the student protestors had to weave their way through the ever-growing crowds sweating in the April sun. As we had just days earlier, the entire student body eventually assembled to wait for word of what was going on. As before, the media arrived, setting up their cumbersome cameras and huge floodlights. As the afternoon passed, community leaders and alumni came and went from the guest house, but we students received no information. Tension grew almost unbearably as we waited and speculated. We hoped against hope that our leaders would emerge to tell us the boycott and protest would continue until the administration readmitted them and the state pledged significant steps toward desegregation. But in that warm April afternoon, even the most positive among us began to falter. When night came, the klieg lights threw a ghostly glare over the ground, rudely illuminating each face. Spirits dwindled. The meeting had lasted too long.

Finally, shortly after midnight, the door of the guest house opened. A tangible sense of foreboding swept over the crowd as Marvin, Don, and Major Johns walked out into the brilliant media klieg lights as if from a darkened cave. They immediately headed for a school bus at the edge of the lawn and climbed on top of it to address the hushed crowd.

"The protest is over," Marvin said haltingly, his voice no longer strong or proud. "We are leaving the university. Now you must end the boycott and return to classes."

"Our effort was not wasted," Donald Moss continued. "We made our point. Segregation is wrong, and one day it will be abolished. But now you must concentrate on the survival of this school and the completion of your studies.

"If we continue in the direction we have started, it has been made very clear to us that Southern University will be destroyed, and all it represents for the black community will be lost. If that happens, all we have gained through this long protest will be lost," Major Johns added, with an uncharacteristic absence of fire or passion. "Go back to your dorms. It's over. Go home."

For a few minutes, no one moved. We stood stunned, staring blankly at the school bus. Disbelieving what we had heard, some of us refused to accept what we were being told. Finally, comments could be heard coming from the crowd.

"What's going on? What are they talking about?

"What do they mean, it's over? How could it be over?"

"Hey, we want to quit too!"

Major Johns heard all this and spoke again. "This is best. If the school survives, we survive."

"But, you're leaving! Are they making you leave?"

"We have reached the decision on our own," he said slowly. "The administration agreed not to dismiss anyone else if we agreed to leave." He climbed down from the bus.

Throughout the crowd, you could hear people crying. What had gone wrong? How could this have happened? It wasn't supposed to end this way. We watched the media people rush to get a statement from Dr. Clark, who smiled as he assured viewers and readers that tomorrow all would be back to normal.

"Normal? Normal! What's normal anymore?"

"Does he expect us to forget all this?"

"WHAT WENT WRONG?"

And then the floodlights clicked off with an echoing suddenness, leaving a shadowy night to engulf the crowd of students. For a while there was no movement, and then one by one we began to drift back to our dorms in the pitch-blackness. The halting, almost pitiful words of our leaders played over and over in our minds, and our own confusions played again and again on our lips. For the rest of the night, we debated; we searched our souls for strength and understanding. Many of us cried. We cried in exhaustion and with a strange and overwhelming sense of irretrievable loss.

The next week was characterized by confusion and feelings of unresolved conflict as we struggled to come to grips with what had happened. On April 4, the nine remaining jailed students were released on bond. Even so, the suspension orders remained in place for all seventeen protesters, and they were ordered off campus, which angered many of us. The reality of it was so much harsher than the words. We had been beaten—soundly, resoundingly beaten—by the forces of segregation. After all, the boycott and protest were over, and it seemed unreasonable and even vengeful that the administration would want more from the students they now ruled. Sadly, any point they were trying to make was lost on most of us; we weren't listening. We still believed in the value and rightness of what the leaders had stood up for, and we knew our shared beliefs remained intact. We didn't blame them for agreeing to halt the protest because we knew they hadn't given in because their convictions had faltered. Much later, we discovered that the pressures they had wrestled with during their almost eight hours of meetings were extreme. They had been threatened and badgered. Administrators and alumni leaders had told them repeatedly that if the protest continued, the school and all it represented for the black community would be utterly wrecked. And they had been told that their own careers and aspirations would be ruined. During the negotiations, the administrators had even gone so far as to phone the families of the leaders, urging them to plead with their sons and daughters to come to their senses.

In the end, Dr. Clark's gamble paid off. But while he may have broken the back of the protest, he also shattered the spirit of Southern's students. Ultimately, most of the students who completed withdrawal forms were not allowed to withdraw without parental signatures, which dared the students to call their parents to secure permission. Obviously, the brave ones who did call their parents were subjected to parental scoldings and demands to straighten up. Adding insult to injury, the citizens' group that had offered to provide transportation money to any student who withdrew from the university suddenly met with Dr. Clark, called back this pledge, and announced that their funds could be used only for bail.

Then Dr. Clark reneged on his promise to the leaders and expelled one more student, closeting himself in seclusion, a nerve-racked and distraught victim of the dialectic of social strife (and social progress) that destroys all middle ground and middle-of-the-road administrators with grindstone pressure. Perhaps developing a backbone under such pressure requires a deep, strong belief.

The rest of the spring of my first year passed in an unfocused blur, not combative but not entirely peaceful either. I tried to sort out what I thought about it all and what it meant to me while I went about the business of arranging dances and holding freshman class meetings. I wasn't sure where I fit in.

I did know the campus had changed. It was no longer an island, a safe, paternal plantation where Felton Clark made everything right. Our trust of the administration and faculty was severely damaged. With our sense of safety diminished, we weren't so quick to nod and smile. Southern had entered the world of the civil rights movement. It could no longer live aloof from outside pressures and realities. It couldn't hide. Southern was now part of the mainstream struggle. And, I thought, as I rode the train home that summer, so was I.

~ 6 ~

Encounters of the NSA Kind

This is to advise that segregation must stay in our schools if we are to have a public school system. I do not know of any place in the Bible or in the Constitution of the United States that says schools must be integrated. I have been working on the development of the public education program in this state for 36 years as well as contributing my efforts and services to the entire South and the Nation. I know of the needs of all people and have helped to develop our educational system to where it is today. I know what is best for both races; therefore, as citizens and Christian people, it is necessary to stand up and see that RIGHT prevails, and that we do not have communistic movements thrust upon us to tear down our way of life. The education of children is important, but it is more important to have OUR WAY OF LIFE and sovereignty of the State saved than to be overrun as many have experienced in other nations. . . . Please be assured that it is necessary to stand firm against these movements to tear down our way of life.

—SHELBY M. JACKSON, STATE SUPERINTENDENT, DEPARTMENT OF EDUCATION, BATON ROUGE, A LETTER TO CONCERNED CITIZENS, SEPTEMBER 12, 1960

IN THE AFTERMATH of the protest, what remained of the student government appointed Paul Lewis, student government president-elect, and me to represent Southern at the National Student Association (NSA) Congress in Minneapolis the following August. The NSA had become a strong collective force on the American political scene. Lobbied and courted by politicians and special-interest groups, the NSA was viewed, like no other student organization before or since, as the premier representative of a growing student constituency. Americans believed, during this period of history, that students did have political views and that their pressing concerns would determine how they would vote or whether they would vote at all. Therefore, political activists of every type fought for support on the NSA convention floor while the national media intently followed the goings-on and swiftly labeled the prevailing liberal or conservative view as the "student voice."

In the early 1960s, the NSA tried to harness the power of these competing interests for different purposes. For the white students, it was a new phenomenon; they were only beginning to recognize their strength. And for the black students, who were outnumbered by whites at the NSA conferences by about ten to one, it was a recent phenomenon in the context of the sit-in movement. Around the country, NSA members had already begun to make their break from the establishment. The stance that the primarily white NSA took on the sit-in movement would not change the movement itself, but its endorsement or lack of endorsement of the movement was important because it would be taken to represent the views of a national student body. If the delegates at the convention voted to support it, they would be presenting the sit-in movement as a *student,* not just a *Negro,* protest. However, if they refused their support, they would abandon their developing power as students and lend credence to the segregationists.

In a few short years, this collective white student body would use the civil rights movement as a prototype for their own protests against the Vietnam War. More than any proclamation by the NSA, the advent of the Vietnam protests that the white students would call their own unified a student movement and made us all, black and white, if not necessarily fighters for the same cause, at least brothers in arms.

Ironically, the NSA—the first sieve through which this newfound student power was poured—was funded through the student government treasuries of all the member colleges and universities, which made it a legitimate establishment organization. And because the NSA was neither renegade nor extremist, it was respected rather than feared. In the mid-1960s, the organization's credibility took a severe blow when it was revealed that the U.S. Central Intelligence Agency (CIA) had been channeling funds and influence through the NSA's International Students operations to manipulate students in other countries. The CIA involvement was largely unknown to the four hundred American campus affiliates, and it would have been unwelcome to most of the NSA's campus student leaders, who strongly opposed the 1950s-era communist witch hunts of the House Un-American Activities Committee and government intrusion into the lives of citizens.

For a few years in the early 1960s—before the more radical Students for a Democratic Society formed—the NSA provided the only political forum where students could meet, reflect, and be creative as both students and American citizens. The SDS carried the student movement sharply to the left of the NSA, first meeting in 1962 in Port Huron, Michigan. There they developed an activist student manifesto known as the Port Huron Statement, which called on students to break with the establishment and their parents' generation with a confrontation -driven movement against nuclear weapons, and racial and economic injustice. They were also building a youthful Left to vigorously challenge the calculated conservative effort to smear as communist anyone fighting for change,

During the pivotal 1960 NSA Minneapolis convention, we enjoyed a special freedom beyond the watchful eyes of our administrators, and at the same time we had an additional safeguard because we were there with our administrators' blessings. I have no doubt that Dr. Clark would have hurried to withdraw Southern from the NSA if he had had any suspicion that his students might return to Southern with radical, disruptive ideas, and I feel sure the same would have been true of the administrators at other southern schools.

By the time I made the first trip to the University of Minnesota, news of the sit-in demonstrations in the Deep South had swept the nation, challenging the very order of American government. Debate raged on college campuses everywhere as students strove to determine the wisdom, legality, and propriety of the surging civil rights movement. This was true in Minneapolis that summer, and, indeed, it was the primary focus of the NSA conference. The mood when I arrived, however, was even more tense than most of us had expected. After the initial wave of sit-ins in early 1960, Curtis Gans, the national affairs vice president of the NSA, had issued a public statement endorsing and supporting the Negro protests. Given the highly sensitive, emotional nature of the protests and the inevitable political impact the endorsement would have, Gans's statement enraged many student leaders, especially those from the South. When we gathered that August, the overriding preoccupation of the congress revolved around a move to censure Gans—a move that, if successful, would destroy any unity of purpose that might otherwise have developed. Students divided into opposing camps, some gathering to organize a complaint against Gans, and others, like myself, participating in liaison meetings with Gans and a small group of East Coast campus leaders. Among these leaders were Paul Potter from Oberlin, the NSA president-elect; Tom Hayden, campus organizer and strategist; and Barney Frank, a fast-moving and hard-fighting Harvard delegate who coordinated the fight against censure.

Now, I must make it clear that I did not go to the convention with any specific objectives in mind. I wanted to go because, quite simply, I had been asked; it was a prestigious thing to do, and it gave me the chance to go someplace new and see what was going on. I carried no torch to Minneapolis, no burning desire to change anyone else's mind or even to speak my own. I was an observer. And when I arrived at the University of Minnesota campus, nothing I saw surprised me much. Those two weeks marked my first experience with one-on-one conversation with whites. Although I realize this may sound like a momentous occasion—and I suppose to some extent it was, if only in the obvious difference in environment—the initial impact on me wasn't great.

The white kids looked, acted, and talked just like I expected them to, just like they did on TV. When I walked into the convention room, I saw hundreds of well-groomed, pale-faced kids trying to live up to their parents' expectations. My stereotype of whites—based on what I had seen in the families on TV, in politicians, and in whites I had worked for—remained intact: they seemed to presumptuously believe that they had all the answers. The students at the NSA convention—even the 80 percent of them from the North—seemed, for the most part, no different. In fact, I found their presumptuousness even more irritating. Here they were, heatedly debating civil rights issues when most of them knew full well the outcome made no difference to them because the only blacks in their communities were servants. They were so arrogant that—despite their profound ignorance of the black experience—they were going to tell all the Negroes within earshot how they should act with *other* white people.

Even so, I still had a lot of idealism and hope, and I gave most of them the benefit of the doubt. I knew they were only human: they had five fingers; they got scared; they drank beer; and they turned red—that last was different, of course, and good for a laugh among blacks. I realized that many of them were just doing and saying what they had been told . Their understanding of me was as set and limited as mine was of them. Open discussion of why we Negroes were the way we were—or even the attempt at such discussion—was brand-new conceptual territory, and some of the students didn't appreciate having to think about it at all. Some quite frankly wished we'd all go back to the Negro schools where we belonged. But, then, the NSA was by majority a white organization. It served an important role in the evolution of white, not black, student activism. Black student activism was already under way and would become an unstoppable force. So we talked—what else could we do? We tried to force white discussion out of the realm of the theoretical and ideal and into the real and the actual. That ours was an awkward, terribly uncomfortable position was not generally appreciated by any of us.

That first afternoon, before I could unpack my bags, I found myself standing in the middle of a group of whites who were all firing questions at me about the sit-ins. It seemed that most northern white delegates were itching to "help," and every southern white delegate was equally anxious to prove the protests were just an unfortunate, overblown misunderstanding— if not merely reckless lawbreaking. The questions droned on, day in and day out, for two weeks: "Is the situation down there as bad as the newspapers report?" "Is it worse?" "What makes you think you can get away with this?" "How do you feel as a southern Negro student?" "Don't ya'all understand you're breaking the law?" While the theme of the congress was expressed in its title, "Students in Action—A World in Transition," the overwhelming topic of discussion was the sit-ins and whether to support the fight for desegregation.

As the convention progressed, I got the definite impression that not only was the general consensus of opinion pro-desegregation, but also that the NSA—at least politically and publicly (if not necessarily in practice in every delegate's hometown)—would come out in favor of the sit-in movement and pass a resolution backing it. But sometimes, in late-night dorm debates or arguments over dinner or a beer in the lounge, this feeling was hard to remember. I tried to remind myself that, regardless of who won any particular argument or what conclusions were drawn, when they got on the airplane or train that was taking them back to school, these white kids were going to be the same white kids they had been when they had arrived. It didn't matter. All we were doing in those late-night debates was bruising each other and banging one another around . . . and we were doing it probably, quite simply, because for the first time in our lives we could get away with it. It was a new experience, and sometimes it felt good. Sure, there was anger and hostility and some yelling and screaming, but not a whole lot was accomplished. That is to say, nothing beyond the interaction was accomplished, and, in retrospect, perhaps the interaction was accomplishment enough.

I remember a short, stocky, combative black delegate from Texas who would tirelessly argue with a crowd of whites until three or four in the morning, if they kept at him. "You white folks have a whole lot of nerve trying to characterize blacks as uncivilized," he said, forcefully, but without malice. "By what right have you appropriated for yourselves a premium on civilization? Remember it was your so-called civilization that kidnapped our forebears and enslaved them by the most barbaric violations of human decency and dignity. Do you dare to censure us for raising our voices in protest of your historic degradation of our people?"

The white students would sit absolutely motionless in the lounge, rapt with attention. One night a white delegate from Alabama responded: "But you folks can't take the law into your own hands. You're breaking the law down there. That's the point. Sure, I'm in favor of desegregation. I don't have anything against colored, but I think y'all ought to have your own schools and restaurants. If the laws are wrong, then the thing to do is to go to the legislatures and get them changed. There are a lot of southern schools in this association, and already of lot of them want to drop out over this thing. It's getting more and more difficult for those of us who support the NSA to keep our schools in." He took a deep breath. "What it boils down to is that this association shouldn't be getting involved and taking sides without knowing all the facts."

"Facts?" asked the Texan. "Okay, let's talk about the facts. Let's take these laws, the very laws you keep talking about, laws you violate with impunity to trample on the rights of our people. Let me explain this to you—listen close. Any of your laws that set secondary and inferior terms for us have no legitimacy," he stated with careful emphasis. "We will not obey them."

"But you are a citizen of this country . . ."

"Being a citizen by birth doesn't make you a member of the club, now, does it?"

"I don't understand."

"I didn't think you did."

One night the topic turned to miscegenation and the fanatic segregationist fears that integration would destroy the purity of the races. After several rounds on that topic, the Texan had had about enough: "Who's to say miscegenation wouldn't do the white race a lot of good? No, seriously. White people go around comparing blacks to monkeys, don't you?" He looked across the table at four puzzled faces. "Sure you do. But now I'm asking you to take a good look at yourself, and a good look at me, and a good look at a monkey and compare similarities. Look at that hair all over your skin. Those thin lips.

You tell me who looks more like a chimpanzee? Why don't you stop putting black people down and take a good look in the mirror?" They were shocked, they were insulted, but they laughed. But one way or the other, their assumptions were challenged . . . many for the first time in their lives.

It was in these kinds of dialogues that the notion of white guilt arose—the idea that if I, a black man, tell a white person the truth about how I feel, then I'm playing on their guilt and trying to make them feel bad. In 1960, though no one used those terms because the experience of interaction was so new, the same feelings were very much present. Later, the same conversations we had that summer would be dismissed as "unfair" because the blacks actually answered the questions they were asked. We would be accused of manipulating white people's emotions by exploiting their guilty consciences. "Don't lay a guilt trip on me" would become a common white defense. It sounds less self-implicating than "It's not my fault," or "I can't do anything about it anyway," but it means the same thing. Of course, in the later 1960s and into the 1970s, as dialogue between blacks and whites became more common, some blacks did exploit the interaction by trying to make whites feel guilty or personally responsible for the black situation (whether real or exaggerated). Blacks frequently took advantage of whites and used them for selfish purposes rather than trying to convert the white person to their way of thinking or their view of the world, which is really the only legitimate reason for that kind of dialogue. The goal is to change someone's mind, not to badger them into giving you something.

So if nothing else, we established a degree of interaction that summer that broke new ground in race relations. A lot of it was unnecessary and painful for most of us: I'm sure that we went back to our colleges with minds unchanged. But at least we had been confronted with each other's prejudices face to face. This sort of sharing for its own sake by representatives of a broad cross-section of America was an unheard-of and wonderful thing.

One white female delegate explained her feelings at one of our last group meetings: "I've never attended an interracial conference before, and I was honestly quite stunned to find upon my arrival that I was rooming with a Negro girl. Here I was, a southerner from the heart of Georgia, complete with my prejudice against Negroes as a race. And in this smug little world of mine where apathy prevailed, I was for the first time exposed to interracial contact on an egalitarian basis. All my life my concept of the Negro had been of a semi-free servant, good enough to ride on the front of trains and the back of buses and sit in the top of theaters. While speaking out for racial equality, I had never really believed a Negro to be my equal on any basis. However, during the conference my roommate became to me a fellow student."

So undoubtedly there were whites who, consciously or unconsciously, gained a greater respect for, or at least a broader knowledge of, the Negroes back home once they had dealt with those of us at the convention who had no particular reason to defer to them. The experience certainly helped me to realize that it was an error to perceive white people as a monolithic group of incorrigible racists.

Racism, I concluded, is not genetically determined. And even where it does exist blatantly or in more insidious forms, it can be undermined. You undermine it, I began to realize, by attacking the system that supports it or the safe assumptions that the bigoted person sets up like a barricade around his life. You do this not only through one-on-one interaction and confrontation but also by keeping the issue in front of him, right there in his hometown, so it becomes very difficult for him to ignore his racial feelings and the consequences of those feelings when they are translated into the real day-to-day world. The NSA convention gave me some satisfaction along those lines. The new experience of conversational interaction gave me a chance to show the whites I wasn't some dumb kid who had just gotten off the boat. Moreover, it helped me to realize that I could look whites straight in the eyes and assure them that the assumptions they were born and raised to hold onto would have to stop at the door when they got to my house.

Although the battle lines at the NSA convention were clearly drawn at the start, and all of us were fully armed with lifelong assumptions about each other, as the week progressed, the one-on-one interaction among the students, the sharing of personal experiences, and the desire for a better world took precedence over fear and doubt. As the *facts* were repeated over and over, those opposed to the sit-ins began listening rather than blindly defending the system. There was nothing idyllic about it, however. The struggle was harsh and the polarization sometimes disillusioning as speaker after speaker took the convention floor.

A panel of guest speakers finally brought the meeting to an emotional peak and resolution. Sandra Cason, who later married Tom Hayden, was the first speaker. A striking white woman from the University of Texas, she had participated in sit-ins in Austin. In a soft voice made weighty by her southern accent, she talked about the rightness of the struggle and of her personal commitment—against substantial opposition and many obstacles—to work for integration and Negro rights.

The next speaker was a white man from the Young Americans for Freedom who took strong exception to the association's support of the sit-in movement. "Thousands of students across this country believe that integration is wrong," he nearly screamed from the podium. "Integration will only hurt both races. Show your support for freedom and for the American way of life, walk out of this convention with me. Stand firm against integration." He received only scattered applause.

Then Donald Moss, one of the leaders of the Southern protests that spring, stepped to the podium. The chamber grew completely quiet as Don drew graphic and striking pictures of the cruel toll exacted from blacks on the altar of white supremacy. Don was tall, curly-haired, and light-skinned, which may have made him appear less threatening than a darker black to many of these whites in their first encounter with a black militant. But when he spoke, his clear voice became relentlessly uncompromising, and his features hardened with passion. All eyes focused on him as he told of the early constitutional compromise when the Founding Fathers decreed that Negroes be counted as only three-fifths of a person, and then he traced the legacy of this decision. He spoke about the destruction of families, police abuses, the absence of schools, the constant scratching for survival. Most especially, he drew into focus—more succinctly than anyone else had—the major issue of the convention, the reason we had all come to Minnesota, and the challenge we would take with us back to our homes and colleges.

"What is it about white folks that makes it so essential for them to deny us Negroes the right to pee in a public place?" he asked with jarring directness. "What is it that makes them feel justified in forcing us to the back doors and back alleyways to eat or get a drink of water?" He paused and surveyed the crowd of young, expectant faces. "I cannot answer that question. But I know that we Negroes in the South have vowed that that day is over."

When he finished speaking, many of us rose to our feet, crying and applauding. We locked arms and stood together, releasing a week of emotion and conflict. For the first time, I realized the overwhelming rational, legal, and ethical force of the civil rights movement. In listening to Donald Moss explain the unavoidable injustice of a legal system—a legal system of the world's most powerful democracy and the freest land, no less—that at its inception chose not to recognize certain of its citizens as fully human, I was moved as no other argument had moved me.

In my freshman year I was young and hesitant. I could call for my fellow Southern students to rise up against South African apartheid, but I could not sit in at a segregated lunch counter in Baton Rouge. Like many others of my race, I did not see an immediate need for participation in the American fight for equality. At that point, the issues were not clear enough or horrifying enough to me personally to put completing my education at risk in order to participate in the movement that would force the recognition of our right to equality. But after the NSA convention, I was a changed man. I felt the universal force of the civil rights movement for the first time. The movement was not based on a series of isolated incidents in backward areas of the country, and its issues were not best left to others or things that would work themselves out. The Negro movement questioned the very structural fabric of the whole country. What I heard at the NSA convention was nothing less than a rational, legal, and ethical call for wholesale change in the condition of the black community. The success of the movement was utterly important, and it involved everyone.

I realized this was especially true if you were a student with a passionate intolerance for injustice. I began to see that I was no different from Emmitt Till, or the high school students in Little Rock, or the women on a Montgomery bus. I had been more directly involved in the convention than in any other student effort. Though perhaps still unknown to myself, I was preparing for action. Two days after the speeches, in an unprecedented action, the thirteenth National Student Association Congress went on record backing the sit-in movement and committing money and manpower to its support.

~ 7 ~

NSA Summer Camp Transformations

When you return to your campuses and someone asks you, "Why are you knocking your head against the wall to take a position on all the challenges facing the world in the 1960s? After all, when we get out of this place, we have to be concerned with those things. Now, ye gods, we've got Chem 313. We've got Saturday night Tri Delt formal and the prom three weeks later. We've got Homecoming and parents' weekend and the carnival. We've got lots of things to be concerned with. Why are you introducing this kind of havoc into our lives?" I wonder what your answer is going to be to them.
—DONALD HOFFMAN, PAST PRESIDENT, USNSA, SEPTEMBER 4, 1960

M Y SOPHOMORE YEAR at Southern passed without a great deal of conflict. You needed a B average to run for student office, and my average came to a B–, so I began working instead as the announcer for the ROTC drill team and writing a weekly column in the *Southern Digest*. I called the column "Campus Exposé," and wrote about activities on campus, occasionally criticizing the administration's policies or attitudes. Also that winter, when Paul Lewis appointed me NSA campus co-ordinator, he and I wrote a series of articles on the issues discussed at the NSA convention. In those articles, I tried to suggest—without being too strident or obvious—the immense discrepancy between the world of the Southern student and the world of those with wealth and power on the outside. "How do you come back to your university and say to your fellow students, 'Students, from our experiences at the congress, we have found we are behind in our in-tellectual pursuits and academic endeavors?' This is something which needs to be said. But will our cries be heard? Will our ideas be understood? South-ern is a remarkable institution, comparatively high in the South in its educa-tional and cultural standings, but we must go higher," I wrote in December.

I didn't want to turn people off by preaching at them, but I wanted so desperately to pass on some of what I had learned. Increasingly, I viewed the student debates in Minnesota as a signal that we needed to broaden our awareness at Southern and become more serious of purpose. But of course, the distractions of college life, just as Donald Hoffman foretold, kept almost everyone occupied with other, more entertaining things.

And certainly I participated in college life just like everyone else, while I used my column to blow off steam—that is, until Dr. Clark decided such a release was no longer needed. My final "Exposé" came out on March 23, 1961. In it, I wrote about the events of a year ago that very week, when the students of Southern had marched on downtown Baton Rouge, exhibiting an unsurpassed spirit of dignity and pride. I asked where that pride had gone.

"I speak of the ROTC band and drill team and their splendid march behind the horses in the LSU Livestock Show parade through downtown Baton Rouge even though it was segregated and degrading to the morals and character of any organization forced to take a position in the rear," I wrote. "As I watched this typical outrageous spectacle, I wondered what had happened to that spirit of dignity and pride which just a year before could easily be seen in the eyes and felt in hearts of every Southern student. Have we cut off ourselves from the real meaning of the 'cause' we envisioned a year ago this week? If so, then would it not have been better if the 'cause' had never occurred? If our campus is again engulfed in conformity and complacency, then what has been our gain?" I asked not for demonstrations, not for violent action, but simply for manly and dignified actions in our daily lives to regenerate the spirit of 1960.

Governor Jimmy Davis, who had been keeping a close watch on Southern since the events of the previous spring, was none too pleased with my article and let Dr. Clark know it. Consequently, Clark called me to his office along with the newspaper advisor, a proud and talented journalist, Thelma Thurston Gorham, and read us the riot act, demanding that I write a retraction of the column. I refused. Exasperated, he told me a couple of times that he had hoped I would be smarter than that. Finally, he said that not only was he changing the name of the column from "Campus Expose" to "Strolling the Campus," but that he would personally approve all future issues before printing. So, for the remainder of the year I wrote harmless columns about fraternity quarrels and cafeteria food while I eagerly followed the news. Every day the headlines traced a growing confrontation over race in the South:

Legal Questions Provoked by Sit-Ins Now Faced by U.S. Supreme Court
February 4, 1961. The sixteen Southern sit-iners were convicted on the
grounds of "disturbing the peace." NAACP attorneys had challenged
the convictions and filed three petitions declaring them unconstitutional, marking the first time that legal tests arising from the sit-in
movement had reached the Supreme Court. The lawyers said the cases
raised the fundamental issue of whether the "State could use its power
to compel racial segregation in private establishments open to the public and to stifle protests against racial segregation." The convictions
were based on a Louisiana statute that makes it a "Crime to act in such
a manner as to unreasonably disturb or alarm the public." The State
courts found that the continued presence of the Negro students at the
white counter might have caused such "unreasonable alarm."

"Hate Riders" Plan Strategy in New Orleans Today
May 24, 1961. American Nazi Party members, traveling in a painted
"Hate Bus," picketed the NAACP and CORE headquarters and a New
Orleans theater showing the movie "Exodus."

Little Rock Gets New Integration—Board to Desegregate Five More
Schools in the Fall
May 26, 1961. The school board announced that they would increase
from eleven to forty-nine the number of negroes in racially mixed
classes. Governor Orval E. Faubus warned that if the NAACP would
settle for nothing less than total integration, "If and when total integration comes, you will have a degrading of the public school system.
. . . School authorities will then find it necessary to employ additional
policemen to keep order and to protect teachers."

Negro Group Issues Freedom-Ride Call
May 26, 1961. In Atlanta, the Student Non-Violent Coordinating Com-
mittee called on student members throughout the South to become
Freedom Riders from Birmingham to New Orleans.

Mississippi Court Fines 27 for Test at Bus Terminal
May 27, 1961. Twenty-seven Freedom Riders were found guilty of
ignoring police orders to leave the white waiting room of a Trailways
Bus station in Jackson. James Farmer, national director of CORE, the
Congress of Racial Equality, was convicted.

Asks I.C.C. to End Bus Segregation

May 30, 1961. Attorney General Robert Kennedy moved to wipe out racial segregation on interstate busses and terminals serving them. In petitioning the I.C.C., he referred to the mob action, violence and arrests in Birmingham and Montgomery, Alabama and Jackson, Mississippi resulting from Freedom Rides. A significant provision of the new regulations would ban the use of signs separating portions of the terminal facilities on the basis of race. This was aimed at ending the widespread Southern custom of labeling one waiting room for "Colored Intrastate Passengers Only" in order to encourage all Negroes, whether local or interstate passengers, to use that room.

Alabama Orders Recall of Guard

May 31, 1961. The thirteen Freedom Riders were charged with breach of peace and are being held on $500 bond in Jackson, MS. This brings the total number of Freedom Ride arrests to sixty-five since the rides began last week. The Freedom Riders said they would fast to emphasize their mission to the public and win Federal intervention in their effort to desegregate transportation in the South.

U.S. Court Enjoins Freedom Riders in Alabama Trips

June 3, 1961. In his fifteen-page order, Judge Frank M. Johnson, Jr. conceded that white and Negro demonstrators might be within their rights, but they caused an "undue burden and restraint on interstate commerce." He ordered Freedom Riders to halt tests of segregation of public transportation in Alabama. He also enjoined Ku Klux Klansmen and others to let interstate buses alone.

As my sophomore year ended, I was invited to attend the NSA-sponsored Southern Students Human Relations Seminar at the University of Wisconsin. Its purpose was to bring together eighteen carefully selected college students, nine Negroes and nine whites, who were all from southern and border states. For three weeks, we were to be isolated in the resortlike cottages and dormitories of the university, where we would live together while we read and studied the questions of race in America.

As I boarded a Delta jet for my first flight, I was at once excited at the opportunity to meet with other southern students on such an intimate basis and, after my experience at the NSA convention, a bit apprehensive about what would actually happen. I wondered what the attitudes of the white students would be, whether they would come to the seminar with open minds, ready to discuss real-world issues, or whether they would be blind to the world around them or even hostile. I wondered if the Negro students would be more politically mature than I was.

From Memphis to St. Louis the ride was smooth and comfortable. I marveled silently that I was more than thirty thousand feet in the air and breathing and eating and looking down at the clouds. Technology was pulling man into a fearless future, I thought, but our fear of each other was holding us back. The last leg of the journey, from Chicago to Madison in a twin-engine prop plane, left me no room for such philosophizing. A few minutes out of Chicago, we flew into a thunderstorm that shook the plane with such force that I forgot everything but my own heartbeat and prayed for the ground.

Eventually I was met at the airport and driven to the university campus, where a meeting was already in progress. The two NSA staff officers who were leading the seminar, Connie Currie and Reverend Will Campbell, were orienting everyone to the program. Connie, a white woman in her thirties, had studied and worked on human rights issues in Atlanta. Will, the leader of the group, was a clergyman from the Nashville area. A balding, gentle man in his late forties, Will spoke with a southern hill country accent and was an avid lover of country music who, it turned out, would frequently serenade us on his banjo. Both were very accessible and nonjudgmental people.

As I walked into the dormitory lounge, however, the first person who caught my eye was a big white fellow sitting with his back to me, one cowboy boot crossed over the opposite knee, slouched down in his chair. His hair was slick and curled back in the pompadour style so popular among rural southerners, and he was speaking in the heaviest southern accent you'd ever want to hear. I cringed when he said thickly: "Ah'm Bob Zellner, from Mobile, Al'bama." Immediately I wondered if Bob and I might not eventually run into some problems.

I tried to put these skeptical thoughts from my mind as I met the rest of the group. Tim Carr, a friendly young white student from the University of the South at Sewanee, Tennessee, was my roommate. Then there were Walter Williams, who later became student body president at Jackson State College and would be expelled for leading protests against Mississippi segregation laws; Sally Hobbs, a southern belle from Duke; Jane Clay, a brown-skinned college coed from a middle-class family in Kentucky; and the rest of the group, all seemingly warm and alert men and women.

Surprisingly, the atmosphere at the seminar was completely different from that of the convention the previous summer. In Minneapolis, the emphasis had been on debate, on winning the argument, which created a combative, hectic atmosphere. Here the program was structured and the pace more leisurely, with the emphasis on learning and discovery rather than preparing for battle. Perhaps this worked because all of us had been selected with openness and flexibility in mind. None of us were blatant white-haters or black-haters on principle.

As the first week progressed, we established a daily pattern of activity. Connie and Will provided us with a variety of books, both racist and liberal, and academic papers analyzing the race issue. After eating breakfast together, we would meet in the mornings to discuss topics based on our readings. Under Will's careful direction, these meetings often became lively discussions that continued for hours, forcing us to analyze our own philosophies in the face of beliefs very different from ours. Although we were an explosive political mixture—including militant blacks, apologetic blacks, sincere liberal whites, and naïve, stubborn whites—our discussions were less attacks on each other than reflections of our own views and why we had them. Sometimes morning speakers would come in. My favorites were Dr. Jim Silver, author of *Mississippi, the Closed Society,* a searing analysis of the racial discrimination that had become an integral part of Mississippi life; Dr. Vivian Henderson, a distinguished Negro economist who discussed the economics of race discrimination and its by-products; and liberal Wisconsin governor Gaylord Nelson. Not only was there a rare give-and-take between these guests and us, but an unusual honesty also seemed to pervade the whole seminar. We weren't giving lip service to our school administrators, our legislators, our parents, or even our race. We were a small microcosm to be sure, but we were trying, usually with success, to deal with each other as human beings. Most importantly, we were doing it for ourselves. We had to wonder where else, in the summer of 1961, were nine blacks and nine whites eating, sleeping, talking, and playing together with such camaraderie.

We'd regularly talk about nebulous and difficult things like what it was like to be black in a white-dominated society, or what it was like to be white and afraid of blacks, or what it would mean if American life really were integrated and whether we were afraid of that and why. We closely analyzed allegations of the genetic inferiority of blacks that conservative extremists and fundamentalists had chosen as their latest weapon in the fight against desegregation. Quietly, almost without noticing it, we became genuine friends. We had a lot of fun because racial antagonism was being neutralized as we gradually let our guards down. In the afternoons out on Picnic Point, a peninsula jutting out into Lake Mendota, we swam, played games, roasted hot dogs, and grilled hamburgers. At night, we would sit around the campfire toasting marshmallows, singing "Kum Bah Yah" to someone's accompanying guitar, listening to Will's banjo, or just watching the night sky, which seemed to have more stars than anywhere I had ever seen.

It was strange, I guess, because we were, after all, whites and blacks who came from segregated environments where this kind of interaction was unheard of. But on the Madison campus for those three weeks, we truly were neither black nor white: we were merely human. By some peculiar alchemy, we achieved that summer a level of communication beyond the conversational. Perhaps it was Will Campbell's gentle, easygoing way—as he directed us to reanalyze our beliefs and assumptions, to dig deeper inside ourselves, and to discover why we felt the way we did—that was responsible. He didn't let us cop out. Perhaps it was through this unusual sharing of emotions and motivations that I recognized for the first time that there were whites who could be real allies, who could honestly feel, relate to, and understand what it was like to be a Negro in America. I realize that I say this at the risk of sounding ridiculous, that the experiences and feelings I describe may now seem incomprehensible. Perhaps it's like that line at the end of the old joke, "you had to have been there."

But I really think that if someone is truly willing to drop all their preconceptions and to view life from the other man's side—to walk a mile in another's shoes, as the saying goes—then it is possible to develop a kind of symbiotic interaction. By the end of the seminar, at any rate, we clasped hands and looked out *together* at the realities of racial conflict in America. We could do this because we lived together, talked together, and ate together as equals. Ultimately, the whites came to trust us, just as we came to trust them. We no longer saw each other as demons or savages, as black skin or white skin stretched over bones, but as human beings and, finally, as friends. To be a friend, you must be able, to some extent, to feel the other's pain. And we did. Sure, it required mental gymnastics—and I guess it does sound a bit far-fetched for a three-week seminar—but it happened. It happened because somewhere inside of each of us we wanted it to. We wanted to be human beings, unlabeled and unclassified, and, at least for a moment, *free*.

As the final week drew to a close, we shared a sense of foreboding about returning to our day-to-day lives. We didn't want to leave. We promised to keep in touch and to continue to support each other. Then at a final meeting, we sat in a circle and told what the seminar had meant to us.

Jane spoke first: "Back home I used to lie out on the docks and try to get darker because I was ashamed of my light skin. I couldn't stand the thought of having white blood because I hated whites." She stopped and looked around at all of us. "I never had to face my anger and hatred until now," she said quietly. "I never had to look at a white person in the face and realize my hatred made me no better than those whites who for no reason other than the color of my skin hated me. You know, I have realized that in the same way each individual person's hatred adds up and makes a difference, so too does each person's acceptance and love. I wouldn't have thought it was possible, but now I can look at whites beyond the color of their skin because I have seen that they can look at the person I am beyond my skin color. And we can be friends."

Bob Zellner, with his southern accent and well-oiled hair, taught me a lesson about judging a book by its cover. He was actually an activist at heart and a strong believer in personal freedom. "Well, ah've decided t'go back ta Al'bama and work with the Student Nonviolent Coordinating Committee," he drawled. "Ah been thinkin' about it for awhile. Ah like thar philosophies, and ah think with mah background, especially afta these weeks with y'all, ah could lend a good hand to thar organizin' efforts. Ah've learned a heckuva lot up here," he said with a slow smile, "but thar's work ta be done." I had to chuckle. But by then I had realized that a guy like Bob could make a difference in areas that the rest of us could never reach.

Sally—the Duke coed with the soft southern accent—was near tears as she told us how the seminar had changed her. "I know I will never be the same person again," she said slowly. "I've been very lucky in my life and never wanted for anything. I think that made me apathetic and uncaring about people who weren't as fortunate. Talking about the things that I was always afraid to talk about . . . being honest about my feelings and hearing the honesty of the rest of y'all has opened me up. I feel so much more aware of myself and the world. It's really a liberating feeling." She stopped for a moment, smiling through her tears and collecting herself. "I want y'all to know that I'm going to go back to Duke, do everything I can to support racial justice, and to wake up all those students who are apathetic like I was."

Each of us spoke in turn, explaining what we had learned and vowing to continue the fight on our home turf. I, like the others, felt my consciousness had been broadened. I no longer clung to the stereotype of the prejudiced white who had paraded in and out of my childhood as the *only* white. I recognized and appreciated that many of these white students felt nearly as estranged by a society based in racial discrimination as I did. Before this summer, I would have thought such a notion preposterous. Whatever else the three-week seminar may have accomplished, it had taken the concept of integration out of the realm of the theoretical and demonstrated it at work in the real world. And all of us, black, and white, were shaken by the realization that, at base, despite all that we had been taught and led to believe, we wanted the same things and were not much different.

It may seem a bit clichéd today, but then the words of the old Negro spiritual resonated among us as we sought to build community strong enough to weather the coming storm:

We need freedom, Lord, kum ba yah
We need freedom, Lord, kum ba yah
We need freedom, Lord, kum ba yah
    Oh Lord, kum ba yah.
Somebody's crying, Lord, kum ba yah
Somebody's crying, Lord, kum ba yah
Somebody's crying, Lord, kum ba yah
    Oh Lord, kum ba yah.
—Traditional Negro spiritual

Walter (left) and D'Army Bailey, ages three and two.

Bailey's Stand, owned by my grandfather, where I spent many afternoons as a child and young man. Drawing by Luther Hampton, reproduced with permission.

My grandfather, D. A. Bailey, and my father, Walter L. Bailey Sr., in front of Bailey's Stand.

My paternal grandmother, Mary Bailey.

Walter and Will Ella Bailey, my parents.

My maternal grandmother, Lureana Robinson.

Nurse Will Ella Bailey.

My father, Walter L. Bailey Sr., at a checkers tournament.

Railroad porter Walter L.
Bailey Sr.

Booker T. Washington High
School principal Blair T.
Hunt and his famous bell.
Courtesy Special Collections,
University of Memphis
Libraries.

Booker T. Washington High
School history professor, writer,
and pioneering radio disc jockey
Nat D. Williams in W. C. Handy
Park on Beale Street. Richard
Gardner/*The Commercial Appeal,*
July 1974.

Booker T. Washington High School newspaper staff, 1959.

D'Army as high school senior.

On break from college during my freshman year.

At right, E. C. "Suge" Jones, one of Memphis's first black policemen. Courtesy Special Collections, University of Memphis Libraries.

Southern University freshman class president D'Army Bailey.

~ 8 ~

Singing in the Tear Gas

What started out as a demonstration against segregation customs imposed by
whites in this old Southern City has taken the peculiar twist of becoming a
conflict between Negro students and the Negro administration of all-Negro
Southern University.
—BICKNELL EUBANKS, *Christian Science Monitor,* APRIL 6, 1960

A S MY THIRD YEAR at Southern quietly began, I felt impatient
with the campus atmosphere. as if I had come down from a moun-
taintop where idealistic people had the luxury of being friendly, to
a hostile land where nothing had changed and defensiveness reigned. All-
Negro was still all-Negro, and the whites in the community were holding
firm. As the classes began, I felt sure that no matter what we did as students
at Southern, the movement was accelerating to the point where we would
soon be affected by it. By the fall of 1961, the American college campus was
approaching its heyday as an arena for political and philosophical activism.

The students who served as campus leaders, NSA organizers, or representatives of the Student Nonviolent Coordinating Committee (SNCC) or the
Congress of Racial Equality (CORE) were the children of an age of doubt,
schooled at a time of moral and intellectual renaissance. We were the children
of Freud and Einstein, of Nagasaki and Little Rock. We experienced the era
of McCarthyism and postwar anticommunism. We were discontented with
the world of our parents, and that discontentment was growing.

I envisioned no immediate role for myself. There seems to be a unique
chemical, physical, and emotional reaction triggered by the racial sensors
within blacks who encounter white prejudice. Our gut churns, blood pressure rises, and emotions tense or generate anger. These prejudices, whether
covert or openly hostile, plague us at times unexpectedly and suddenly, often
dampening our most pleasant experiences. The unfairness of this, I think,

helped make me more compassionate for others. At the same time, it stirred my own hopes and dreams and fueled my passion to resist. I was discovering that this quick passion could be controlled and transformed into practical action for good—good that is always thwarted unjustly. Whatever else it may be, this passion is part of my inner core.

Inevitably, at the start of my junior year, I was changing. Like nineteen- or twenty-year-olds in any period of history, I was questioning my life, my meaning, my ambition. I was wondering if I could make a difference, wondering if I could make others see things my way. Nevertheless, by all visible indications, I was just going about my business as usual, enjoying the distractions of being nineteen. I continued testing the waters with my weekly column. I was in love with a beautiful young lady from New Orleans, Joyce Palmer, and I enrolled in advanced ROTC. During the football season, I served as half-time announcer for the ROTC drill team, which allowed me to travel to out-of-town football games at the school's expense. I was managing to have my share of fun.

But in my more contemplative moments, I looked around the campus or at the students in casual conversation or playing ping-pong in the student union and wondered if we were, as Descartes claimed, truly blank slates. If this were true, I asked, where had the passion come from that had made some of us activists and others onlookers, some of us change-makers and others graspers after the past? I knew in my heart that I was not an onlooker. I was a philosopher, an idealist. I saw the way, but was I willing to take risks to show it to others?

I was encouraged to see that there were some new freshmen and sopho- mores on campus who seemed to be change-makers and risk-takers, who seemed to be rushing forward to meet the future and make it theirs. They were a different breed, more restless, searching, and potentially more vola- tile than the students of previous years. One new leader, Patricia Tate, had transferred from Spelman College in Atlanta after being involved in civil rights efforts there. The freshman class president, Ronnie Moore, was an honors student in political science, as well as a minister.

Things began to change early that fall, when two field secretaries from CORE set up a Baton Rouge chapter and began hanging out on campus, meeting with Pat and Ronnie and talking with groups of students. Soon, when Ronnie was appointed chairman of the local chapter of CORE and Pat was named secretary, word began circulating throughout the campus that they were planning initial strategies for another Southern protest. This time there was a major shift as the movement broadened its focus from challenging lunch-counter segregation to a more fundamental challenge to job discrimination against blacks by Baton Rouge merchants. In early December 1961, I learned that they had begun distributing fliers listing Baton Rouge businesses that practiced segregation and job discrimination and writing letters to managers of various department stores requesting the opportunity to meet with them to discuss their hiring policies. Slowly but surely, they began nudging the community and waking us up.

Even as we were preparing to renew our student struggle, aftershocks from the struggle of 1960 reverberated in Washington as the U.S. Supreme Court issued an opinion that overturned the criminal convictions of the sixteen Southern students arrested in the sit-ins of March 28, 1960. Seven years after writing the landmark *Brown* decision outlawing school segregation, Chief Justice Earl Warren again handed civil rights forces a major victory, reshaping the law and prohibiting Southern authorities from arresting peaceful sit-in demonstrators. In the Court's unusually swift December 11, 1961, ruling, *Garner v. Louisiana,* Justice William O. Douglas took special note in his concurring opinion of Louisiana's racial history:

> But in Louisiana racial problems have agitated the people since the days of slavery. The landmark case of *Plessy v. Ferguson,*—the decision that announced in 1896 the now repudiated doctrine of "separate but equal" facilities for whites and blacks—came from Louisiana which had enacted in 1890 a statute requiring segregation of the races on railroad trains . . . as the first Mr. Justice Harlan stated in dissent in *Plessy v. Ferguson,* "in view of the law, there is in this country no superior, dominant ruling class of citizens. There is no caste here, our constitution is color blind."

The Southern University students arrests also evoked a strong concurring statement from Justice John Marshall Harlan that placed peaceful student sit-ins squarely within the protections of First Amendment free speech:

> There was more to the conduct of these petitioners than a bare desire to remain at the "white" lunch counter and their refusal of a police request to move from the counter. We would surely have to be blind not to recognize that petitioners were sitting at the counter, where

they knew they would not be served, in order to demonstrate that their race was being segregated in dining facilities in this part of the country.

Such a demonstration, in the circumstances of these two cases, is as much a part of the "free trade in ideas" as is verbal expression, more commonly thought of as "speech."

In extraordinary historical irony, the four days after the *Garner* decision would see student demonstrations and arrests in Baton Rouge that would later bring the Supreme Court to issue a second Louisiana decision signaling another major breakthrough for civil rights forces. The day of the December 11 ruling, Baton Rouge CORE representatives organized twenty Southern students to sit in at the white lunch counters at Kress and McCrory's to test the new decree. Lunch counter operators refused to serve them, but there were no arrests.

Three days later, on December 14, more than fifty students picketed the two stores carrying signs saying: "Don't Buy Here, This Store Discriminates," "Have Money, Will Buy Elsewhere," and "We Tried to Talk, Now We Walk." Twenty-three were arrested, including CORE field secretary Dave Dennis. As he was being taken into the jail, Dave told reporters: "We were not doing anything to agitate. We are just doing all we think is possible to eradicate the problem of segregation. CORE feels picketing is one of the most lawful methods left to help solve this problem." District Attorney Sargent Pitcher issued a warning that police and sheriff's deputies were prepared to enforce all laws in the face of the demonstrations. He urged whites and Negroes to ignore the demonstrators.

That same afternoon, Pat Tate asked me if I would help CORE lead a march from the campus to downtown Baton Rouge. The plan was to march seven miles into the city and stage a protest rally in front of the jail. She did not have to ask a second time; I agreed immediately.

Almost a year earlier I had written my last "Campus Exposé" to ask what had happened to the spark and pride that had made Southern students march before. Now, it seemed as if that spark had been rekindled, and as if I were the kindling: I was ready. Obviously, I could no longer sit around campus, read my books, and go to class while my fellow students were going to jail. Even so, there was nothing rash or emotional about my decision. For two years I had bided my time, established what I thought was a fairly sound educational base, and developed my own beliefs. As a freshman, I had been young and cautious. College had been new; leaving my home in Memphis had been new; and as a freshman, I could not see risking my future for a cause I did not completely understand. But by the fall of 1961, I had plowed the intellectual ground for two years: I had gone to conventions, talked to people, written my column. Seed time had come and gone; it was time to harvest. Now was the time to alter my course and work for results.

By then I had thought out and rethought the options, and I saw none. If change were going to occur in America, if the eyes and ears and minds of ordinary Americans were going to be opened, some dramatic act of civil disobedience was necessary. It was that simple. We couldn't carry the citizens of Baton Rouge up to Wisconsin's Lake Mendota in groups of eighteen; we had to do it here. So, on December 15, 1961, I put down my books, ending one evolutionary process that had started when I spent the morning sitting in at the doors of the boardroom at John Gaston hospital, and beginning another, when I marched at the head of two thousand Southern students to a rally in front of the Baton Rouge jail. The resulting confrontation not only engaged the nation but would later be reviewed closely on film by members of the U.S. Supreme Court and provoke minute analysis and sharply divided opinions among the High Court on what had happened that day.

Well I woke up this morning with my mind, stayed on Freedom,
Oh Yeah, I woke up this morning with my mind, stayed on Freedom,
Oh Lord, I woke up this morning with my mind, stayed on Freedom,
Hallelu—Hallelu—Hallelu—Hallelujah.
—Civil rights movement freedom song based on a traditional
  Negro spiritual

I certainly had not planned to be at the front, but the momentum of the previous twenty-four hours put me there. The day of the arrests, Pat had taken me to meet with Reverend B. Elton Cox; another CORE field organizer, Ronnie Moore; Weldon Rougeau; and several other campus leaders. They needed help in spreading information about the planned march, so I quickly began combing the campus, organizing dorm meetings, and telling students what was going on. That night, following a basketball game, we held a rally in the gym where we told at least five hundred students of our plan.

Inevitably, on the morning of December 15, the administration was in a panic. The governor was already on the phone to Dr. Clark, demanding that he maintain control. When approached by student leaders, Dr. Clark refused to dismiss classes for the march and threatened anyone who participated in it with "harsh disciplinary action." No one seemed to care. Once again, almost two thousand students boycotted classes and massed on Swan Street, near the railroad tracks at the edge of campus. Although the university refused us the use of its buses, Scotlandville blacks volunteered their own buses, cars, and taxi cabs to get hundreds of us downtown while others walked the seven-mile distance. Ronnie Moore was arrested at the campus entrance while parked in a car equipped with a loudspeaker and charged with violating an antinoise ordinance. As the march of students flowed down the highway, Reverend Cox, a tall, handsome man in his mid-thirties, Pat Tate, and I were at the front.

Once I had decided to join the movement, I joined, body and soul. I had taken a stand when I agreed to help Pat, Ronnie, and the others: silently, perhaps even intentionally, I laid everything on the line. At the time, I didn't realize what an important line it was or, for that matter, its strangely magnetic force—you don't worry about things like that when you take your first step across it. You don't worry about consequences because you can't.

For four hours, we marched into the city singing songs like "Oh Freedom."

> Oh freedom, oh freedom,
> Oh freedom over me,
> And before I'll be a slave,
> I'll be buried in my grave,
> And go home to my Lord and be free.
>
> No segregation, no segregation,
> No segregation over me,
> And before I'll be a slave,
> I'll be buried in my grave,
> And go home to my Lord and be free.

As we marched we also sang "Go Tell It on the Mountain," "The Battle Hymn of the Republic," and another famous civil rights song, "We Shall Not Be Moved":

> We shall not, we shall not be moved
> We shall not, we shall not be moved

Just like a tree that's planted by the water,
We shall not be moved.

We're fighting for our rights
we shall not be moved
We're fighting for our rights and
we shall not be moved
Just like a tree that's planted by the water,
We shall not be moved.

We're on our way to victory
We shall not be moved
Segregation is our enemy
We shall not be moved
Just like a tree that's planted by the water
We shall not be moved.

Even though the morning was drizzly and cool, with a chill wind whipping at our overcoats and umbrellas, with two thousand black voices raised in united resistance, I hardly felt it. State police—whom we had contacted and told of our intentions the day before—drove slowly alongside us, blocking two lanes for the march, but I truly felt no fear. My elation and the whirlwind of song blocked out all other feeling. I was standing at the head of a mass of my people, leading them to oppose a great wrong. I felt like the ancient Christians being led singing into the arena to face the lions, knowing we'd win in the end. I couldn't imagine being anywhere else.

When we were about halfway through the seven-mile journey, the Scotlandville buses and cabs picked us up and carried us the rest of the way into town. We arrived close to noon and massed around the stately Old State Capitol Building. The moment was at once exhilarating, uncertain, and tense. None of us could predict what would happen, but we knew we had broken too many taboos and stepped on too much white pride for it to be good.

Baton Rouge police cars slowly patrolled the almost empty streets. In the time that it had taken us to gather at the old Capitol, the citizens of Baton Rouge had been informed we were coming, and a great many had hidden themselves indoors, basically closing up downtown. An unnerving air of doom hung in the deserted streets, as if some disaster had been planned and everyone but us had taken cover. I noticed whites peeking from behind curtains and window shades, gazing at our singing procession with awe and horror. Their age-old way of life, and with it the centuries of racial assumptions they embraced, were being vitally threatened right before their eyes. They were terrified by these uppity niggers, yet they could do nothing, or so it seemed to us at the time. We continued to sing "Hold on, hold on, keep your eyes on the prize, hold on."

Subsequently, the streets of downtown Baton Rouge belonged to two thousand singing Southern students marching on the jail, and to the Baton Rouge police who shadowed our movements along the way. Soon after our line started moving from the Old State Capitol toward the jail, the police stopped us. Captain Font of the city police department and Chief Kling of the sheriff's office approached Cox as I stood beside him: "I'm Sheriff Kling of the Sheriff's Department," he said. "You all are going to hav-ta stop this marchin' and gwan back home. Now, uh, I see that you are a man of the cloth, and so am I. I, I don't wanna be unreasonable about this thing, but you know this just ain't right what y'all are doin'."

Cox stood placid and expressionless, maintaining eye contact with the two lawmen. Kling continued: "Look here, now, we've already arrested one of your group for usin' them loudspeakers and disturbin' the peace. I, I don't want it ta haf-ta come ta this now, but if you don't stop this thing you're awl gonna end up in jail."

Cox waited a few extra seconds before he said, matter-of-factly: "As you can see, Sheriff, we are a peaceful, organized group. We are completely within our rights to come downtown and make our protest known."

Kling mumbled something as he stared with obvious surprise and confusion at Cox's calm face, and then, with some agitation, the two lawmen walked away. We resumed the march: Cox smiled, perhaps at the thought of the police trying to put two thousand of us in the city's small jail. Had they chosen that route, we were prepared to go peacefully and pack the jails.

We had just turned the corner into St. Louis Street, which fronts the jail, when we were stopped again, this time by Police Chief Wingate White. I couldn't take my eyes off the helmeted deputies and city policemen who stood in double rows along the street behind him. They were all heavily equipped for battle, holding riot guns, revolvers, submachine guns, tear gas canisters, and two snarling German shepherd police dogs. My mouth grew suddenly dry and my stomach churned as I looked at their hard, masklike faces. *Sharpeville,* I thought. To them, this was war. It was as real as it ever was going to get. Obviously, even though not one of us held a weapon, we threatened their very existence. Such was the force of peaceful civil disobedience, I thought, that grown white men had to come armed to the teeth to confront a well-behaved mass of singing black students and their community leadership who were challenging their ability to force us into submission.

Chief White was angry, and maybe just a little afraid, too. He obviously didn't know where this thing was going. "Now, y'all have had your say, and now I'm gonna have mine," he said slowly. He was shorter than Cox, about five feet ten inches, with a soft, pudgy build and a jowly, pasty face. His baggy, wrinkled suit seemed to mirror the bags and wrinkles in his face, giving him a lost, hangdog appearance. When he spoke to Reverend Cox, he started off in a loud, irritated voice and waggled a finger in the other man's direction. Even so, without saying a word, Cox intimidated him. I think Cox's bearing, his height, his calm expression, and even the large silver cross dangling from his chest truly frightened the police chief. He quickly dropped the wagging finger, lowered his tone, and averted his eyes with the sighing relinquishment of a man both frustrated and ashamed of himself.

"I'm gon giy y'all jus' two minutes ta turn around or we'll arrest you all," he said.

Cox didn't flinch. "We'll be glad to disband peacefully and go back, but after we have finished our march. We plan to hold a rally in front of the jail," he said simply.

The cheif shook his head in disbelief. "Go right on ahead, then. Have it your way."

As we continued to move onto St. Louis Street from St. Phillip, I saw the whole block lined with eighty to a hundred city and state policemen and sheriff's deputies, firemen, and a fire truck. Up to three hundred white on-lookers stood between the line of policemen and the jail building itself jeering and taunting us. Reverend Cox began singing, "We Shall Overcome," and we all joined in with him until the street was filled with the whirlwind of our strong, young voices:

> We are not afraid
> We are not afraid
> We are not afraid today
> Oh deep in my heart
> I do believe
> We shall overcome someday

Three deep we lined the sidewalk opposite the jail on St. Louis, St. Phillip, and Lausanne streets. We sang, the hecklers screamed, and the jailed students cheered. It was as if pandemonium had been unleashed. We were faced off, black against white, staring across the street at each other, almost motionless for a time. It was plain to see that we outnumbered them seven to one. No wonder the white crowd was agitated. The situation was overwhelming: even my senses were numbed. Then Reverend Cox walked to the center of the street, raised his arms calling for silence, and spoke. In the hush that followed, his loud, clear baritone spoke of the struggle that defined a black man's life in America, and of the struggle that was the legacy of his children:

"We are citizens of this country, yet we do not share in the freedoms that make this country what it is. We are charged the same dollar a white man is charged for food or for entertainment, yet we are made to endure second-class service, to enter and exit through back alleys, and to sit in the worst seats. Louisiana must be brought into the modern age, an age that acknowledges all human beings—black, white, brown, or yellow—as equals. If we stand as equals in God's eyes, what mortal man dare say that we should not stand as equals on earth? No man can say that. And no law of man, either."

His voice echoed against the granite buildings.

"We must give these arrested students any support we can. We must stand firm with our silent, nonviolent demonstration. We do not hate those in authority. But if others have the right to picket and protest against what is wrong, then we have that same right."

When I stared at those armed men who seemed anxious to act, I couldn't help wondering what would happen if the police opened fire. Do we run? Do we fall on the ground? Could they really do that? Would they?

"If there is any violence, we will help break it up. If we go to jail, we will go without bail. If they give us tear gas, then we will take it and fall honorably."

"Don't worry, nigger, we'll make you fall so you won't never get up!" jeered an onlooker. And then another screamed, "We'll make you wish you was still a slave, preacher man, while we teach you respect for the law!" And others joined in: "GIT OUTTA HERE NIGGER, GO HOME!"

Cox was unfazed. "We know we have friends. We know there are many who believe in our cause, but they are scared to do anything, like a lot of Negroes are scared. But, we must remember we are strong."

We all cheered wildly, and then suddenly the jailed students began singing "We Shall Overcome" from their cells.

"Sing for FREEDOM!" Reverend Cox hollered. He turned and saluted the jailed students, and then turned back toward us. It brought tears to the eyes of some of us. A bone-chilling mist hung in the air as we shivered from the damp cold, nervousness, or both.

"Now, children, let us continue what our brothers and sisters have started. It is almost one o'clock, and we are hungry. Let us go and eat at the downtown lunch counters. If they will not serve us, we will sit there an hour, all the while saying that WE ARE HUNGRY!"

All this was apparently too much for Sheriff Clemmons, who climbed onto the top of a nearby patrol car and began screaming through a portable loudspeaker: "Attention! ATTENTION! We have given you the opportunity to demonstrate here, but now you are creating a disturbance. THIS IS ALL. NOW BREAK IT UP!"

We kept on singing, ignoring his order to disperse. It was amazing how these strong, young, black voices resonated in those small and confining streets and grew stronger and stronger, blotting out everything else.

Even so, as I kept my eye on Clemmons I could barely make out his final order. "MOVE 'EM OUT!" he screamed through the loudspeaker.

And then I heard the distinct hiss and pop of the first tear gas canister as it bounced across the asphalt.

~ 9 ~

Arrested Development

Freedom is not a gift, but freedom is a merit that is acquired only through determination and sacrifice.
—CORE FLIER DISTRIBUTED IN BATON ROUGE, DECEMBER 1961

I T IS IMPOSSIBLE to describe what it feels like to be shot with tear gas. I could say it makes your skin sting and burn so badly you think it is peeling off your hands and face. I could say it makes your eyes feel as if they have been set on fire, and then it makes your eyes water so steadily you cannot see. I could say that when the harsh, pungent gas fills your lungs, it is as if two great hands have reached up and squeezed your diaphragm and then placed a bag over your head so you cannot breathe. But these descriptions, while accurate, don't convey the full effect of the experience.

Even more difficult to explain is that the anger I felt that December afternoon, as the tear gas canisters exploded throughout the streets of downtown Baton Rouge was of an intensity I had never before known. All the hellish years, all the indignity and injustice, all the times a white person had refused to acknowledge me, all the times I had been insulted welled up inside me. All those feelings and memories broke through the walls of restraint I had built around them and came together in one hard mass of anger, and some part of me said, "No more." Some part of me said, "I will not live my life in the back alleyways of the world." And I hardened myself to the fact that, though my purpose was good, if I stood by it, anything could happen.

*

MOB (mäb) n. 1. a disorderly and lawless crowd, rabble
—*Webster's New World Dictionary*

The instant Sheriff Clemmons hollered "move 'em out!" one of the deputies threw a tear gas canister that struck Reverend Cox on the ankle as it exploded, knocking him to the ground. As several students rushed to carry Cox to safety, canisters exploded in quick succession up and down St. Louis Street.

Confused and hysterical, we all began running, blindly trying to escape the swirling gas. Shoes, umbrellas, and purses littered the streets. I could hear the unmistakable barking of police dogs and the whining of the sirens mixing with the almost overwhelming noise of students' screams, scattered singing, and the sharp explosions of the tear gas canisters.

Of course, there was nothing to do but run, to run as fast as you could, and to try not to wipe your eyes because—as I found out too late—that made it worse. As I ducked down the nearest alley, I reminded myself that I had known this was a possibility before I had agreed to come. I reminded myself that the police could and would get away with whatever they decided to do.

I tried to convince myself that I had known and expected these things, but I hadn't—not really. I hadn't known I would be so afraid. I hadn't known about the dogs, or about not being able to breathe. I hadn't known what it would feel like to wonder, as I ran with the police at my back, if they might use those shotguns, and if the bullets might hit me. But I ran anyway. I ran down alleys and tried to catch my breath in the doorways of buildings; when a cloud of gas overwhelmed me, I closed my eyes and groped my way along the nearest wall. I ran looking for safety and fresh air, and I felt that, though I might eventually find some air to breathe, I would never be safe anywhere. I hated that feeling, but I hated the white police more.

When I was nearer to the old State Capitol, in an alley just off Third Street, I met up with Pat Tate and a large group of students she was leading.

"D'Army! Are you okay?"

"Yeah, I'm all right. A little shook up, but I'm making it. I wasn't really expecting the gas."

"None of us were. Or at least not so much of it. And the goddamn dogs. I guess we're all dangerous criminals now, huh?" We looked at each other.

"I feel dangerous," said another student menacingly. He had lost his shoes but still carried an umbrella. "I'd just like to see those bastards come at me again."

"And what are you going to do? Shield yourself with the umbrella or beat them up with it?" asked Pat.

"I dunno. Something. We gotta do something." His voice was desperate. About twenty of us stood in the alley. All movement had stopped.

"Yeah, Pat. What are we going to do?" I asked her quietly. "What's the plan now?"

"Well, we're all trying to get back to the old State Capitol so we can regroup."

"So that's all? asked a female student. "We run away from their dogs and their tear gas to give them another victory?"

"Yeah! If we run away now, the police are gonna think they won. They haven't won nothing from us," said someone else.

"Where's Reverend Cox?" I asked.

"They got him to a car. I guess they're taking him back to Scotlandville. I don't know. He's hurt," said Pat.

"Have y'all tried any of the counters?"

"No . . ."

"Has anybody?"

"I don't know," she said slowly. "Everyone went in a different direction. . . . Hey, listen." Suddenly, Pat looked up and raised her voice. "Reverend Cox told us to eat lunch, and that's what we're going to try to do."

"Yeah!"

"Then, let's march!"

"I stood next to Pat as we moved out of the alley onto Third. We soon discovered that the store managers had anticipated our arrival. At McCrory's, a guard was posted at the door next to a sign reading "Closed to Negroes." Kresge had its lunch counter roped off and was admitting only white patrons. Rosenfield's had signs posted announcing their lunch counter was closed to all but store employees. Soon after this last visit, we spotted a group of policemen moving toward us.

"Start singing!" Pat hollered, and the group again launched into "We Shall Overcome" as we moved slowly up the street.

"Pat, this time we're gonna stand our ground, right?" I asked her.

"Right," she responded, looking at me seriously.

"I mean, we're just going to stand here in complete peace, look them in the eyes, and dare them to shoot, right?"

"Yeah, right. No more running. Things have gone far enough."

"We looked at each other and smiled. "No more running."

Less than a minute later, we were face to face with the police. A carload of them pulled across our line of march, jumped out, and pointed tear gas guns at us. For a few seconds, no one moved. Echoing in my mind were words we had been singing all day, *Deep in my heart. I do believe. We shall overcome some day.* Somehow they were comforting, strengthening words.

We shall overcome. I fought an overwhelming desire to hit them, slap them, or scream them into realizing we were all the same.

We shall overcome. I fought a deep, gut-wrenching need to run. I looked at Pat.

Deep in my heart . . . I breathed deeply.

I do believe . . . We will stand peacefully. We will stand here peacefully until they let us go forward.

We shall . . .

They began shooting tear gas. When I turned, the group behind us had already started running.

Hours later, we were back in the relative safety of Scotlandville. The first gas canister had been thrown before one o'clock, and we were hounded and hunted until late afternoon, many of us not making it back until six or seven that night. As we rode or walked home, word passed among us that we were gathering at the Camphor Memorial Methodist Church to regroup and devise a plan for our movement.

The stench of tear gas hung heavy in the air that night. It clung to our clothes, hair, and skin, a constant reminder of the wrong we were up against. Hysteria in Baton Rouge was growing, and the news was exaggerated to the point of pure fabrication. The only violence we witnessed came from the police, yet we were the ones being portrayed as aggressive hoodlums and vandals.

As I looked around the church, I saw students who had been beaten and bruised. I heard stories of others who had gone to the hospital to be treated for dog bites and head gashes. But the overall feeling in the air was calmness. We were strangely, grimly calm, like people who have come though a great tragedy or loss and who realize that now they must take stock of their lives. We had been through our baptismal fire. We had survived our rite of passage from idealism into real-world, nonviolent political action. Now we were ready to move forward again. And most of us were merely eighteen, nineteen, or twenty years old.

Our main student leader, Ronnie Moore, was in jail. Pat Tate, a few others, and I met with Reverend Cox in the pastor's study off the main auditorium to discuss the rally and strategies for keeping up the momentum of the movement over the weekend. Word came to us that the district court had issued a restraining order prohibiting any further CORE demonstrations in Baton Rouge. And then Shelby Jackson called an emergency session of the State Board of Education to decide how to deal with the arrested students. Angry and exhausted, we felt as if we were under siege. We didn't understand.

By now it was getting late. The church was packed, and hundreds more stood outside waiting to hear what to do next. Those of us who gathered in the little room were the steering force of the moment now, and as such we were expected to pull the movement back together, to realign it, and to lead it. Outside the church, students were putting up loudspeakers on the church walls so they could hear our speeches. We could feel the excitement building like a pulsating drum as we prepared to go out to the podium to lead the rally.

"Let's reassert our strength," Pat said. "We know we're right. Nothing's changed. Where's our dignity?"

"It's right here in this room, and it's all over this church," said Cox. It's our job to remind them they've still got it. Got it?"

Then Cox drew me aside. "D'Army, I want to ask you something."

"All right," I answered quietly.

"Dave, Jerome, and Ronnie have been arrested, and all these others. We've got to get them out of jail, first. And we've got to be ready to fight these businesses to end their discrimination. We've got a lot of fighting to do, D'Army."

I nodded, wondering what he was getting at.

"And it's gonna be hard, and it's gonna be bitter. Do you realize this? Do you understand what I'm saying?"

"Yes, sir, I understand. I know."

"Good. Because I want you to stand with me in this thing. I want you to help me lead this movement, D'Army. I've been watching you, and I see fire in you. I know you can do it." He looked me straight in the eyes. "Will you stand with me in this?"

I was shocked. Me? Stand with him? I was new at this. I had spent a day running from dogs and tear gas—did that make me a movement leader? For a moment, I was afraid. But a moment later, as the day's events and the inescapable reality of my new anger and my new commitment welled up inside me, I knew it was the only logical thing for me to do. When I looked to the others gathered in the small room, they voiced their support. Yes, I thought,

I must do what must be done. I have a chance to unleash the passion, and I've got to take it.

"Yes," I told him, "I'll stand with you. I'd be honored."

For the second time that day, I felt an overwhelming sense of rightness. Before, we had been just another group of students, most of us undirected, unmotivated, and largely apathetic toward our world. Now, here we were, fired with a sense of mission, burning with the idea that we could change things, that we possessed power and control over our destinies. Then, only minutes before we were going to begin the rally, about a dozen deputies descended on the church and filed into the back hallway. Two men burst into our little meeting room.

"Reverend Cox?" asked one of the men in a booming Louisiana drawl.

"I am B. Elton Cox." His voice revealed no reaction, no alarm, just a non-plussed admission of fact.

"We are from the East Baton Rouge Sheriff's Department, and we have a warrant for your arrest."

"With what crime am I charged?"

"Inciting to riot and breach of the peace. Bail will be set at the court-house."

"I see. And who is bringing these charges?"

"Sheriff Bryan Clemmons and Mayor-President John Christian."

"I see."

The man who had been speaking glanced at the other deputy with a quiz-zical expression. I could hear the students clapping and singing out in the church. Then the other man spoke in a high, squeaky twang: "So, uh, if you'll jus' come 'long with us peacefully, we'll uh be takin' you on down-town."

"Young man, everything I have done today has been done in peace," he said quietly, with the same calm expression he had used in speaking with Chiefs Kling and White, and Captain Font that morning. "I will peacefully go with you to the jail now, but I cannot walk. My ankle was bruised by one of your tear gas canisters."

The deputies exchanged quick glances, the man with the deep drawl opening and closing his mouth like a hooked fish. The other one grabbed him by the shoulder, whispered something in his ear, and stared at him sternly, as if daring him to disobey. Then he looked around at us and said:,"We'll, uh, carry you on outta here, then."

Reverend Cox nodded his head once more and said, "Fine."

After a few more minutes organizing the endeavor, they lifted Cox shoulder high and passed him from deputy to deputy, through the crowded church, to the police cars waiting outside. The others in the group turned to me to lead the rally. Charged by Cox's arrest and by the cheering of the crowd, I took the microphone, not knowing until I spoke what I was going to say.

"Today, we have seen the most barbaric events," I began, my voice slow and clear, my body trembling slightly with emotion. "White policemen—who are sworn to protect us and observe the laws—turned against us with brutal force. They are in league with those who want to deny us the most elemental of human rights. They and those like them in the white community of Baton Rouge want to keep us going to the back door and walking with our hats in our hands." The energy in the air was tangible. Hundreds of young minds and spirits were turned to one goal. Affirmations rang out in the auditorium as we echoed each other and pumped each other up. Yes, this is good, this is right.

"Well, it's a new day in Baton Rouge," I continued. "All the police dogs, all the tear gas, and all the guns in the world won't stop us. They can fill their jails, but they won't bend our spirit. We want all of the white people in this city to know that we black people in Louisiana have had enough."

Stand firm, I thought to myself. It's time for a face-off. The day's events ran like a newsreel in my mind. "We want the walls of segregation broken down downtown," I said. "If they can take our money, then we're good enough to sit at their lunch counters. There'll be no more sitting at the back of the bus and no more going through the kitchen. We are prepared to stand up and fight. We are going to stand behind our fellow students who have been arrested, and we are going to stand behind Reverend Cox." Cheers and applause burst from the crowd as if from a corked bottle. The excitement and anticipation were almost unbearable. Then they quieted once more, waiting for me to finish.

"The university's administration has been doing everything in their power to stop our protests. They have not cooperated with us, and have threatened to expel those of our leaders who have been arrested. Well, I say, tonight is the time. It is time for us to know where the university administration stands. Do they stand with us, or do they stand with the white lawmakers of Louisiana? So, we are going to leave this church tonight, and we are going onto the campus to march to the home of President Clark."

Cheers broke out again. "We want to know where he stands." My voice was challenging, almost combative. "We want to know if he supports our just struggle to end the practice of racial discrimination, and whether he'll stand behind our fellow students who have been arrested and refuse to throw them out of school."

Finally, I had an outlet for some of the aggression, betrayal, and humiliation I had been feeling all day long. I got some of it out, and in doing so I gave focus and direction to hundreds of people who felt the same way. The crowd was instantly on its feet, cheering and clapping, ready to march. As the news swept out from the church, we were surprised to find the campus police and the Scotlandville police clearing the way from the church to President Clark's house. Within minutes, over a thousand students were filing away from the church and beginning the peaceful mile-and-a-half march to the white Victorian house on the Mississippi River that was the historic home of Southern University presidents.

We assembled in the front yard, not knowing what to expect but feeling that our presence there was a victory in itself. Because we knew we were treading on forbidden ground in standing up to the university and its president, our daring made us even bolder and more fervent.

The other leaders and I went directly to the front steps of the president's house and rang the bell. When he appeared dressed in a neat grey suit, his dark, straight hair combed to one side, he seemed entirely composed. As we chatted briefly, he showed no signs of antagonism, which surprised me. I had been expecting belligerence, or at least defensiveness, from him. But he stood there under the porch light, occasionally swatting at the moths and mosquitoes and calmly matched my gaze as I told him why we had come.

"Dr. Clark, we have marched here tonight because a group of Southern students has been wrongfully arrested for standing up for human rights. Today we have been chased by dogs and shot with tear gas for openly showing our support for our friends and colleagues in jail. We are asking you and the university to stand behind them with us and call for their release."

I kept my voice determined and respectful. I saw myself as the spokesman for all of us, and as spokesman it was my job to make our demands clear to him. I have never been inclined to voice animosity unless it was for a calculated purpose, and since I neither had any such purpose that night nor felt that kind of emotion, I did not sound angry or act angrily. I was just measurably determined. I was determined to secure the support of the university, determined to demand that Dr. Clark take a stand that night on the porch steps.

He nodded his head very slowly as I spoke. In the artificial yellow light, his face seemed suddenly thinner, paler, and more drawn.

"We must know tonight that the university will support us," I continued, trying to keep my voice even. "I have been chosen to ask you to speak to us tonight and to tell us you will not expel our friends who have been arrested. Dr. Clark, we know we cannot win this fight alone. We will not leave tonight until we know the university will call for the students' release." I looked out over the near silent crowd. "We are asking you to support us in our protest against laws you must know are wrong."

"I understand," he said solemnly. "Yes, of course, I'll speak." Megaphone to mouth, he began, his familiar voice echoing almost godlike across the crowded lawn: "I have been monitoring your protest today and discussing it with state officials. There is a great deal of pressure on me to expel the students who were leading the protest." A murmur, almost a groan rippled through the crowd. He held up his hand for quiet. "But I want you to know that I think your protests are right. Even though the state officials do not understand or agree with what you are doing, they are the people I have to work with. But I understand. I think what you are opposing is a great wrong."

He paused and cleared his throat. Standing next to him, I was fairly shocked by his sudden outpouring of seemingly heartfelt support. I could have sworn that there were tears in his eyes. It was if he had been rent apart by conflicted emotions and was suddenly at one with himself.

"I want each and every one of you to know," he continued, "that before I will expel or suspend any of the student leaders who were arrested in the protest, I will resign as president of Southern University. I will not support the wrong you are fighting. Moreover, Southern University will intercede in any way we can to speed the release of the students who are in jail."

The crowd erupted in spontaneous applause, and, even though I was more than a little skeptical about this sudden change in attitude, I joined in. I even took the megaphone and led the crowd in a "Yea, Dr. Clark" cheer, partly to cement his commitment to us and partly because, doubts aside, after a day like this one, we needed a victory, something to celebrate. After several rounds of the cheer, Dr. Clark smiled and waved and then went back inside the mansion. We broke up, heading to our dorms and apartments for a much-deserved sleep.

As I lay in bed, my thoughts and emotions wandered. I was buoyed by Dr. Clark's show of support, but I was at a loss as to what it could mean. It would be wholly unlike him to risk his position at the university for a protest whose methods he had never before approved of. It would, in fact, be tantamount to a complete personality reversal. And that was hard to understand. But I wasn't complaining. On the whole, I was pleased with the way the day had ended. We were unified, I reminded myself as sleep overcame me. We had survived the tear gas and the dogs. And Dr. Clark, wonder of wonders, hadn't come out against us.

~ 10 ~
An Offensive Christmas

The first rule of education, in all lands, is never say anything offensive to anyone.
—VOLTAIRE (IN THE *Southern University Digest,* OCTOBER 1961)

THE NEXT MORNING, Dr. Clark closed school four days early for the Christmas holidays. And the *Baton Rouge State Times* ran a long article under the headline "Board of Education Issues Warning to Negro Students, Courts Ban Demonstrations." The board's statement declared that any student arrested or jailed would automatically be suspended and forbade students living on campus to take part in demonstrations not sanctioned by the institution.

"Those who live off the campus and take part in demonstrations not sanctioned by the institution shall not be allowed to return to the campus," the resolution stated. Lewis Doherty, a member of the East Baton Rouge Parish School Board, asked the State Board to screen out-of-state applicants to state-supported institutions. He asked school authorities "to exercise more prudence in the invitation of guest speakers." And he asked that any individual who is connected with a tax-supported educational institution and who is found guilty of violating any state and local laws should be permanently expelled.

The article also included a description of how police were forced to use tear gas to "quell 1,500 Negroes" and a restatement of District Court Judge Gordon West's restraining order against any CORE-led or CORE-sponsored activity.

None of this surprised us very much. We had no reason to assume or even hope the board of education would act any differently than they had in

1960. We knew CORE was wearing on the local bureaucrats' nerves, and we expected to have to do some battling in court. The only thing we needed in order to pull off protests against the board and the courts, the local businessmen and bureaucrats was Dr. Clark's support. All we needed was Southern to stand behind us in opposition to the expulsion orders. With that, we felt sure we could win.

When Dr. Clark announced the early closing of the school, we weren't sure how to react. Maybe he was biding time—getting us off campus and out of town in order to get the board off his back, so he could think this thing out. Clark was astute enough to recognize that while his announcement of support had brought a certain amount of bewildered satisfaction to the minds of his students, it had not eased the tension that overwhelmed the campus. Tension was what he wanted, understandably, to avoid. But none of us could be sure what Clark would do when push came to shove. We had no positive precedent to point to. Moreover, it remained to be seen whether he had actually learned a lesson from the events of 1960.

An uncertain nervousness hung over the ten of us who were the remnants of the Baton Rouge CORE and Southern leadership—now called the Student Freedom Committee—and who gathered at Pat Tate's small two-bedroom apartment in Scotlandville. It was the nervousness that comes from knowing there is something you should be doing, but you can't remember what it is. It was like constantly looking over your shoulder only to find no one there. Although we tried to support each other and give each other hope, tempers sometimes flared—understandably in these circumstances. We knew that, instead of heading for our various hometowns, we had to stay near the campus to maintain a visible presence and keep our momentum alive. It was hard: there were ten of us camping out in a small apartment, sleeping on the floor or upright in chairs, fixing meals in a cramped kitchen. We handed out fliers, worked on money-raising schemes, kept in contact with the national CORE office in New York, visited the jailed students, and met with lawyers to plan for the first round of hearings.

The liberal leader Allard Lowenstein—who was then at Stanford University and whom I had met at the National Student Association convention— stopped off to visit and offer us encouragement. He was on his way to New Orleans to visit his fiancée, Cokie Boggs, daughter of the Louisiana political leader Hale Boggs. Our goals during this wintry and turbulent period were threefold: to achieve desegregation of public facilities, to pressure the South ern administration to work with us, and to arrange the release of the jailed students and their reinstatement at Southern, thereby achieving a certain triumph over the repressive police and legal authorities. Corollary to all of this was our radical idea of full racial equality: equality in hiring, in political influence, in free speech, in education, in police treatment, and in the opportunity to lead a full life. And, yes, we were serious. We saw no reason why we shouldn't demand these things and have them. We knew we would have to work, but work was the one thing we weren't scared of.

I think it is important to note that, in the winter of 1961, Baton Rouge was really the only place in the country where these kinds of protests were going on. Many protests occurred in the South before and after this one, but at this time things elsewhere were quiet. Consequently, we received extensive press coverage. Once Baton Rouge and New Orleans media had covered the initial arrests of the students at the lunch counters, national newspeople were dispatched to Scotlandville to gather more stories. The march downtown, the meeting at the church, and the march to Dr. Clark's house were fully publicized across the country. From December 15 on, we were constantly being photographed or interviewed or being asked what we were going to do next. Gaining publicity was strategically important on the one hand, and a source of unrelenting pressure on the other.

Not only was all of this very new to me, but I was also amazed and impressed by the power and influence that the media attention gave us. But as the days passed, I never once felt as if I existed for the reporters and the TV cameras: on the contrary, I felt the media existed for us. It existed to be manipulated: we served their purpose in manipulating them because it helped to make a story. Klieg lights and cameras, reporters' notebooks and microphones became an often stressful yet necessary part of our daily lives and figured prominently in our plans. Much to the growing anger of the politicians, businessmen, white supremacists, flaming segregationists, and Ku Klux Klan members, we were intruding ever more deeply into their lives through television, radio, and newspaper coverage.

Two days after the march, the Baton Rouge authorities increased bail on the Southern students to a total of $116,000 and then brought against many of them the more serious charges of "criminal anarchy" and "criminal conspiracy," which carried possible ten-year sentences. The CORE national office offered to step up their fund-raising efforts and to appeal to several national foundations in the hope of getting the students released by Christmas. Indeed, our protest at Southern became one of CORE's first major civil rights undertakings of the 1960s, and a surprising number of wealthy New Yorkers opened their pocketbooks and gave. Civil rights was a new cause that was fast becoming chic. Even so, the process of receiving and channeling the money was slow. A week before Christmas, it was clear we would not get the students out in time for the holidays.

The campus was deserted. All protests had come to a screeching halt. And notwithstanding our efforts on their behalf, most of the jailed students stayed locked up for over a month. The segregationists had won yet another victory.

Those of us who stayed on tried not to let that fact dishearten us as we passed the last few days before Christmas making bold plans for our January resurgence and daily treks to the East Baton Rouge Parish Jail to reassure our colleagues. But the word from the jail wasn't good. Many of our leaders had been put in with the rougher criminals and were being threatened, forced to stay awake, and beaten. When they complained to the guards, they were either met with more abuse or they were simply ignored. During a visit from one of our workers, Weldon asked for a razor blade to conceal in his shoe.

"I know they are going to hurt me if I don't get outta here. I got to have something, man—these dudes are serious. They're *criminals,* this is what they *do,*" he said looking and sounding more like the panicked nineteen-year-old he was than the conspiring anarchist he was supposed to be. Eventually, someone brought him a razor blade.

After being refused several times, I was finally allowed to meet with Ronnie Moore. Originally, Ronnie had been arrested for using loudspeakers and charged with "annoyance." CORE paid the $1,500 bond, and Ronnie was released only to be rearrested on the jailhouse steps and charged with "conspiracy to commit criminal mischief." His bail was set at $3,500.

"This place is so overcrowded, you wouldn't believe it," he said. "They've got us in with the real criminals, the murderers, and the rapists. Are we dangerous? Have we done *anything* at all to deserve this?"

"How's Cox?"

"I don't know. It looks like they're not going to tell me how he is"

"What do you mean?"

"I've been really worried about him. You know, his ankle was really bad, and he never saw a doctor before he got in here. I know there's no way in hell a doctor's going to see him now. So, I kept asking the guards if I could see him, until I found out he was in solitary confinement and on a fast. But I will keep asking anyway until that bastard jailer screams, 'Hell, no! I wish that motherfucker would die!'"

"That's it?"

"End of conversation. The upshot is, I really don't know where he is."

"How are you?"

"I don't know. Tired . . . weak. I've been coughing and noticing blood in my spit. I was asking the guards if I could see a doctor. But about the third time I asked, this guard picked me up by my shirt and slapped me in the face, so I quit asking. I think the only thing to do in here is to take the path of least resistance. You can understand, D'Army, I'm getting really angry. It's hard in here, and we're all getting real angry."

Eventually, some black jail workers got word out that the physical abuse was becoming more and more common. CORE field secretary Jerome Smith was knocked out by a judo chop to the neck for merely inquiring about his lost property receipt. When Dave Dennis sought to talk to Sheriff Clemmons about the brutality, he was yanked out of the cell block, hurled against the bars, and placed in solitary.

Armed with this report and Ronnie's testimony, we lodged a complaint with the local FBI, which launched a halfhearted investigation. Of course, when the guards were questioned, they denied practicing any violence or mistreatment, and the investigation ended there. Ronnie later told us that after the FBI came through, Warden Edwards called all the jailed protestors together and said: "Lemme get one goddamn thing straight. I run this jail, and no one is going to tell me to reprimand an officer. Furthermore, there's going to be no more damn singing, no more damn hunger strikes, and no more damn beating on the walls."

It wasn't a very merry Christmas for any of us.

~ 11 ~

Eye to Eye with the Enemy

Friday's March on downtown Baton Rouge was a deliberate agitation, led by outside people who stirred a substantial minority of students of Southern University to come to Baton Rouge to protest the enforcement of the state anti-picketing laws by mass violation of these laws.

. . . Police permitted Friday's demonstration to proceed peacefully. But when its announced purposes had been achieved and when the mass demonstration threatened to turn into mob action, they stepped in to disperse the crowd and restore order. . . . The explosion of tear gas bombs amidst crowds of people runs counter to everything in which we all believe. But it was an action by the police which was necessary to prevent results which would have been infinitely worse. . . .

Baton Rouge, like all cities, has enough problems on its hands without permitting a group of university students to create more.

—EDITORIAL, *Baton Rouge Morning Advocate*, DECEMBER 18, 1961

M OST OF THE LEADERSHIP returned to Scotlandville very early in January and gathered at Pat's to decide what to do. Outside, the sky was a dreary slate gray, and low-hanging clouds spat a sticky mist. The bail money was rolling in, and it looked like we'd have everyone released by the time school reopened . . . but then what? From all indications, the board was sticking by their decision to expel all of them. And Dr. Clark? Well, he had promised support, closed school early, and disappeared. We had no guarantees. Our whole movement hinged on Dr. Clark and the university. We were reduced to waiting and hoping, our momentum diminished, our foe shielded by that most impenetrable of all armors—bureaucracy.

We wondered if Dr. Clark would recognize, as we did, that the wrong we were fighting was rooted in the blindly presumptuous white legislature, in the thoughtlessly arrogant white children of thoughtlessly arrogant white parents, and in the swelling white ignorance that is so close to hate? Would he realize he could remove himself from that system, thereby disempowering the whites who orchestrated it? Would he recognize that we didn't want to fight our university, that we wanted to fight to change the structure that made the university what it was? Would he recognize that any change we made would be a positive change not just for us, but for him? Or would he this time, as he did in 1960, maneuver himself between us and the white establishment, much like a grown-up child defending an abusive parent, so that instead of attacking the establishment, we Negroes would rain blows down upon ourselves?

We decided, however, that waiting and hoping wasn't good enough. In a daring gambit, we decided that we would meet with the white establishment ourselves rather than counting on Clark to be our emissary. First, we contacted Acie Belton, a top black political leader in the area. Acie not only organized blacks to register to vote but also often told them which candidates to vote for. Over the years, he had built up a position of authority and influence in the black community while also garnering the respect of white officeholders, who saw him as a valuable spokesman for the black community. Not surprisingly, there were many white politicians in Louisiana for whom race was a matter of expediency and nothing more. We hoped that if they could be convinced it was in their own best interests to come down on our side of the fence, they would. Acie recognized this and capitalized upon it. When we told him we wanted to meet with a white lawmaker in person, he immediately suggested that he set up an appointment with Shelby Jackson, one of our major adversaries. Acie, a Jackson insider, laid the groundwork for us and scheduled the meeting at Jackson's offices at the State Capitol Building.

Pat, Thomas Peete, Willie Bradford, and I, along with a couple of others, were going to the meeting: needless to say, we were all a little nervous. We were going to meet the opposition face to face and eye to eye—a daunting prospect for youthful college students. But when we were introduced to Jackson, he was all southern cordiality, very pleasant and polite. He was unquestionably a shrewd man, if just in the fact that he had come to the meeting. I imagined he had made a career out of shrewdly and successfully walking the thin line between two conflicting constituencies. He had the assured, reserved air of a man whom you might assume ran into this sort of confrontation every day, if you didn't know otherwise. But I did know otherwise—Negroes didn't do this kind of thing in Louisiana in 1962—and I wondered if he was self-possessed enough to handle the truth.

As soon as the opening pleasantries were exchanged, I took a gamble and cut right to the point. "Look, Mr. Jackson, we are just students trying to get what is due to us as citizens of this country," I said slowly. "We are just trying to get the State of Louisiana to recognize us and treat us like human beings. Those students who were arrested were just peacefully standing up for what they believe in. That's not unreasonable, is it?" As I said this I visualized the policemen jumping out of their car and looking at Pat and me standing there calmly, without weapons, without hostility, and then raising their tear gas guns and firing.

"In the schools we are taught that we live in a democracy. We are taught that the laws and principles of the country are that people are to be treated as equals and that fundamental fairness is a basic fact. Yet racial discrimination is open and apparent."

"*G'wan home, nigger. G'wan home, nigger.*" Images of "Colored" and "White Only" signs flashed in my mind.

"It's just like the words on the emblem on the back of your chair there. Truth, Justice. Honesty. Those are the things we are striving for. We aren't criminals. We aren't violent. We aren't destroying anyone's property. We don't want to hurt anyone. We just want equal rights under the law." I took a deep breath. "Give us help, sir. Try to understand what we're doing."

When I finished, we looked at each other for a long moment, and then Jackson's eyes moved slowly over the faces of everyone in the room. I was surprised at the close attention he paid to what I was saying, that he looked me square in the face and didn't interrupt. For a moment, I thought he really did understand what I was saying, that we were of one mind and wanted the same things and that he would help us get them. He leaned forward in his chair, placed his hands flat on the desk in front of him, and spoke in a Louisiana drawl heavy with the weight of humid afternoons, rocking chairs, and sweetened tea. Though a year earlier Jackson had fought to keep Louisiana schools segregated, his rapport with Belton and other black leaders gave me hope.

"Sure, I understand what you're talking about. I know you and the other students are right. And I know goddamn well that segregation is wrong. I don't have a thing in the world against blacks. I work with them all the time, and I've enjoyed their political support. Acie here and I are good political friends." He stopped and surveyed the room again. "I'll tell you what. I'll let all those students back in, and I won't expel another one of you if you can guarantee me that when I run in the next election I won't get defeated because of it. If you can show me you've got enough votes to help me win the next time, then I'll let those students back in. But if you can't, then I'm afraid we're not going to be able to help you."

I stared at him, fighting the knowledge that I had heard him right. This was the moral fiber of our nation? My mind reeled. This was the kind of man who was deciding how young people should be educated? I didn't want to accept that. As we left his office, my emotions tumbled and slammed up against each other. I was shocked, hurt, angry, confused. I thought politicians were supposed to be open to reason, that they were supposed to listen to all sides of an issue, think about it honestly, and then pass judgment on it. If a judgment was reached that something was wrong, then, in my incredibly naïve concept of democracy, the politicians would stand up, say it was wrong, and do something to change it. I don't like to think that I was ever so simple-minded as to believe that the world could be so clearly defined or that people always operated in such crisp categories. But, in our hearts, what drove us was the hope that even with the most calculating foe, if we could look at him and talk to him one on one, we could touch his heart.

Although the reader may find it hard to believe that I could still be so naïve at age twenty, this was actually my first eyeball-to-eyeball encounter with a white politician, and it was an eye-opening experience. If this politician could ignore the moral rightness of something when it was presented to him simply and directly by the people he was supposed to represent, then I supposed others could, too. I supposed Dr. Clark and all the rest of Southern's administration could . . . again. I realized then that I had to change the way I was looking at this whole thing.

If reason and a direct moral appeal would not reach a man, then what would move him to initiate change? All my experience with whites through the NSA had been based on the idea that there were systematic, logical, moral, legal, and ethical arguments for the civil rights movement and desegregation, and I had trained myself to think about the movement in these terms. After my encounter with Jackson, however, I realized that the system was not going to be changed without determined, ongoing, and uncompromising struggle. *Battle.* If my morality wasn't going to move the keepers of the system, then it was my job to figure out a way to kick their asses and get their attention. Subsequently, that became part of my philosophy.

This experience marked the beginning of a real period of growth for me, a time when I realized that, if I had any intention of winning at their game, I had to start thinking like the big boys. If I didn't plan to lose the game—or be maimed or killed—I had to jettison my childlike assumptions, along with the rest of those knights-in-shining-armor illusions, and view the world as it was, not as I would have it be. I realized, too, that if I planned to keep on playing their game, I had better plan for the stakes to get higher. There is a certain point, in games of this sort, from which there is no return.

As in Memphis, black lawyers played a central role in offering us guidance and legal support. One of Baton Rouge's earliest black attorneys was Johnny Jones, a slight, brown-skinned solo practitioner who was cagey and unafraid. Briefcase in hand and bent slightly to the side, Jones walked hurriedly—whether into a meeting or into the courtroom—and didn't shy from helping us take on the powers that be. The other black solo practitioner in town was Murphy Bell, a dark brown-skinned man of medium height, slightly chubby with a modestly receding hairline and a face that bespoke intensity of purpose. Bell was a deliberate man who analyzed with us our different courses of legal action and was at the ready when our students went to jail. Giving their legal representation was the way these lawyers were offering their commitment and support to our struggle.

Before the opening of school on January 12, due to the combined efforts of CORE, Reverend Jemison, and attorneys Jones and Bell, all the student demonstrators were released. We held our breath, hoping against hope for an announcement of their reinstatement to the university.

But Dr. Clark did not keep his promise. We heard he had been holding almost daily consultations with State School Superintendent Jackson and District Attorney Sargent Pitcher (also chief legal advisor to the Louisiana Association of the White Citizens' Councils), and the three of them had reached a compromise. Instead of all the arrested protestors being expelled in accordance with the state board's original edict, only seven leaders (among them Ronnie Moore, Weldon Rougeau, and the key leaders of the Baton Rouge CORE group) would be dismissed.

On the surface, it might seem better to have seven expelled than the entire group, but to us it was another white victory. We believed that Dr. Clark should have stood by his promise: either all students would be reinstated or he would resign. He should have joined the protest with us and put real pressure on the governor; he should not have capitulated by sacrificing our strongest leaders. Even so, his inaction did not surprise us: it seemed characteristic of his wishy-washiness, his lack of follow through-on his commitments, and his lack of communication with the student body. As he announced the expulsions, he never mentioned his promise to resign before any students were expelled, and he never explained what had changed his mind. For several days, he said nothing.

In fact, the entire administration remained aloof and noncommittal, so we never knew where they were coming from and never understood what they really thought. Most of the faculty, it seemed to us, were simply too afraid for their jobs to openly support us. Evidently, they couldn't see beyond their Southern Heights front yards to the big picture that we were struggling to write ourselves into. They seemed to think that a 1,500-square-foot house was big enough.

We clearly didn't understand. We could not accept their apparent apathy and their fear of committing to change, change we saw not as an option but as a necessity. Weren't *they* supposed to be pulling us along? But it just wasn't that way. Southern's own students were being steamrolled by the judicial system. They faced serious criminal charges, long jail sentences, ruined careers and aspirations . . . and for what? What was their crime? Was standing up for rights equal to those of whites a crime? It galled me that these older, supposedly wiser and more educated blacks would stand by and pay lip service to this blatant and unlawful white domination. Couldn't they see that they were being exploited as much or more than we were? Yet, they did nothing. I wanted to shake them, just as I had wanted to shake the white police—shake them and wake them up. If saving their school required the sacrifice of seven black leaders, what would they have saved?

On January 12, we held a rally at the off-campus house on Swan Street and called for a boycott of classes until Dr. Clark explained himself. Class attendance the next day was scattered. The leadership group had begun meeting every morning at Pat's house and holding morning and afternoon rallies at different points on and around campus. Each day, more students stayed out of class. The feeling on campus was tense, expectant, and emotional. We felt betrayed by Dr. Clark, and our movement was faltering under the weight of *his* fear. It seemed to us as if he was allowing the segregationists to claim another victory. We were determined not to give in.

The pressure throughout this period, from December 15 on, was intense. The press wanted to know what we were going to do next: they were pressuring us to keep up the action, to keep the news coming. We also felt pressured by the legislature to withdraw our protests and shut our mouths about the police, the arrests, the jail, and the expulsions. Then there was the pressure from the local whites, who wished we'd vanish from the face of the earth. Since we had no way to estimate what the extent of their violent response might be, theirs was the one pressure we could never shake or ignore. We lived in real fear of physical violence, real fear that they might come around and shoot us. Certainly that kind of retaliation was not unknown. The mere fact that there were violent precedents to point to created a kind of manic group paranoia as we shuttled back and forth from Pat's house. Even as the situation escalated on campus, Dr. Clark initiated a "crackdown" on students who were boycotting classes, urging professors to "talk sense" to us. Students on scholarships were threatened with loss of their scholarships. The administration even called our parents: this insidious mental pressure finally got to me, and that feeling I had had as I ran from the tear gas and the police dogs became a constant. I was in constant fear of the moment, of physical violence, and, more importantly, of aloneness, of having nowhere to go, of never being safe again.

On January 15, we resolved to end our frustration and our inaction and confront Dr. Clark. We called him but succeeded in reaching only his secretary and his wife. We left word that we had organized a student delegation and wished to speak with him about the expulsions. He never returned our calls. Then we explained that we were willing to march to Dr. Clark's house and sit in his yard until he spoke with us. He did not respond. In the meantime, the boycott and the daily rallies continued. Word got out that I planned to speak on the steps of the administration building the next afternoon.

That night my brother, Walter, and I were unexpectedly called to meet with Ulysses Jones, the dean of men. As we walked to the small, white frame house on the edge of campus, I became increasingly apprehensive. It must be ultimatum time, I thought to myself. Had I finally come to that point of no return that some part of me had been dreading all along? If pushed, would I turn around? Would I go back, or would I go on?

When I opened the door to the screened porch, we were immediately greeted by a yelping little terrier. "Well, hello, D'Army, Walter. Don't mind Trixie—she's all yap and no bite. How are you boys?" asked Mrs. Jones warmly.

"Fine. Fine. And you?"

"Still recovering from Christmas, I think. But doing all right. The weather sure is cold."

"Yes ma'am."

"Let me take your coats. Dean Jones is sitting in the living room."

The simple conversation calmed me as I breathed in the comfort of the quaint little house. As we walked into the living room, Dean Jones rose to shake our hands. He was a tall, muscular man with a full head of coarse white hair. He enjoyed the confidence of the administration because he was not a boat-rocker, but a solid, dependable administrator. Like few of the faculty at Southern, he not only demanded respect, but he gave it in return. I think he honestly believed in students and empathized with our passions, struggles, and desires. While the students were jailed for more than a month, he made it a point to check on them and helped see that some of their personal needs were met. Dean Jones made establishing a rapport and trust with students a personal priority.

"D'Army, I know how strongly you feel about this boycott, and I sympathize with you. Believe me, I do. You're right. The situation is bad. And you young people are doing the right thing in standing up to mistreatment of blacks. But, you've gone downtown and marched, and you've had your demonstrations, and you've made your point. You've gotten press coverage from all over the nation in this. But, D'Army, politicians are jumping all over the state to try and get us to stop this."

Apparently, the white constituents and the white legislators had had about enough of our uppity behavior; they were growing increasingly aggravated that we weren't being kept under control, especially since Southern was a state-supported school.

"D'Army, we just can't let those students back in school, not now. It's no use calling up Dr. Clark and badgering him and making speeches because we can't do anything about it. If we did, the governor and the state board would be all over us in a minute. And we can't afford that." He took a deep breath. "In time, maybe we can let them back in, after all this blows over. But not now. Why don't y'all just call off the class boycott before things get further out of hand?"

I listened to a clock ticking on the wall above the fireplace. I looked at my hands, at the grain in the wood floor. "Well, sir, I respect your position," I said calmly, looking up at him, "but at this point we can't. We are committed to what we are doing, and we have gone too far to stop now. It was wrong for those students to be expelled. Dr. Clark promised he would not expel them: he even said he would resign first. Instead, he expelled them anyway. He promised us university support, yet the university has fought us every step of the way. We know we are doing what is right, and we won't back down."

Dean Jones then turned to Walter. "I've talked to your parents, Walter. I've told them that D'Army is on the verge of being thrown out of school if he doesn't halt his activities. They weren't too happy about that. They suggested that maybe you would talk with him and remind him of the importance of a college education."

"Well, Dean Jones," said Walter slowly, after clearing his throat several times, "I don't think I could change D'Army's mind if I wanted to. In addition, I don't want to because I agree with his principles. I think they are right, and I think the protests should continue. I respect what he is doing too much to step in the way of his judgment," he explained, his voice serious and even.

Although he had not assumed a leadership role in the protests, Walter always attended our rallies and offered me support and advice. They assumed he would be the weak link in the two of us. After all, they had brought him there on a football scholarship; athletes weren't supposed to be interested in this sort of thing. They had hoped they could convince him that my behavior would cause us both all kinds of misfortune and misery. Obviously, they wanted to play on the "big brother knows best" psychology. But none of it worked.

Dean Jones was silent for some time, his eyes moving from Walter to me and then to the floor in front of him. He seemed truly conflicted and distressed by what he had to say, but I knew it was coming: "D'Army, I know you are planning to speak tomorrow at noon on the steps of the administration building. But if you do, we will have no choice but to expel you from the university. Furthermore, if you ever speak on this campus again in relation to anything that is going on now, you will be immediately expelled." His eyes and face had taken on a masklike hardness. "Do I make myself perfectly clear?"

"Yes, sir," I said and was quiet because there was nothing left to say.

At 11:30 a.m. on January 16, I left my dorm and began slowly walking toward the administration building perched on the Mississippi River bluff. I was cold, deep-down cold, inside and out. My thoughts raced.

At least what Dean Jones had said hadn't come as a surprise. I had known it was coming from the night I stepped up to the podium of the church in

Scotlandville, the night of the tear gas smell and the march to Dr. Clark's house. As every day passed and every rally ended, I knew this was going to be part of the price I would have to pay for staying in the game. I decided that I could handle it, that I was ready to go on. I knew that if I turned back then and did not speak, I would be turning my back on everything I claimed to believe in. And that the cost of that—having nothing left of myself to believe in—would be greater than that of being thrown out of school. *I can handle it,* I told myself. *I shall overcome.*

That morning, the CORE leadership met at Pat's, and we decided to carry through on our threat to march to Dr. Clark's house. So, at noon on January 16, a miserably cold day with an icy wind slicing across campus and turning the Mississippi frothy brown, over one thousand students gathered in front of the administration building. Standing atop the granite wall bordering the steps, I addressed the crowd. From there, Jerome Smith, Dave Dennis, Ronnie, Weldon, Pat, and I led the group the short distance to Dr. Clark's front lawn, which was right next to the administration building. We waited through the afternoon and into the night for him to come out. There, under a cluster of moss-draped oaks, we huddled together in sleeping bags and under bedspreads and blankets through the early-morning hours, meditating, praying, and singing. I huddled with my girlfriend, Joyce. She was a pretty brown-skinned girl with flowing shoulder-length hair and an engaging smile. We shivered into the night. In spite of all, there was something lovingly reassuring on that cold ground, arm in arm, almost as if God had sent this woman to help me through the night.

> I'm gonna sit at the welcome table,
> I'm gonna sit at the welcome table one of these days,
> Hallelujah!
> I'm gonna sit at the welcome table,
> I'm gonna sit at the welcome table one of these days.
> —Traditional Negro spiritual

Eventually, Dr. Clark sent out a messenger, who told us: "There can be no communication in a mob situation. Dr. Clark will not speak to you."

That night, we restated our commitment to boycott classes until we received a response. "We must make it unavoidably clear to Dr. Clark that we will not be ignored!" Ronnie shouted to the crowd. "Our movement must continue until we can sit side by side with whites at every lunch counter in Baton Rouge."

"We must hold him to his promise of support and remind him that we are not just his students, we are his own people. We are fighting for the rights of all Negro people!" hollered Dave.

"We shall overcome! We have overcome the police and the tear gas. And we shall overcome the courts, the white bigots, and even Dr. Clark and this university!" Ronnie shouted again. "Let's stand together. Boycott classes tomorrow. Stand up for what you know is right!"

"We do not want to fight against our own people. We want to fight against the white legislators who make unjust laws," I explained. "We want to change those laws so all men are free!"

The next morning, Dr. Clark called a special, campuswide convocation. And I received notice to be in Dean Jones's office at 11:00 a.m.

~ 12 ~

Expulsion, Dismissal

The right to peaceful assembly is a guarantee of our Constitution. It is not however, a right to promote the infringement of laws of the land. So when a point has been made by a demonstration, it is then time to quit the demonstration. There is a very thin line between an assembly of peaceable persons and an unruly mob. Moreover, when one group assembles in behalf of a certain issue, another group is likely to assemble also at the same place and create an explosive situation.

The right of the Negro group to demonstrate on Friday was recognized. . . . This demonstration was tied in with the sit-in attempts at various lunch counters. There are state laws designed to prevent one person from trespassing on the private property of another without invitation. These laws were taken to the nation's highest court and were not ruled upon. . . . So, the right to peaceable assembly has to stop short of violation of the state law.

As of now, the points in this issue have all been raised. People are aware of them. We've had demonstrations enough.

—EDITORIAL, *Baton Rouge State Times*, DECEMBER 18, 1961

D EAN JONES'S OFFICE was on the upper campus, near the administration building, and separated from the student union and the gym by Lake Kernan. I wondered, as I walked under the moss-draped oaks, if I would ever walk this path again, and if I would miss it. When I arrived at the cluster of administrative offices, Dean Jones was in no way hostile, but he was brisk and direct. "You have violated the university's direct order, as explained to you on January 16, that you not speak on this campus again," he said. "Dean Harvey is waiting in his office to speak with you."

As we entered the dean of students' office, he stood, as customary, and then asked us to have a seat. Dean Harvey was a short, portly man with a receding hairline and a protruding belly. This afternoon, as always, he held a pipe. "D'Army, you have no idea how I hate that this moment has come," he said in a businesslike tone. The quintessential college administrator, Dean Harvey always spoke in a faintly patronizing tone that struck a note somewhere between boredom and disdain. "I respect you and what you are trying to do," he continued. "I understand it. When I was young I struggled, too. I sat down in the street in protest in the 1940s, and I was arrested. I know what it's like. Your cause is not wrong—that's not the problem. The problem is that you don't know how to compromise." He paused and tapped his pipe in his palm. "You don't know how to stop."

Okay, I wanted to ask him, when is it permissible to turn away from wrong instead of fighting to change it? Just sometimes? Just in this case? If we don't try to make our future better, who will? When, if not now, do we begin to take control of our own lives? I thought all of them were forgetting their responsibility. I thought they were copping out.

Dean Harvey filled his pipe. "I am afraid that Dr. Clark has decided you are to be expelled from the university," he said. "As you know, all the other students who have been expelled were arrested first, which is covered under a university rule that says a student who is arrested can be expelled before he is brought to trial."

I had no idea what he was getting at. I watched him light the pipe.

"You have obviously not been arrested, and your grades are fine, so I think that it is only fair to explain that, since we must have grounds for your expulsion, we are citing violation of Rule 18 in the student handbook." Rule 18 read, "Southern University reserves the right to sever a student's connection with the university for general inability to adjust to the patterns of the institution."

"In actuality," he explained, somewhat apologetically, "this rule was designed to allow for the expulsion of students who are found to be homosexuals. But it was as close as we could come, in terms of its wording, to a rule violation to base your expulsion on."

Perfect. I hadn't broken any university law, but I hadn't adjusted to the system. Evidently, the unwritten laws—the ones they don't mention at freshman orientation—said my thinking was supposed to adjust to the university, along with my politics and my outlook on the world. Since I remained an individual, mine didn't. As a result, the system threw me out in an act of self-protection.

Dean Harvey dispatched this news as if it were just another part of a busy day. But Dean Jones wouldn't look at me, and I knew he was profoundly hurt. A wave of understanding washed over me as I realized that he, of all the administration, surely felt just as helpless as I did.

"I cannot overemphasize how important it is that you remain off campus," Dean Harvey continued as he puffed on his pipe. If you are found on campus, you will be subject to arrest. Do you understand?

"Yes, sir."

"Walter is being moved to an off-campus apartment, so you won't be tempted." He looked at me over his pipe. "I'm sorry this had to happen, D'Army. I had hopes for you. I always thought you could have been a good student."

While the two deans were dutifully protecting the university on one end of the campus, Dr. Clark was adamantly defending it on the other. In a speech in the woman's gymnasium that I did not witness, but that was described to me at length, Dr. Clark officially announced the expulsion of the seven student leaders whom he described as "vandals and anarchists." He derided all students who participated in the protests as "vicious hoodlums" and branded us as "culturally void."

"We at Southern are interested in education and nothing else," he informed faculty and students. "This misdirected protest has created a reign of terror on this campus, and it must end." He demanded that the faculty stand by him and warned them that the dog that bites the hand that feeds it is soon no longer around. He reprimanded us all for our lapse of "straight thinking" and our apparent inability to follow the "party line."

All in all, it was probably one of the most abhorrently anti-intellectual speeches ever delivered by a university president. Lacking leadership, lacking conviction, lacking any apparent understanding of the backgrounds, experiences, or beliefs of his young black student body, Dr. Clark assumed the role of patriarch and disciplinarian, demanding obedience and allegiance. But every word, despite his firm stand, was tinged with desperation. His position was unsound. His reasoning was less reasoning than a string of illogical insults and irrational proclamations. All had to be accepted without question simply because he demanded it.

When I entered the gym, he was nearing the end of his address.

"I have made every effort to restore order to this campus," he stated for the umpteenth time. "But you choose to listen to the rabble-rousers rather than listening to me. This boycott is threatening the survival of the university. A university cannot be run by mobs and vandals. The student rebellion must end. Therefore, today I am closing Southern University indefinitely."

A murmur of shock passed through the crowd.

"You have until five o'clock today to have all of your belongings packed and to clear off campus. The highway patrol will take over the campus at five o'clock, and any of you remaining here at that time will be subject to arrest."

This I hadn't expected.

"I cannot tell you at this time when the university will reopen," he continued. "But when it does, some of you will not be allowed to come back because of your protest activities. All students will have to reapply for admission, and the university will send letters to those of you we want to return. If you do not receive a letter, you are not, I repeat, you are not to return."

Suddenly, everyone was on their feet in a roar of panic and confusion. Hundreds of Southern students lived out of state or in outlying areas of Louisiana: telephone lines were jammed for hours as students called home and tried to make arrangements to get off campus before the five o'clock deadline. Some of us were hurt and felt strangely, intensely insecure; it was as if part of our family had just rejected us, or as if we had just been told we were orphans. Others were angry— blindly, ferociously angry at everyone and everything. But most of us, I think, were merely numb. We were numb with the slow realization of the present moment and numb with fear of the unknown. What was going to happen to us now?

I immediately searched for Weldon and Ronnie, finally finding Weldon in the student union.

"I've just been expelled."

"What?" He stared at me. "On what grounds?"

"Lack of adjustment. It's a rule for expelling sissies that they're adapting for me. Ha! Can you believe it?"

"Man, this is crazy, absolutely crazy."

"But it's the principle of the thing, man! Clark's blowing a golden opportunity for all of us, and he's playing right into the hands of every white asshole in this town!"

"So what the hell can we do now? Will you look at this shit?" Weldon motioned out into the union lobby. The low-ceilinged, tiled room was filling to capacity with students crying, hugging, talking, yelling messages at each other. Twenty or more people were lined up at each pay phone.

"What are we going to do?"

"We're going to have another rally this afternoon."

"We could get arrested, man. Clark'll have police crawling all over the place."

"Who cares? The school is closed. We'll lose everything, if we don't keep the students together. Right? C'mon, Weldon, right?"

"Right. Okay. Right. So, we need to get the word out. When are we gonna do it?"

"How about three o'clock on the gym steps? Get Ronnie and tell him what's going on. We'll all speak, okay?"

"Okay, good."

"Hey, Weldon, meet me there about five minutes early."

For the rest of the afternoon, I watched long, winding lines of students streaming off campus like refugees, carrying everything they owned in suitcases, boxes, and bags. Small cafés, the movie theater, the bus station, and the streets of Scotlandville were filled with students trying to arrange a ride to a place to stay. I rushed from dorm to dorm, urgently telling everyone I saw that the protest was not over. We were having a rally at three o'clock: the movement was not dead. I urged them to wait another hour to leave campus, to come to the rally, to stay with the movement and the fight for freedom.

It was just before three o'clock when I began making my way toward the gym. I had talked to a lot of students and felt sure at least a couple hundred would come. My heart was beating fast, and my adrenaline soared as I walked quickly along the sidewalk.

Up ahead, I saw Weldon waiting for me, and I waved. Weldon waved back, and then I saw Ronnie join him. I was maybe twenty feet away from them when a police car pulled right up in front of the gym. I stopped. Two policemen got out, a few words were exchanged, and then they immediately handcuffed both of them and led them to the car. I turned around and walked the other way. My emotions were torn, but I knew it would not help our movement for me to volunteer to join them in the back seat of the trooper car.

By five o'clock, the campus was almost deserted. Showing uncharacteristic mercy, the administration had relented and allowed the handful of students who could find no place to stay to spend the night in their dorms without being arrested. The highway patrol surrounded the campus, imposing a complete blockade. To get on or off campus, we had to pass through a highway patrol checkpoint. Campus security officers were posted at each inhabited dorm, and some sheriff's deputies patrolled the grounds.

As the hours passed, the campus grew ghostly dark and quiet. When I looked out my dorm window, only a solitary light here and there indicated any other life at all. So this is what it's like to feel alone, I thought. I wondered if Weldon and Ronnie would be placed in solitary. I wondered what it was like in jail. I wandered around the dorm, not knowing what to do with myself. A couple of students sat in the lobby and stared dejectedly at the TV. No one said anything. I couldn't concentrate.

I asked myself how I felt, but I didn't know. I tried to pack. I couldn't. I stared at the walls, my mind wandering. Our leadership group had met earlier in the evening to reaffirm our commitment, to maintain the protest, and to get Ronnie and Weldon out of jail. I told myself to hold onto that, to look ahead. I had been expelled; that was a fact. Even if the university reopened, I wasn't coming back. I needed to get on with my life, with what I believed in. This was just an interruption of my education, a detour, nothing tragic. Maybe I could find a place where I didn't have to "adjust" to mysterious "patterns." Maybe there was a place where you could be black, an individual, and a fighter for equality all at the same time. Maybe.

Finally, about nine o'clock, I decided it was time to call home. The events at Southern were national news at this point, and I knew my parents would be worried. They wouldn't lecture, and they wouldn't judge; they'd just want to know if I were okay. Down in the lounge the television was still on, same as always. It made eerie patterns and shadows on the dark walls. I put my nickel in the pay phone and called Memphis collect. My mother answered.

"Hello, Mama, this is D'Army."

"D'Army! It's so good to hear from you."

"How are y'all doing?"

"We're doing fine, just fine. Your father went out of town tonight, to Chicago. How's your brother?"

"He's fine. He was over here earlier. He's gone back to his dorm room now."

"And you?"

"Well, that's what I wanted to talk to you about. It's about my situation here at Southern."

"Yes, honey, what is it?"

"As you know, we've been having our protest demonstrations, and I was one of the leaders. The dean had ordered me to stop speaking at protest rallies, but I wouldn't, so they expelled me today."

"Yes, I know, son. There was a story on the evening news, and I heard that you were expelled. But how are you doing? Are you doing all right?"

"Yes, Mama. I'm really doing fine. I'm all packed, and tomorrow I'm moving off campus to a downtown hotel. CORE is sending us some money to help put us up for a while, and this black hotel is going to give us a special rate."

"Do you need anything, any money? Do you want to come home?"

"Not right now, Mama. We've got a lot left to do. I think I need to stay around here for a little while longer, get these other students out of jail, and keep the movement going."

"Well, son, you know your father and I have confidence in you; we respect your judgment. If that's what you want to do, and that's what you think is best, you know you have our support. Just please be careful, you hear?"

"I will, Mama."

"And if there is ever any time you need us or want to come home, you remember we're just as near as the telephone."

"Yes, I know that, Mama, and I appreciate it. You know that's part of what helps me to go on, knowing I have y'all's support."

"Just be careful, will you?"

"I will. Give my love to Daddy, and thank you, Mama."

"All right, I will, son. Good-bye."

I went back to my room and sat for a while in the darkness, which had now transformed into a comfortingly empty quiet, and then I went to bed.

The same dark evening Professor Adolph Reed was up late drafting a letter to Dr. Clark. Professor Reed was not a believer in the sit-ins because he did not believe any social changes of consequence would result from them. He took a more uncompromising approach toward protest, believing as he did that nonviolent demonstration would not change anything. He felt that America did not deal with important issues in terms of morality or conscience but in terms of dollars and power. He who wields the power wins.

Some agreed with Reed, and some of us didn't. I tended to think the country was more malleable than that and that eventually it could be manipulated by means other than brute force. But then I was an optimist and an idealist, believing that peaceful confrontation would force change, and Reed was a pragmatist and skeptic. Consequently, although Reed didn't march alongside us, he never told us we shouldn't be doing what we were doing or discouraged us from our goals. In fact, he maintained a fairly low profile until Dr. Clark unleashed his ill-fated speech upon us and closed the school. By that time, Professor Reed had had about enough.

The fourteen-page letter he drafted in the days immediately following Clark's speech was a masterfully witty, well-documented, and sane analysis of the president's behavior since the very first demonstrations in 1960. The sheer intellectual and rational force of Reed's criticisms was irrefutable, and his understanding of the complicated, multifaceted issues was both enlightening and inspiring. Here was an older, educated black man standing up uncompromisingly for what he believed. In my opinion, he was what educators were supposed to be: people of principle and courage.

The letter was reprinted in part by several newspapers and covered on the local news. We quoted from it during later rallies and distributed as many copies of it as we could. In one of the letter's finest points, Reed wrote: "In our situation at Southern, you utilize what is tantamount to the Adolf Eichmann attitude—that there is no administrative alternative than to carry out the evil designs of perpetrators of an evil social system. This intellectual-administrative position can be projected into some horrifying eventualities. For instance, where is the line drawn, if it is drawn?" He continued:

> In fact, Dr. Clark, if you were to explain to your superiors that you cannot control the currents of history, and that young people called Negroes can no longer be expected to read of and to be told of the platitudes in what Myrdal refers to as the "American Creed" and to simultaneously observe that the creed is a mirage as it relates to themselves, the faculty would likely support you to the hilt. To the hilt means that if you were removed from your position as president as a result of explaining this historical, sociological, psychological fact to your superiors, the faculty would in all probability walk off in protest. But there is a dramatic absence of direction and leadership on your part.

Reed then went on to explain that education cannot exist in the abstract, separate from people and issues: "The intellectual position that 'education' somehow exists divorced from human relations begs careful reexamination. Your repetition of the phrase, 'We at Southern are interested in Education and nothing else,' places a peculiar connotation on the word 'education.'"Can education realistically exist in the abstract?" He also criticized Clark for the inconsistency in his emotion-charged accusations of students: "Certainly as a professional psychologist, you could not have meant 'culturally void.' By definition, no human being is culturally void. Indeed, most of us as Negroes are culturally deprived, but then we do not establish the social order and value system which renders us culturally deprived."

Reed wrote that if Dr. Clark saw even the slightest merit in his position, he would be pleased to discuss or debate the issues in a faculty group, public forum, or any other setting. Professor Reed was summarily fired. Only later, as I remembered Professor Reed, did his broad impact on our tumultuous years come into focus. Several of the first group of sit-in protestors at Southern had been students in Reed's political science class. Similarly, my brother and I had heard of Reed's thought-provoking lectures and enrolled in his class. Reed lamented the "ruling class's" dividing poor and working class people by race, and focusing their attention on the wrong enemies. He decried American militarism and spoke of the complicity of the news media, religion, and the education system. He sharply rebuked those Negroes in administrative and authority positions who accommodated and ran interference for white-controlled authority.

After Reed's death in 2003, I learned that his activism dated back to the 1940s in New York in the American Labor Party, and to 1948, when he was a delegate to the Progressive Party convention that launched Henry Wallace's presidential campaign. In addition, he was among the thousands who had attended the famous September 1949 concert in Peekskill, New York, expressing solidarity with the great singer and black political activist Paul Robeson, and protesting the right-wing mob attack against Robeson supporters at his Peekskill concert weeks before. It was Reed's humanity, courage, and progressivism that helped light the flame of our rebellion. For that I will ever be grateful.

~ 13 ~
Turning the Page

December, 1961, it was Southern University in Baton Rouge, and April, 1962,
it is Lincoln University in Jefferson City, MO. In Lincoln, when Negro and
white students protested, 9 were suspended following continuous demonstrations against segregated bowling alleys. Following suspension, members of
the Missouri State Youth Conference of the NAACP burned an effigy of the
university president. Reason: "To protest with vigor and determination the
dictatorial attitude and policy of the Lincoln administration." Apparently
there were two antagonists in both situations—the people "downtown" and
those at home.
—ARTICLE IN *Southern Digest,* APRIL 4, 1962

O N JANUARY 19, the *Baton Rouge Morning Advocate* ran a long story
under the headline "No Word Is Given on Re-Opening of Southern
University":

Aides close to President Felton G. Clark, who is reportedly ill with
influenza, told newsmen the president is not available for further
comment on the closing which was announced at a student-faculty
convocation yesterday. . . . State Supt. of Education Shelby M. Jackson,
who said yesterday the announcement of the closure was a surprise to
him, said he did not know if the State Board of Education would take
up the issue when it meets today. . . . After the formal announcement
of the closure, sheriff deputies arrested two Negro student leaders
with the Congress of Racial Equality upon request of the university.
Arrested were Ronnie Moore, local CORE chairman, and Weldon
Rougeau, another CORE official. They were arrested in a group which
was forming near the gymnasium and charged with trespassing and

disturbing the peace. The pair was apparently ordered off campus earlier this week by a disciplinary board.

Later that day, we found out that Ronnie and Weldon were locked up together in an isolated cell. Bail was set at three thousand dollars. That was a lot of money in 1962, when a new Corvette, for example, could be purchased for five thousand dollars.

On January 20, the *Morning Advocate* ran the headline "Southern University Plans to Resume Classes Jan. 29 ": "A university spokesman said second semester classes at Southern will begin on Jan. 29. Registration will begin on Thursday, Jan. 25. Notices to students of the reopening will be in the mail Monday. It was indicated that there will be a screening process based on 'Scholastic and other requirements.'"

When James Farmer and the New York CORE office put up the funds, about twenty of us—including Dave, Jerome, Thomas, Willie, me, and eventually Reverend Cox—moved into the Lincoln Hotel located at 400 South Thirteenth Street in Baton Rouge. In the early to mid-1950s, the fifteen-year-old, four-story hotel had been *the* hotel in black Louisiana. With a spacious restaurant on the first floor, modern carpeted rooms along L-shaped corridors, high ceilings, and chandeliers, the hotel had been a stopping-off point for top-name black entertainers. But those days had long since passed. In January 1962, the once grand hotel was very nearly empty. Water stains showed on the carpet; the wallpaper was faded and peeling. The hotel was now to become Baton Rouge's first official civil rights headquarters. And as such, we were its first inhabitants.

We immediately began picking up the pieces of our movement. We held meetings with black community leaders. We sent out fliers warning of the discrimination and segregation practices of local stores: Kress, Goudchaux's, Woolworth, J. C. Penney, Montgomery Ward, Rosenfield's, Three Sisters, McCrory's, Sears. We wrote letters. We appealed to citizens, clergy, and businessmen for donations. We met with attorneys in Baton Rouge and in New Orleans in preparation for a series of court hearings that were coming for the student protesters and Reverend Cox. Also providing valuable legal support were three black civil rights lawyers in New Orleans: Bob Collins, Nils Douglas, and Lolis Elie. A handful of us made regular visits to their New Orleans law office, where they briefed us on their legal strategy to defend those who had been arrested, and on their efforts to get us back into the university. The lawyers were very supportive and reassuring, and we'd top off our visits with delicious fried-chicken dinners at Dookie Chase, New Orleans's fancy, premier soul food restaurant on Claiborne Avenue.

The New Orleans and Baton Rouge lawyers were backed in their efforts by CORE's New York general counsel Carl Rachlin, and Jack Greenberg, who succeeded Thurgood Marshall as general counsel of the NAACP Legal Defense Fund. Douglas, Rachlin, and Greenberg ultimately battled three Southern University protest cases all the way to the U.S. Supreme Court. The Court declined to hear one case, the conviction of SNCC activist Dion Diamond, who was arrested while trying to rally campus students, but it rendered landmark decisions in *Garner,* and later regarding the demonstrations of December 15.

The only support we received from the white community came from a civil rights organization in New Orleans, the Southern Conference Education Fund. Its leader was Dr. James Dombrowski, a sincere man in his fifties, tall and of sturdy build, but bent forward on crutches, his mobility limited, but not his spirit. He came to the Lincoln Hotel to see about us, to give modest financial help, and to offer encouragement. The following year, Louisiana police raided Dombrowski's offices and those of the group's treasurer, New Orleans civil liberties attorney Benjamin Smith, as well as the offices of Smith's law partner, Bruce Waltzer. These were the only white lawyers I knew of in the state who were helping the civil rights cause. The files and records from both offices were seized, and the men were arrested under Louisiana's Subversive Activities and Communist Control Act. Dombrowski sued the governor and state officials, charging them with intimidating and harassing citizens who supported the rights of blacks. A three-judge federal court in Louisiana threw the suit out, and the Dombrowski case went to the U.S. Supreme Court. In response, the High Court further reined in Louisiana authorities, finding the Louisiana statute unconstitutional and expanding First Amendment protections for those fighting for civil rights. In that important decision issued April 1965, *Dombrowski v. Pfister,* the Court ordered the Louisiana federal court to enjoin the prosecutions of Dombrowski, Smith, and Waltzer as a violation of the First Amendment and ordered the return of their files and records.

While it was common for southern authorities to accuse civil rights supporters, particularly whites, of being communists, in my years of political activism I have never had a supporter either identify himself or herself as a communist or invite my participation in any activity that I in any way suspected might be communist. We had too many battles to fight against white racists to spend any time investigating the affiliations of supporters who, though on the political left, were offering open, lawful, and much-needed support.

As with most movements that have reached their high point of intensity, it is necessary to keep fighting even when the opposition bears in and gains ground. We were determined not to allow the white segregationists to claim victory, and we were not about to give up. We began planning strategies for reigniting the fires of protest on Southern's campus when university registration began that Thursday. We were determined not to allow the white segregationists to claim this victory, and we were not about to give up.

Beginning the Thursday the university was to reopen, we held a series of rallies on and around campus. We chanted, "We want freedom!" and "Freedom now!" We sang hymns, and we reminded students of the goals we had set forth in December. We spoke of pride, dignity, and justice and of the freedom to work for the same wages as a white man, to ride in the same bus seats, to drink from the same water fountain, and to eat at the same table.

"If you don't demand a better future, you will not get it!" Dave shouted from the balcony on Swan Street. "Tomorrow will be as bad as today or worse. You must hold strong to what is right! Equality is right!"

As we should have expected, student support was scattered and hesitant. It was obvious that the campus community was afraid. The night before the campus was to reopen, Thomas Peete and Willie Bradford—who had been expelled in the original seven—and I planned our attempt to register. We called the media and staged the event, fully expecting to be arrested since we had been banned from campus. Even so, we knew that was all part of the game we were playing. We were willing to go to jail if that meant more media attention that would put us back in the forefront of the public consciousness. Our rallies and occasional pickets weren't enough to keep the spirit of the protest from lagging. We needed a media boost.

So on the bright morning of January 26, we walked out of the Lincoln Hotel and caught a black-owned cab to Scotlandville. I had to admire the courage of that cab driver, who knew from our conversation in the cab that we were driving into a police confrontation. We were apprehensive about what would happen when we got to Southern because we knew the place would be swarming with officers from an alphabet soup of agencies. Thomas and Willie had already spent three weeks in jail, and they weren't exactly anxious to go back.

"If y'all end up back in jail so soon, the real criminals are gonna think you missed them," I said with a smirk, trying to break the nervous quiet. "I'm beginning to think this life of crime isn't such a bad way to go," I said.

"Huh?"

"Hell, you get your meals, a nice cot to sleep on—"

"Right," said Willie, "and all kinds of dudes telling you stories you don't want to hear. Bailey, you just wait, man. You don't know a thing about it."

"Now, hold on, Tom, what about Sugarboy, that old man with no teeth? I thought y'all got along good. Or Cleveland, that fat guy who loved his Mama."

"He killed her."

"Yeah, but he reeeeeally loved her."

We all laughed. "And he's gonna luuuv Bailey, too," added Willie. "I just can't wait for y'all to meet."

"C'mon, we're not going to jail," I said, a little nervously. "We're just gonna get on the evening news."

"You love that TV, don't you, Bailey?" Willie chided. "Can I wave to the folks at home?"

"No," Tom replied with mock disgust. "But I sure hope to God you wore two pairs of underwear."

"Finally, the cab turned onto the campus and pulled up in front of the Registrar's office. Frantically, we looked out the windows. No cameras, no press.

"Where the hell are they, goddammit?" I felt myself beginning to panic.

"Maybe they're tired of filming our ugly faces," said Tom.

"Dr. Clark probably paid them off." I think Willie was trying to joke, but at that point, almost anything was believable.

"No, no way, man," said Tom, deadly serious. "How would he know we were coming?"

"Someone could have told him." We looked at each other, almost believing this was true, that we had been set up. I quickly scanned the grounds around the cab for police. News coverage often prompted the police to be more cautious than when they weren't being watched. I shuddered. If our attempt to register wasn't recorded, the whole purpose would be lost, and we might get hurt. "There's just no way," Tom said again. "Come on."

We got out of the cab, and a few minutes later, as we stood there wondering what to do, a student supporter rushed over to us and said the newspeople were waiting on the upper campus on the steps of the administration building. When he volunteered to go get them, we hung back and slunk around, hoping we wouldn't run into anyone important. Ten minutes later, they approached us, cameras clicking and buzzing away as they asked who we were, what we were doing, and why we were doing it. They followed us into Registrar J. J. Hedgemon's office and listened and filmed while he told us we couldn't enroll.

"You have been expelled by the Southern University Disciplinary Board. You know as well as I do that you cannot register."

"We were expelled on illegitimate grounds," I replied.

"Go see Dean Jones," he said tersely. And back we went, entourage in tow, to the administration building.

We made quite a show, traipsing into Dean Jones's outer office, with reporters, cameras, and supportive students filling every available space. "D'Army Bailey, Willie Bradford , and Thomas Peete are here to see Dean Jones and ask to be readmitted," I told the wide-eyed secretary. "Please wait here," she said curtly as she hurried into the dean's office and closed the door.

Just then a breathless student burst into the outer office and pushed his way through the crowd. "The po-lice! The po-lice! They're all outside. State police and sheriff's deputies are pulling up by the carloads. They have the building completely surrounded!"

Willie, Tom, and I were frightened; there was no use hiding it. The worst had come to pass. Clearly, the rules of the game were getting tougher and tougher. "Well," I said at last, forcing air into my tightening chest, "We'll just wait to see the dean and then go outside and be arrested. That's what we're here for." "Riiiight," we said to each other with weak smiles as we braced ourselves as if for a tornado.

Minutes later, the chief campus security officer shoved his way past us and into Dean Jones's office. A buzz of speculation passed through the group. We had no idea what was up now. Momentarily, the security officer emerged from the dean's office to a cicadalike whirring and clicking of cameras. "Dean Jones has instructed me to escort D'Army Bailey, Willie Bradford, and Thomas Peete to my patrol car and drive you off campus," he said. "He does not wish to speak with you. However, he has told me if you come with me now, you will avoid being arrested because you will remain in university custody until you are off the campus. Do you understand?"

We stared at him. The room was suddenly quiet at this unexpected generosity of the university.

"Follow me."

As we left the building, we stepped out between double lines of police and newsmen, who converged as we moved quickly to the patrol car. Reporters yelled questions at us, and flash bulbs blinded our eyes with the possibility of notoriety. Lines of sheriff's and state troopers' cars escorted us off campus. After a solemn procession fit for the funeral of some dignitary, we arrived on the other side of the railroad tracks, and the chief security officer let us out. As the police continued swarming the area impotently, we walked into Scotlandville and took a cab back to our hotel.

"I guess Dr. Clark doesn't want us back, after all," said Willie in obvious relief.

I couldn't respond. I was overwhelmed by thoughts of the significance of the moment, realizing this January morning marked the end of one era of my life and the beginning of the next—whatever it may become. No, Dr. Clark didn't want us back. We weren't going back, or at least I knew I wasn't. I didn't know where I was going, but one thing was certain, I wasn't going back to Southern. I began to turn my eyes outward, to the rest of the world.

> We'll never turn back
> No, we'll never turn back.
> Until we've all been free
> And we have equality.
> We have walked through the shadows of death.
> We have walked all by ourselves.
> But we'll never turn back.
> —Traditional Negro spiritual

~ 14 ~
A Siege Mentality

One has to search the repressive codes of the most loathsome Communist and
Fascist tyrannies to match Louisiana's latest device for trying to curb the
integrationist movement. This is to charge active advocates of civil rights who
run afoul of the law with "Criminal anarchy."
—"LOUISIANA LUNACY," EDITORIAL, *New York Post,* MARCH 16, 1962

T HE IMPORTANCE OF media coverage to the growth of the civil
rights movement cannot be overstated. Transmitting the immediate
drama of sit-ins, marches, and arrests to millions of readers, viewers,
and listeners, it was the fulcrum around which the movement turned. People
who had never thought about the hardship and degradation brought on by
segregation now had these realities broadcast directly into their homes. The
consciousness-raising we had worked to bring to one southerner at a time at
the Wisconsin human relations seminar was now being brought to the masses.

Once we figured out that this was our movement and we could call the
shots, we staged events and confrontations—like our attempt to register for
classes—pickets, or boycott rallies in order to be ensured of media coverage. We
realized that our only protection, such as it was, against limitless retribution
was the whirring and clicking cameras and the scribbling pencils of reporters.

On Saturday, January 27, we held another rally from the balcony of the
house on Swan Street, just twenty feet from the campus, overlooking what
was considered the gateway to Southern University.

"We cannot abandon the movement!" I hollered in my most rousing voice
to a crowd of about four hundred. "On behalf of the expelled students, for
Ronnie Moore and Weldon Rougeau, who are still in jail, and for all of you
who have marched and who have gone to jail and who have fought to end
segregation in this city, we must not give in! We are calling on you today to

boycott classes on Monday. Do not attend any classes or university activities until every student is readmitted. Do not bend to the will of the segregationists. If a boycott means Southern will be closed again, then, hell, let's close it. Let's close it rather than give the bigots a victory. We have let people trample on our freedom too long!"

Several people spoke on and off throughout the day, trying to summon up the old energy. We were deadly serious and brutally intense in that heated moment. But it wasn't a self-serving intensity staged for our own aggrandizement. We weren't trying to be paragons hogging the spotlight; we hardly had time to catch the news or read the papers ourselves. In a moment-to-moment, day-to-day sense, we didn't see what we were doing as particularly courageous or self-sacrificing. We just did what we did because it was, quite simply and honestly, all we could do.

We had no idea if our efforts were having any effect. State police and sheriff's deputies still owned the campus. Black-clad officers manned security checkpoints as they had since the university had been shut down: The university imposed stringent curfews that were rigidly enforced by uniformed police. Not surprisingly, the student body was afraid, and with good cause.

On Monday, January 29, the *State Times* ran another long story under the headline "Classes Are 'Normal' at Southern U":

An attempt to promote general student boycott of classes at Southern University appeared this morning to be a failure.

Early morning classes appeared to be well-attended and one university spokesman noted that class attendance seemed to be about normal.

Meanwhile, Dr. Felton G. Clark, president of Southern University, was contacted by the *State Times* today for comment on the signing of a petition by 102 faculty members calling for a "constructive reappraisal of the present policy" in dealing with student demonstrations.

But Dr. Clark was reluctant to discuss the issue. He said "anybody had a right to express his opinions." But the president added when asked if the petition would mean any further discussion of a policy reappraisal that might readmit expelled students, "I really don't know much about [the petition]."

Clark was asked whether he would seek the readmission of the students as a result of the petition, but said he could not answer that question. He said this was a matter of policy established by the State Board of Education and the university. He concluded, "I think I have said about enough."

According to the article, the Louisiana State Conference of the American Association of University Professors had expressed concern over the expulsion of students without following academic procedures. Dr. Henry L. Mason, secretary-treasurer of the conference, said it had not been clearly determined whether the students were outside their legal and academic rights in taking part in the demonstrations: "The denial of the right of students to readmission to a university seems to us clearly an evasion of the necessity for an academic hearing. Such denial is an abuse of academic authority, depriving citizens of the United States of their right to an education merely because of their exercise of basic American freedoms." Shortly thereafter, fifty additional students were denied readmission.

Though the boycott had fallen through, we did not give in. On Tuesday night, following a well-attended rally, three mysterious fires broke out on campus that brought in the FBI, beefed up security, and gave the media something new to cover. Though the fires were attributed to CORE, our Lincoln Hotel group had nothing to do with them, and to this day I don't know who started them.

Then, on January 31, Dion Diamond, a field secretary with the Student Nonviolent Coordinating Committee, led a rally at the Student Union shortly after one o'clock. "I'm asking all of you to walk out of classes this afternoon," he shouted to a crowd of about three hundred who milled around the lawn. In an obvious effort to intimidate the crowd, university maintenance crews blocked off all streets leading to the area. "If you don't have the courage to stay out all week, just walk out this afternoon. Don't bend to Dr. Clark's orders. He is wrong. Don't be a coward like he is—stand up for yourself! Police or no police, we're gonna march through these classrooms, and we're gonna boycott classes until every student who has been expelled is allowed back in school!" Dion then led over a hundred students in a noisy march through several classroom buildings shouting, "We want freedom!" and "Segregation is over!"

Later that afternoon, Dion was escorted off campus by security officers. The next morning he was arrested and jailed for "vagrancy and trespassing." His bond was set at $4,000. On February 12, as CORE prepared to put up the bail for the release of Ronnie and Weldon, the charges for all three of them were changed to "criminal anarchy." Ronnie's bail was increased to $12,500, which was the price of a good-sized house in Scotlandville in those days. In addition, Weldon's bail was set at $7,000 and Dion's changed to $13,000. The police denied all three mail and visiting privileges. On February 17, Chuck

McDew, the SNCC chairman, and Bob Zellner, the SNCC field secretary and my old friend from the Wisconsin NSA seminar, were arrested and charged with "criminal anarchy" simply for trying to visit Dion. McDew attended the NSA Human Relations Seminar the year before Zellner and I had. According to the authorities, they were carrying "subversive" literature in their briefcases.

February was not a good month. On the first, the same day Dion was arrested, the *Morning Advocate* ran the headline "Rev. Cox Starts Jail Term Today."

> The Rev. B. Elton Cox, Negro field secretary for the Congress of Racial Equality, today began the first of three jail sentences he received for disturbances growing out of anti-segregation demonstrations here.
>
> The High Point, N.C. minister drew 21 months in jail terms and $5,700 in fines upon conviction of three misdemeanors. The jail terms don't overlap.
>
> Johnny Jones, Cox's Negro counsel, argued the Negroes were doing nothing more than exercising their constitutional rights to free speech, and they had permission of authorities to hold the demonstration.
>
> District Attorney Pitcher told the court "it would have taken all but the pop of a cap to have created one of the worst race riots in history." He said Cox was in charge of the demonstration and that he came to the South to "create as much trouble as he could," and that CORE was using "techniques that have been used by the Communists for many, many years."
>
> Cox had to go to jail despite a defense notice that two of the sentences would be appealed to the Louisiana Supreme Court.

District Judge Fred Le Blanc Jr. found Cox guilty of "impeding the administration of justice by holding a demonstration near the courthouse." He said that the 1950 state law under which he convicted Cox was almost identical to a federal statute that was passed to stop Communist demonstrations near federal court buildings. He said that having 1,500 Negroes go into the white business district is "calculated to incite violence." Judge Le Blanc further explained that Cox had created a situation that forced him to leave the courthouse and neglect his duties:

> I know, especially of late, there is tension between the races. I think I felt apprehensive that trouble or violence could erupt from such

a situation. I didn't want to be near it. I have a feeling that there is some subtle intimidation of me, of us who have the responsibility of upholding the laws of Louisiana, of segregation. I feel there was some intimidation intended in defense counsel Jones' making an issue of the courtroom's policy of segregated seating. I knew as well as Jones did that to desegregate the courtroom suddenly would be asking for trouble.

If Reverend Cox had not been our hero by then, the actions of the court certainly elevated him to heroic status. He had a spiritual strength and defiance that awed us. He sent us messages telling us to keep working and fighting. Over and over, he urged us not to give up.

Subsequently, Cox's conviction was appealed to the U.S. Supreme Court and once again the High Court was faced with examining the constitutionality of the conduct of the Louisiana authorities. The appeal of Reverend Cox's conviction was argued before the Court exactly one week before the Court hearing in Dr. Dombrowski's case. However, the Cox convictions created much more contentious and difficult issues, sharply dividing the Court and resulting, in 1965, in the extraordinary issuance of two separate opinions. Among themselves, the justices had very different views on what had happened on December 15 in downtown Baton Rouge. While the majority was approving, or at least sympathetic, to our march and demonstration, dissenting Justice Tom Clark was sharply critical. Three Cox convictions were before the Court, one for breach of the peace, the second for obstructing public passages, and the third for picketing and parading near the courthouse. Seven of the nine justices voted to overturn the convictions for breach of the peace and obstructing public passages. In contrast, the High Court overturned the courthouse picketing conviction by only a slender 5-4 majority.

Louisiana officials argued that the jailed students' singing of freedom songs from inside the jail and our cheering in response to them were evidence of a breach of the peace. On this the Supreme Court wrote:

The cheering and shouting were described differently by different witnesses, but the most extravagant descriptions were the following: "a jumbled roar like people cheering a football game," "loud cheering and spontaneous clapping and screaming and a great hullabaloo," "a great outburst," a cheer of "conquest . . . much wilder than a football game," "a loud reaction, not disorderly, loud," "a shout, a roar," and an emotional response "in jubilation and exhortation." Appellant [Cox] agreed that some of the group "became emotional" and "tears flowed from young ladies' eyes." . . . Inspector Trigg testified for the State that "from their actions, I figured they were going to try to storm the Courthouse and take over the jail and try to get the prisoners that they had come down here to protest."

The Supreme Court overturned Cox's breach of the peace conviction, with Justice Arthur Goldberg writing for the Court:

The State argues, however, that while the demonstrators started out to be orderly, the loud cheering and clapping by the students in response to the singing from the jail converted the peaceful assembly into a riotous one. The record, however, does not support this assertion. It is true the students in response to the singing of their fellows who were in custody, cheered and applauded. However, the meeting was an out-door meeting and a key state witness testified that while the singing was loud, it was not disorderly. There is, moreover, no indication that the mood of the students was ever hostile, aggressive, or unfriendly. Our conclusion that the entire meeting from the beginning until its dispersal by tear gas was orderly and not riotous is confirmed by a film of the events taken by a television news photographer, which was offered in evidence as a state exhibit. We have viewed the film, and it reveals that the students, though they undoubtedly cheered and clapped, were well-behaved throughout. . . . The singing and cheering do not seem to us to differ significantly from the constitutionally pro-tected activity of the demonstrators in *Edwards v. South Carolina* who loudly sang "while stamping their feet and clapping their hands."

Wading deeper into constitutional waters, the Court ruling then shot down another argument of the state:

Finally, the State contends that the conviction should be sustained because of fear expressed by some of the state witnesses that "violence was about to erupt" because of the demonstration. . . . Others felt the atmosphere became "tense" because of "mutterings," "grumbling," and "jeering" from the white group. . . . Here again, as in *Edwards,* this evidence "showed no more than that the opinions which [the students] were peaceably expressing were sufficiently opposed to the views of the majority of the community to attract a crowd and necessitate police protection." Conceding this is so, the "compelling answer . . . is that constitutional rights may not be denied simply because of hostility to their assertion or exercise. . . ." Yet, a "function of free speech under our system of government is to invite dispute. It may indeed best serve its high purpose when it induces a condition of unrest, creates dissatisfaction with conditions as they are, or even stirs people to anger. Speech is often provocative and challenging. It may strike at prejudices and preconceptions and have profound unsettling effects as it presses for acceptance of an idea. That is why freedom of speech . . . is . . . protected against censorship or punishment. . . . There is no room under our Constitution for a more restrictive view." *Terminiello v. Chicago*

The Court had little trouble overturning Cox's conviction for obstructing public passage. The Court observed that the statute itself made an exception allowing labor unions to have demonstrations that obstructed public passage, and that testimony showed that at other times officials had allowed meetings and parades that obstructed public traffic. Because the statute set no objective standards for who could and could not hold public events, and because of the labor exception, the Court ruled the statute was discriminatory and gave too much discretion to local officials. The Court further stated: "But here it is clear that the practice in Baton Rouge allowing unfettered discretion in local officials in the regulation of the use of the streets for peaceful parades and meetings is an unwarranted abridgement of appellant's [Cox's] freedom of speech and assembly secured to him by the First Amendment."

The toughest and most contentious issue presented for the Court, and what caused a separate bare majority decision, was Cox's conviction for violating a Louisiana law prohibiting picketing or parading near the courthouse. Though Goldberg's slender five-member majority reversed Cox's conviction, all members of the Court seemed to agree that Louisiana had the right to prohibit the demonstration at the courthouse.

In point of fact, most of the students were probably like me—focused on the jail where the students were held and not thinking about court proceedings that had not yet begun or, for that matter, about the issue of the courthouse being located at the jail. For the U.S. Supreme Court, however, demonstrations at the courthouse touched a sensitive nerve. The Court referred to the public outcry from lawyers and the public to picketing of the federal court more than a decade earlier protesting prosecutions of leaders of the Communist Party. The right to free speech was outweighed where the courthouse was concerned: "The constitutional safeguards relating to the integrity of the criminal process attend every stage of the criminal proceeding, starting with arrest and culminating with a trial in a courtroom presided over by a judge. There can be no doubt that they embrace the fundamental conception of a fair trial, and that they exclude influence or domination by either a hostile or friendly mob."

Since the Court seemed to be strongly in agreement on prohibiting demonstrations at a courthouse, we might ask how the majority then came to reverse the Cox conviction on leading this courthouse demonstration? In my view, it was a stretch. The Court acknowledged that the police stopped us twice en route to the jail and were rebuffed by Cox's persistent resistance and determination to continue. But the majority ruled that the police had in fact consented to the jail protest by then giving the demonstration a limited time to protest in front of the jail and by restricting where the protestors would be.

Having been at Cox's side at the time and having heard the conversations, I know that the authorities had attempted to stop the march. But given our disobedience, they either had to begin arresting us or stand by while we continued our protest. Since Cox testified that he had had consent, and the evidence being in conflict on this point, the Court voided the courthouse picketing conviction. Four of the justices would have upheld Cox's conviction for picketing the courthouse. Justice Hugo Black, who had joined in reversing the other two convictions on free speech and due process grounds, wrote: "Justice cannot be rightly administered, nor are the lives and safety of prisoners secure, where throngs of people clamor against the processes of justice right outside the courthouse or jailhouse doors." He concluded that even if the officials on the scene had given permission for the protest as claimed by Cox, they did not have the authority to consent to such a violation of state law, and in any event such permission would have been revoked when the police ordered the protesters to disburse.

The strongest dissent came from Justice Tom Clark:

the appellant [Cox], in an effort to influence and intimidate the courts

and legal officials of Baton Rouge and procure the release of 23 prisoners being held for trial, agitated and led the mob of over 2,000 students
in the staging of a modern Donnybrook Fair across from the courthouse and jail. . . . Finding that he could not stop them without the use
of force, the Chief told Cox that he must confine the demonstration
to the west side of St. Louis Street, across from the courthouse. . . .
The administrative determination upon which this Court turns the
present case was in actuality made, if at all, in the heat of a racial
demonstration in a southern city for the sole purpose of avoiding what
had the potentialities of a race riot.

In the spring of 1962, even before the *Cox* decision, we still harbored hopes
we could fight the legislature and the courts. We still believed jails, trials,
cross burnings, mob violence, and even politically inspired local court rul-
ings could not stop us. Against all hope, we still believed—despite Dr. Clark's
effective deflection of the force of our movement by his cowardly retreat and
his refusal even to entertain the "constructive reappraisal" of his policies his
own faculty suggested—we could win.

As a result, it should be noted that our university community and city
launched the decade of the 1960s with events and challenges that tested us
all, redeemed our confidence, and sharply engaged the highest forces of state
and federal authority. We could not have known that in this brief span of two
years, our witness in the battle for freedom could have generated so much
transformation.

The spring passed quickly at the Lincoln Hotel, but it was never easy.
With so much bail to pay for our friends, our funds for living expenses began
running disturbingly low. Finally, we were forced to take fewer hotel rooms,
at one point even resorting to lining up chairs beside the beds and sleeping
four across them. By necessity, we rationed lunches and cooked dinner on hot
plates in our rooms.

From the Lincoln Hotel we continued our rallying and occasional picketing, and even began a door-to-door campaign to get the city's twenty-eight
thousand unregistered Negroes to register and vote. We also painted houses
and worked at hard physical laboring jobs to add funds to the treasury.
Somehow it was strengthening to go door to door or to picket when we had
paint and blisters on our hands.

Despite everything, for the most part our morale remained high. Because we were outcasts of sorts, not only were we thrust deeper into the movement, but our resolve was also strengthened. Had we still been nestled in the relative safety of the university, I have no doubt that we wouldn't have thrown ourselves headlong into the confrontation the way we did. Our commitment perhaps wouldn't have been as strong because we would have had something else to fall back on . . . and something left to lose.

As it was, we were alone. And in being alone against the world, with the last thin filter of university life peeled away, we could truly see the world for what it was. Finally, we could come up against the civil authorities and all their raw segregationist power. We steeled ourselves to the recognition that in the game we were playing anything could happen. While we hoped for the best and feared the worst, we counted ourselves lucky because the bond of love and dedication among us made the fear easier to handle.

~ 15 ~
The Journey Home

Let's not forget that these students are going to jail not only for their freedom, but for yours and mine; not only because they have been hurt by the indignities of segregation, but because we all have been hurt. As I watch them, as I see the movement spread from college to college and city to city, I am deeply stirred as are millions of other Americans. What is it we feel? What do we hope for? I can answer only for myself; For me it is as if the NO EXIT sign is about to come down from our age. It is the beginning of new things. Of a new kind of leadership. If the white students will join in ever-increasing numbers with these Negro students, change will come; their experience of suffering and working together for what they know is right, the self-discipline, the refusal to act in violence or think in violence will bring a new spiritual life not only to our region but to our entire country.
—LILLIAN SMITH, "ONLY THE YOUNG AND THE BRAVE," OLD SCREAMER MOUNTAIN, CLAYTON, GEORGIA, EARLY 1960S

I F THE LINCOLN HOTEL was our haven, such as it was, from the constant perils of Baton Rouge, and if Reverend Cox was our mentor and spiritual guide in facing those perils, then CORE certainly was our link to the rest of the world. Baton Rouge could become very insular; it was easy to become cut off because of its resistance to the changes happening elsewhere. Ever since Dave Dennis arrived at Southern and started drumming up interest in another sit-in, CORE provided our movement with vital financial support, guidance from the headquarters in New York, and a much-needed link with people from other areas of the nation.

CORE was founded in the 1940s and was the first organization to conduct mass demonstrations against segregation. For over two decades, it had been the only outlet for political, action-oriented blacks. The other national black groups, the NAACP, headed by Roy Wilkins, and the National Urban

League, headed by Whitney Young, were reluctant to embrace activism as a way to promote change. These groups were more inclined to encourage quiet infiltration, social service, and self-help over agitation. Therefore, CORE—based largely in the Northeast and backed largely by white donations—was for years the legitimate, national protest-oriented organization.

Then, in the early 1960s, the Student Nonviolent Coordinating Committee (SNCC) was formed as a branch of Dr. King's Southern Christian Leadership Conference (SCLC). Under the spiritual guidance of Ella Baker, a dynamic black woman who had old-line ties to radical movements in the past, a contagious, youthful enthusiasm, and a belief in protest today, the younger, more aggressive, and less compromising members of SCLC formed SNCC. Their goal was to become the battering ram of national civil rights protest. SNCC members were willing to sit in, to march, to take the beatings and abuse, and to do whatever it took to be heard. In attracting Julian Bond, John Lewis, Jim Forman, Rap Brown, Stokely Carmichael, Marion Barry, and countless other leaders like them, SNCC eventually did become the torchbearer for the movement. A SNCC pamphlet from the mid-1960s titled *Rebels with a Cause* explained:

> The SNCC rebels are intense, nervous people who know the insides of many jails, people who have seen the bottomless cruelty of man, people who have seen their best friends beaten to a pulp and killed, people who have been tested, who have looked on death and despair a long lonely time. . . . What sustains these rebels is a mystique of total commitment. SNCC workers take vows of total commitment. SNCC workers take vows of total poverty and total devotion. They identify themselves totally with the people—i.e. the poor, the despised, the downtrodden, the humiliated.

But when we were embroiled in our protest in Baton Rouge in 1962, CORE, led by James Farmer, was just as progressive as SNCC, and at the same time more well-known, financially stable, and national. They sent Dave to us first, so we became identified with CORE. Our protest was a "CORE protest." Many in our group paid membership fees and became strong advocates and supporters. Ronnie, Weldon, and Pat, who would all three endure almost a year of court battles, were chairman, vice chairman, and secretary of the local chapter, which further strengthened our CORE identity in the national press. To a significant degree, we viewed the members of other organizations and their methods as suspect.

Even so, I found it all a bit unnecessary. While I certainly identified with the passion and commitment expressed in the SNCC and CORE literature, I wasn't in the movement as a tool for filling up the treasury of a national organization. I was protesting for me and for others like me, not for CORE to improve their national profile. From the beginning, I insisted on student identity more than organization identity. I was beholden to no one and represented no one's views but my own. Perhaps it is just another symbol of my hardheadedness, but I entered the protest not as a CORE person, but as an individual and a student, so I did not join CORE. Moreover, I did not subscribe to the belief that the civil rights organizations were in competition with each other and thus could not work with one another. So, when we were contacted by SNCC workers in Atlanta who wanted to know what was going on with Dion, Chuck McDew, and Bob Zellner and how our boycott efforts were progressing, I went to Atlanta to brief them. For a day and a half, I met with Jim Forman, Julian Bond, John Lewis, and Ella Baker, discussing what was going on across the South and learning their strategies for increasing the movement's impact.

My bookcase still contains the small black vinyl notebook I carried to record my solo journey:

Began Baton Rouge: Stopped at Greyhound, Baton Rouge, 3:10 P.M.—3 waitresses—no service—Friday, March 23
8 customers 2 waitresses all served *but me* 3:27 P.M. Left at 3:40 P.M. spoke to manager of bus station spoke to female manager of Post House said that I would be served when waitresses were free from dish washing, table cleaning, etc.
waitresses finished, stood up, but no service

New Orleans 6:00 P.M. 3-23
Coffee and sandwiches at Post House coffee counter
No trouble

Mobile, Alabama,
12:30 A.M. to 12: 40 A.M.
had coffee in restaurant
no trouble

Montgomery, Alabama 5:30 A.M.–6:00 A.M.

Breakfast in Post House
No trouble

SNCC Atlanta 3-24-62
Cooperation among various Civil Rights organizations
Uniqueness of SNCC
Youthfulness of SNCC allows mobility and initiative
Theory—Practice
Representative from each protest body making up SNCC
elect exec. Committee by state

Send plan of Washington Demonstration
Letter to Len Holt asking that omnibus suit be filed in Baton Rouge

Androcles and The Lion George B. Shaw
Get financial needs of girls in detail
Send to Mrs. Ella Baker—41 Exchange Pl. S.E.

I maintained contact with the SNCC office, much to the growing annoyance of Dave and Ronnie. They suspected me of some kind of underhanded collaboration with the organization (just what, I cannot imagine), and even confronted me in Dave's hotel room one day, demanding to inspect my correspondence. Needless to say, I refused. Loyalty was of utmost importance to them, and they feared I was straying from the fold. But that had nothing to do with it. The only loyalty I felt was to the movement; I wasn't in this to push CORE or SNCC or boost or tear down anyone's career. I resisted being categorized or identified by a label. I was a Negro student fighting for my rights as a human being, and that, in my opinion, was label enough.

By the end of May, CORE had filed a federal suit charging that expelling us without disciplinary hearings was a violation of due process. However, the suit was compromised in court and voluntarily dismissed by CORE attorneys, who could not expect to raise the financial backing for what they knew would be a protracted case.

Later the compromise was explained to me. Southern agreed to readmit all of the expelled students except Ronnie Moore, Pat Tate, and me if the suit were dropped. The lawyer explained that, according to Dr. Clark, not long after the march downtown on December 15, I had called his home to ask for a meeting between him and a student delegation. Dr. Clark told the lawyer: "My wife answered the phone and told him I was not in. But that wasn't good enough. He then asked my wife to tell me that if I were trying to avoid talking with a small group of students, he had a much larger group of students who would march to my house and wait until they saw me. And that's exactly what he did. Can you believe the disrespect in speaking to the wife of a university president that way?" The lawyer said Dr. Clark considered my telephone conversations an insult to his wife and gave that as his reason for refusing to allow my readmission.

Between 1960 and 1962, hundreds of student leaders were expelled from Negro land grant colleges in the South. At Southern, Jackson State, Alabama State, and other Negro schools, administrators felt a great deal of pressure from white southern legislators to quash the student protests by any means necessary. Also during this time, northern white students were following the events in the South and were beginning to organize sympathy pickets and rallies on their campuses.

In Worcester, Massachusetts, in the spring of 1962, sympathetic white students and the one black student enrolled at Clark University began a scholarship fund campaign. They washed cars, held bake sales, and sponsored benefits until they raised $1,500. Finally, the university agreed to match the money, so the students raised another $1,000. Then they began soliciting applications from southern students who had been expelled from school. Among the students they contacted was Walter Williams, a friend from the Human Relations Seminar in Wisconsin. Though he, too, had been expelled as protest leader while student body president at Jackson State, his plans were then to go into the military. As a result, he told them about me.

I soon received a letter, the appropriate applications, and a catalog. I had never heard of Worcester, Massachusetts, much less Clark University. The Eastern Seaboard was a faraway, foreign place to me that I imagined as white, rich, and cold. I had never lived in a white, rich, cold place, and—though I was embarrassed to admit it—it scared me that I didn't know what it would be like. Of course, the catalog did nothing to allay my fears. How could it? It wasn't written for me. It was full of pictures of smiling white kids lounging under trees, playing in the snow, and holding beakers and test tubes.

It was not exactly an environment I could see myself blending into. The range of course offerings was mind-boggling, like nothing I had ever imagined. More than 80 percent of the faculty had Ph.D.s. As I read on, the campus seemed more and more alien. Clark was the only school in the country where Sigmund Freud had lectured while still developing his theories. Dr. Robert Goddard, inventor of the rocket, had close ties with the university and had conducted many of his early experiments in Worcester. The school's geography department was world renowned. *Geography department?* How could I succeed in an environment like this? There was more chemistry equipment in one picture than I had seen my whole life. Just reading about Clark's "rich progressive tradition in the northeastern United States" gave me chills. I wasn't part of that tradition, whatever it was, and I didn't see how I could be. And, in truth, I didn't want to be; some part of me really wanted to stay at Southern. But I applied anyway.

Ultimately that turned out to be an excellent move on my part because, although I was clinging to the past, Southern was pushing me away, forcing me to give it up. I had outgrown Southern's rules and codes of behavior. It was not lost on me that if President Clark had replaced me with someone else, then I had replaced that Clark with another Clark, Clark University. It was an amusing, ironic serendipity.

With the lawsuit dropped and with almost everyone acquitted or tied up in court proceedings, the movement—effectively demoralized and diminished by Felton Clark's acquiescence to the demands of the white establishment—lost all momentum. Southern University became the local torchbearer for the segregationists, validating their criminal actions and undermining our just, godly ones. A surface calm returned to Scotlandville as blacks once again began shopping at the downtown stores and as Southern students began doing what students ought to do, going to classes. I packed my bags and prepared to go home.

I waited at the Greyhound station for a bus into Hammond, as I had waited so many times before. Unexpectedly, this evening was different. This evening, I sat at the lunch counter. "White and Interstate Passengers Only" read the sign on the wood and glass door. The sign in front of the kitchen entrance still read "Colored Passengers," and most Negroes, whether traveling interstate or solely within the state, still used that little hot room in the back. But under the law, we didn't have to.

Resentment was heavy as I entered the previously white domain. The gaze of twenty pairs of eyes seared into my skin. The sneered comment, "Colored ain't allowed in here," the mumbled insults, rang in my ears. I tried to ignore them. I am here, I reminded myself over and over. That is the important thing. Blacks and whites are eating in the same place, sitting in the same room. I hadn't seen any kind of integration whatsoever since the NSC seminar in Madison. And God, I thought, I have learned a hell of a lot since then.

I glanced around the shabby lunch counter again and then looked through the kitchen, thinking about the first time I'd gotten off the bus and sat on the other side and looked through the kitchen into this seedy room. So much suffering, so many arrests, so many beatings all over the South, in city after city, for the privilege of sitting at this grimy counter with a white man.

As if in a dream, I was miraculously there! We had accomplished something—all of us—I thought. Our protest at Southern wasn't a failure, after all. We had planted seeds that will never be uprooted. That is true change. Whatever happens, we will always have that.

I had been sitting at the counter for more than ten minutes, and no one had come to take my order. The restaurant may be opened up, I thought, I may be allowed in here by law, but the whites aren't going to recognize me. I felt my face tensing. Three white waitresses stood in a huddle across the room. They were obviously talking about me and kept looking back over their shoulders in my direction. Perhaps, I thought cynically, they hoped I would disappear.

Finally, one of them walked back into the kitchen and came out with a black girl whom she pointed in my direction. This young black woman hurried over to where I sat, her face strained between apology and embarrassment. "Your order, sir?"

"I'll have a cup of coffee," I said slowly, trying to meet her eyes. "Thank you."

She looked up and all her quiet, lonely outrage seemed to well up and burst like a soap bubble and fall to the floor between us. "Thank you," she said.

I drank the coffee and started my journey home.

Downtown Baton Rouge S. H. Kress department store, where the first Southern University student sit-ins took place on March 28, 1960. Courtesy Baton Rouge Police Department.

Reverend T. J. Jemison escorts two of the jailed Southern students after raising bail funds to secure their release. *Morning Advocate,* April 15, 1960. Capital City Press, Baton Rouge, La.

The two-story house and storefront on Swan Street just off the Southern campus where students rallied to hear protest organizers from the balcony after the rallies were banned on campus. *State Times,* April 1, 1960. Capital City Press, Baton Rouge, La.

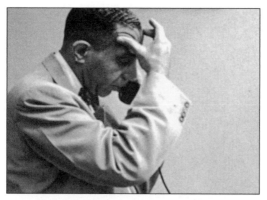

Embattled Southern University president Felton Grandison Clark trying feverishly to contain student discontent. Courtesy Southern University, John B. Cade Library Archives, Baton Rouge, La.

Some of the two thousand peaceful protestors who marched from the Old State Capitol to the East Baton Rouge Parish Prison on December 15, 1961, to protest the arrests the day before of their fellow students for picketing. The demonstrators were tear-gassed in front of the jail, and German shepherds were set upon them. *State Times,* Dec. 15, 1961. Capital City Press, Baton Rouge, La.

Mug shot of Reverend B. Elton Cox taken upon his arrest on December 15, 1961. His case went to the U.S. Supreme Court, where his conviction was overturned in 1965 in the case of *Cox v. Louisiana.* Courtesy East Baton Rouge Sheriff's Office.

Southern University dean of students Martin L. Harvey.

Anxious students crowd the hall outside the auditor's office to withdraw funds to get home after President Clark abruptly closed the university indefinitely, telling them they had to be off campus by 5:00 P.M. *Morning Advocate,* Jan. 19, 1962. Capital City Press, Baton Rouge, La.

Black-owned Lincoln Hotel in downtown Baton Rouge, where banned student leaders stayed for weeks. Courtesy Southern University Law Center.

Baton Rouge civil rights attorney Johnny Jones was fervent in his representation of student protestors. *State Times,* June 14, 1972. Capital City Press, Baton Rouge, La.

As the university reopened on January 25, 1962, three of the ousted students, D'Army Bailey, Thomas Peete, and Willie Bradford, appeared at the registrar's office but were denied readmission and were later escorted off campus. *Morning Advocate,* Jan. 26, 1962. Capital City Press, Baton Rouge, La.

I began my junior year at Clark University, Worcester, Massachusetts, on September 21, 1962, after sympathetic Clark students raised scholarship funds to back a student expelled for civil rights activities. Courtesy *Worcester Telegram & Gazette.*

From the 1963 Clark year-
book. The caption beneath
reads: "The Black man must
be a professional Prometheus
/ Shackled by his skin to
a boulder of blasphemy. /
I would join his chorus of
defiance."

As jeering crowds look on, Baltimore police arrest hundreds of civil rights protestors, including me, at the segregated Gwyn Oak Amusement Park, July 4, 1963.
Walter McCardell/*Baltimore Sun*, July 4, 1963.

Allison Turaj of Washington, D.C., continued her march through Baltimore's Gwyn Oak amusement park despite a cut over her right eye caused by a rock thrown from a mob of angry whites. Over 100 protestors were arrested that day in addition to the 283 arrested on July 4 at the park. Courtesy Associated Press.

James Meredith, who had broken the color barrier at Ole Miss amid violent mobs eighteen months earlier, visits with Worcester Student Movement members D'Army Bailey and Henry Chaiklin at Bailey's apartment before speaking on the Clark University campus, February 27, 1964. Courtesy *Worcester Telegram & Gazette.*

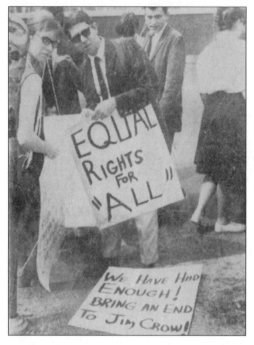

Worcester Student Movement members picket Wyman-Gordon manufacturing plant, protesting racial discrimination in hiring and promotions, May 7, 1964. Courtesy *Worcester Telegram & Gazette.*

Clark students counterpicket against civil rights protestors at the Wyman-Gordon plant. Courtesy *Worcester Telegram & Gazette.*

~ 16 ~

Radical Is as Radical Does

First, we should actively conceive of ourselves as the radical wing of the civil rights movement. This is the traditional role of students in all broad struggles. Relatively free of vested interests, of family obligations, and economic ties, we can experiment with new techniques (always in the hope that they will later be adopted by those stronger than ourselves). We are in a better position to speak out against unprincipled or fruitless compromises. We are less susceptible to temptation than many of our elder colleagues. In short, we are more strongly committed to disruption of the status quo.

—THOMAS KAHN, "THE POLITICAL SIGNIFICANCE OF THE FREEDOM RIDES"

"SIR, COULD YOU please let me know when we're close to Wor-kester?"

"That's Woo-ster, son."

"Wooster?"

"Three more stops to go."

I sat down again, dazed, as if the conductor's kind correction had shot lightning through my skull. How could Worcester be Woo-ster? I looked dejectedly out the window. At this point, I'd been on the train almost twenty-four hours. It seemed weeks since Mama had bundled my box of chicken, and Daddy and I had struggled with my footlocker up the stairs of the Memphis train station. Riding on Daddy's complimentary railway pass, I had to take the routes that accommodated Illinois Central employees: north to Chicago, east to New York, and then on to Boston. But I didn't mind it, really. I was comfortable. More comfortable, I thought, than I'd be at a school I'd never heard of, in an area of the country I'd never been in before, in a city whose name I couldn't even pronounce. Next thing I knew, the train was screeching and groaning to a halt in Woo-ster. I thanked the conductor on my way out.

"Darmie! Darmie!" A redheaded kid was waving, pointing and nodding at me from across the platform. I waved back and then made my way over to him. "Hi! I'm Fred. Fred Jealous," he said in a thick, nasal accent.

I extended my hand. "D'Army Bailey. Nice to meet you."

"Oh. D-army. I'm sorry." He smiled and shook my hand. "Unusual name, D-army. Meet Bob Miller."

I turned to the tall, brown-haired guy standing next to Fred. "Glad you're here," he said as he shook my hand. "Say, is that a particularly southern name, D-army?"

I was amazed. They both seemed so openly, boyishly curious. "No, actually it's a family name," I said simply, intending to stop there, but his expression was so eager I went on. "My grandfather's name was Darmy, and I was named after him. But people always mispronounced it, so when I was in twelfth grade, I changed it and added an apostrophe and a big *A* in hopes people would pronounce it right."

"Oh." He stared at me with amazement. "You can do that?"

"Sure, it's just a name." Bob and I began lugging the footlocker toward Fred's car.

"I just thought maybe in the South . . . it was different," said Bob carefully as we wrestled the locker into the trunk.

"Why should it be?"

"I don't know."

"Listen," Fred said as we pulled out of the parking lot, "you guys can't have these heavy conversations all the time if we're going to be roommates. D'Army, you have to excuse Bob. He can't help it, he's from Rhode Island."

We laughed. I wasn't exactly sure where Rhode Island was, but that didn't seem to matter. Fred was from New York, which was close to Rhode Island, or in the same general area. They were full of questions about Memphis and Baton Rouge and seemed at least as ignorant about the South as I was about the North. Somehow, from that very first afternoon, we got along. In the two years I spent at Clark, I had some of my best and most comfortable times with these two.

The next day I met with Dr. Robert Campbell, the dean of the college and a friendly, accommodating man. He went out of his way to emphasize that race was not an issue at Clark. "Whatever problems you have had in the South, D'Army, you will not have them here," he assured me. "And if you feel even the slightest hint of racial conflict or mistreatment, you let me know immediately. Don't hesitate and certainly don't feel embarrassed. If problems occur—and I'm certainly not anticipating any—but if something comes up, just talk to me about it. I'll investigate it and get to the root of the problem." *"Hint of a problem?"* I wondered cynically. What qualifies as a hint? And *the root of the problem?* That would be an awfully long root now, wouldn't it? How deep into American history would this root delve? To the sale of the first slave? To the survival of Jamestown? To the signing of the Constitution? I thanked him for his support and went out into a world of smiling white faces, alone.

On September 13, the campus newspaper, the *Clark Scarlet,* ran a front-page story under the headline: "Expelled Louisiana Student Is Awarded Anniversary Scholarship at Clark—Senator Javits Applauds Clark's Efforts":

> The scholarship, intended for a southern student expelled from college because of participation in non-violent civil rights activities, was established, supported, and conceived entirely by undergraduate students. After receiving heavy support in a student referendum last September, the scholarship proposal became a reality and fund-raising efforts were undertaken. To this date, $1,938.36 has been collected by the various fund-raising groups.

The article went on to explain that the scholarship had received widespread media attention. It included an editorial entitled "Cheers for Clark" that had appeared in the July 21, 1962, issue of *Ave Maria National Catholic Weekly:*

> The student body, supported by the President of the university, Dr. Howard Jefferson, and by the Dean of the college, Dr. Robert Campbell, has appealed to the citizens of Worcester for the scholarship funds on the grounds that expelled Negro students "are being unjustly denied their right to an education." I strongly commend the Clark University administration and student body for this excellent project and very much hope it is widely emulated throughout the country.

And then, on September 22, a photograph of me smiling as I leaned over an open textbook graced the top of the front page of the *Worcester Evening Gazette.* The headline read "Got His Experience First-Hand, Clark Student Knows Civil Rights Issues." The article presented me, I thought, as something of a worldly wise exotic in the "Now, isn't that something" vein of after-dinner conversation.

D'Army Bailey, 20, should be able to get an A on any examination which asks: How to stage a sit-in demonstration, form a picket line, set up a mass rally—or how to get expelled from college for doing so. . . . Bright, fast on his feet, whether it's answering a question on civil rights or running from tear gas bombs, Bailey's civil rights career began and his southern college career ended during December and January of last year.

Worcester had rescued me from the big bad Land of Cotton, and they were feeling mighty proud of themselves. They were generous, they told themselves. They were liberal; they were progressive; and they were, of course, unprejudiced. Oh, they were thrilled to have me—a real, live Negro activist. They had taken me out of all that turmoil and danger. They had saved me from the incarceration that was life in Dixie and brought me up North, where I could relax, where I could forget all that racial nonsense and concentrate on my lessons. But as they were soon to find out, my career as a civil rights activist was far from over. My eyes and ears were finely tuned to the signs and sounds of bigotry, hypocrisy, and injustice. Obviously, just how they really felt about their new Negro celebrity remained to be seen.

During my train ride to Worcester, I had told myself over and over again that the Clark students were the ones who wanted me. It was all their idea. It wasn't like I was coming uninvited. I reminded myself that I had been out of the South twice before and lived with white students from this area of the country. I told myself that they wouldn't be hostile, that they wouldn't have gone to all of this trouble if they were going to be hostile. And if they were hostile, it couldn't be any worse than in Scotlandville. And I was right.

However, what I, in my naïveté, didn't expect was the celebrity that swiftly overtook me. I couldn't walk from one end of the campus to the other without being followed by a swarm of students anxious to hear about racial problems in the South or to get a two-minute synopsis of "what it's like to be a Negro." I couldn't sit down to eat lunch without having my brains picked. I couldn't raise my hand at a lecture without the burden of the "Negro response" hovering audibly, like a whisper, over the class.

I went along with it all, and I was friendly because they were friendly. Consequently, for a long time, I never felt like me. I was a composite, a representative, a living newsreel—not a person. To these students—most of them from upper-middle-class white communities—I was "Negro America," a curiosity, and therefore conveniently interesting.

They couldn't have cared less about D'Army Bailey, human being. Ultimately, it began to irritate me that I had been thrust into the role of conscience-soother. They wanted to hear about all the bigots in the South so they could congratulate themselves on being different. They wanted to hear just exactly how backward it was "down there" so they could pat themselves on the back for being progressive. They wanted to hear what it was like to "be a Negro" so they could say they understood. They wanted to talk to me so they could tell their folks back home that they had a Negro friend.

Hostility was one thing: it was blatant, loud, mean, and ugly. This was another: it was insidious, sweet, and charming—it snuck up on you. As the weeks passed, I became more and more aware of the tenuous balance that must be maintained by one of the only blacks in a white environment. There was one other black student at Clark; beautiful and poised, Marie was the daughter of a judge in Detroit. While she was cordial, I found her somewhat distant. In this situation I soon realized that the trick to survival was first to recognize that I stood out and not fight it. The next step was to acknowledge that because I stood out, they would project their fantasies onto me. Some whites felt kindly toward me, some felt uncomfortable, some felt awe, some felt guilt: I was *reacted to* constantly.

If I fought it or tried to deny it, I knew I would be miserable. By the same token, when I raised my hand in a class, when I was the only black kid in a room full of whites, I couldn't get away from the fact that I was *The Black Kid,* and that I carried the whole world of the black experience on my shoulders. Before too long I realized that I couldn't let the experience become a burden. I had to cast it off and make the whites have to deal with it.

By 1962, I had the maturity to understand that blackness, as perceived by whites, was a political condition. I knew it was possible to have friends personally and not feel the pressure of that blackness. So I decided not to care how the white students reacted to me when I walked across campus or raised my hand in class. I decided to be a person, not a political symbol, and say what I damn well pleased. So when my questioners began getting on my nerves, when I began questioning the legitimacy of blaming the South for all the country's racial problems without looking at the inconsistencies and contradictions in Worcester itself, I began to ask a few questions of my own.

On September 14, the *New York Times* ran an article about Mississippi governor Ross Barnett invoking the historical doctrine of interposition in an attempt to block James Meredith's enrollment at the University of Mississippi.

Though Ole Miss was under a federal court order to admit Meredith, Barnett proclaimed all public schools and institutions of higher learning would be operated under the authority of state officials and would enforce only state laws. He said: "I hereby direct each said official to uphold and enforce the laws duly and legally enacted by the Legislature of the State of Mississippi and to interpose the state sovereignty and themselves between the people of the state and anybody politically seeking to usurp such power. . . . No school will be integrated in Mississippi while I am your governor. I assure you that they will not be closed if this can possibly be avoided, but they will not be integrated. Every public official, including myself, should be prepared to make the choice tonight whether he will submit or whether he is willing to go to jail, if necessary, to keep faith with the people who have placed their welfare in his hands. . . . If there is any official who is not prepared to suffer imprisonment for this righteous cause, I ask him now to submit his resignation."

Then, on September 28, the *Times* ran the headline "U.S. to Avert Violence, Calls Off Effort to Enroll Meredith; Sends Hundreds More Marshals." A fourth attempt to register Meredith was canceled after it became apparent that this would endanger his life. Federal officials feared that with an escort of only twenty-five marshals, Meredith would be overwhelmed by the two hundred armed policemen, an undetermined number of state officials, and a crowd of over 2,500 angry, defiant whites that ringed the campus.

Alabama governor John Patterson sent a telegram to President Kennedy asserting that if federal troops or marshals were sent to Mississippi, "our action would establish the Federal Government as a dictatorship of the foulest sort." Without qualification, Governor Patterson said that Governor Barnett was right and the federal government was wrong.

President Kennedy issued a statement saying it was "crucial to the American system that there be respect for the law and compliance with all laws, not just those with which we personally agree." He said the course that Governor Barnett was following was "incompatible with the principles upon which this union is based," adding, "I hope that this matter will be resolved peacefully and without violence or further action by the Federal Government. However, if this is not to be, the Federal Government will see to it that the orders which are presently outstanding are maintained and enforced, whatever action that may ultimately require."

That Friday afternoon I was walking across campus, headed for history class, when a student approached me wanting to talk. Everyone on campus had been closely following the events in Mississippi. But as the situation worsened on the Ole Miss campus, I began to tire of the constant barrage of questions and commentary. It was all too self-congratulatory, too blind. Also I was tired of nodding and agreeing, tired of going along with the party line.

"Hey, D'Army! Wait up!" I stopped and turned. I decided suddenly this conversation was going to be different.

"Have you read the paper? I can't believe it, but Meredith had to turn around again. It's incredible. Over two thousand whites were there waiting for him, sitting in their trucks with bats and guns and stuff. You know, I've been wanting to get your impressions on what's going on down there, since you've been there and all. I mean, how do those whites think they can get away with it, treating an intelligent Negro like that?"

"Well, it shouldn't be too difficult for you to understand."

"Huh? What do you mean?'

"Just look around Worcester."

"But, no, I'm talking about the South, the civil rights movement, the reason you're here. You know. Come on."

"No, you come on. I'm really getting tired of all this talk about Alabama and Mississippi. We don't live there. We live here. Let's talk about Worcester."

"What do you mean?"

"I mean, you ever wonder why when you go into a department store or a bank you never see any Negro clerks or tellers? You ever notice that all the Negroes in this town live in one run-down neighborhood?"

The white student stared at me. "No."

"Do you think things are this way because there aren't any *intelligent* Negroes in Worcester?"

"No. I don't think that. I'd never say that."

"Do you know that the Negro community is just as isolated in terms of basic living conditions as it is in the South? And in some ways it's more isolated."

"What are you talking about? It couldn't be."

"At least when I was growing up in Memphis there was some interaction between Negroes and whites in the sense that some poor whites lived in relative close proximity to Negroes. I think there is even greater racial isolation residentially here."

"But D'Army, it's not like we're lynching people up here. We don't have segregated lunch counters and drinking fountains. We're not bashing students' heads in and throwing them in jail."

"Just because no one is protesting doesn't mean there is nothing to protest."

"I don't understand you. You're trying to invent problems where there aren't any."

"No. I'm just trying to point out that the difference between the racial conditions in the North and in the South is one of degree, not of kind. The problems are the same; they're just not as blatant."

"Uh-huh. Go on."

"What does your father do?"

"He sells insurance."

"Where?"

"Boston."

"Have you ever been to his office?"

"Sure, lots of times."

"Are there any Negro secretaries or clerks or typists?"

He slowly shook his head.

"Have you ever seen any Negroes working at your father's office?"

"Sure, uh, there's Mr. Wilson, the maintenance man. And a couple of Negro women clean up the bathrooms."

"Uh-huh. And why do you suppose up here in the North whites aren't hiring Negroes to do other kinds of jobs?"

Long pause. We had walked to the hall where my lecture was held. I was standing at the entrance of the room with my hand on the doorknob.

"I don't know." The white kid sounded defeated.

"Maybe we could talk about that some time."

Needless to say, as I began to realize that the difference between the North and the South was essentially one of degree, as I began to understand the North wasn't miraculously more rational or egalitarian than the South, and as I began to analyze Worcester from that perspective, my fellow students became less and less appreciative. It was no longer fun to talk to me; it was an overt challenge.

I don't think the students or the administration at Clark had ever considered that if they set up a scholarship for a student who had been expelled for his "radicalism" in the South, he probably wouldn't change his radical ways just because he had changed addresses. Perhaps they thought their northern enclave was so idyllic that the need for protest and agitation would never arise. They were wrong.

~ 17 ~

The L-Word

I WAS PLEASED TO discover during my first month in Worcester that many white students throughout the Northeast were aware, if not of what was going on in their own cities, at least of what was going on in the South, and wanted, with an intensity verging almost on desperation, to become a part of the movement. Protest-oriented organizations such as Friends of SNCC, CORE, and the Northern Student Movement (NSM), which was headquartered at Yale, began organizing sympathy protests on their rich, ivy-covered campuses. Many of these white students believed passionately in human rights and took their opposition to segregation very seriously. I watched with interest and surprise the news reports of northern student boycotts of Woolworth's, Kresge's, and other chain stores that were refusing to desegregate their southern facilities. As my first semester at Clark wore on, I met students who had gone south as volunteer organizers, often risking jail sentences and nearly always putting their personal safety on the line—for often the southern white segregationist reaction to white integrationists, or "white niggers," as they were called, was harsher than to the Negroes themselves.

When Meredith's enrollment hit the news, student response was immediate and fervent. The various northeastern organizations banded together to hold a mass rally at Springfield College in Springfield, Massachusetts. NSM invited me to speak at the rally.

At Clark, the student government pitched in by financing a chartered bus to take students to the rally. On that bright October day—a day that ultimately would mean as much to me as the day I became freshman class president at Southern—the sky was a brilliant fall blue and the air refreshingly light and crisp. Jerry Ernst, a New Yorker who had quickly become a good friend, and I were planning to drive up the turnpike in his car. We were finishing up some business on campus when we heard a loud commotion out in the main parking lot. A group of students opposed to the rally were sitting on the pavement in front of the bus protesting: "We don't need troublemakers at Clark!" and "The student government shouldn't pay for this bus!" In response, the students in the bus were hanging out the windows, screaming at them to leave. Eventually the bus driver maneuvered around them and drove away, but it didn't silence the opposition.

Over the next several months, the coalition of conservative students at Clark became an increasingly outspoken voice against civil rights efforts. They were insulted by the implication that race relations involved them, and they found protest distasteful. As Jerry and I began our drive through the breathtaking beauty and color of a New England fall, we talked about our surprise at seeing such passionate opposition to the movement.

"Do you think this qualifies as a *hint* of racial conflict?" I asked sarcastically.

"Only if you're the kind of guy who uses a sledgehammer to test his reflexes."

"Maybe we should ask Dean Campbell which kind of guy he is."

"Maybe we should take a look at his knees."

When we arrived at Springfield, Jerry and I went to the field house and were taken through a back entrance to the stage. More than fifteen thousand people crowded the huge gymnasium and the grounds outside. Television cameras and lights rimmed the stage, and radio and newspaper reporters were everywhere. As I took a seat on the stage and listened to the other speakers, I looked out at all the white faces, more white faces than I had ever seen in one place before, and I was overwhelmed with a sense of fortuitousness. Here was a golden opportunity, a chance to address a white audience directly about the race problem. It was an opportunity that, just months earlier, I couldn't have imagined ever having. I walked to the podium, every cell in my body alive with the power of words.

"Ladies and gentlemen, friends and fellow students, it is an honor and a great privilege to be here to speak before you today on the great issue of civil rights, which is now the most burning issue before the nation. All over the South there is rebellion and debate over whether the racial segregation of the past is going to continue. For too long in this nation we have allowed a wrong and inequitable system of racial discrimination to go on, and we have allowed the Negro American to languish without realizing his full rights of American citizenship."

I paused and breathed deeply. Did they understand what I meant? Was it ludicrous to hope that these white kids, so many of whom were raised in racial isolation as profound as that in the South, would accept it? Most of these kids came from segregated upper-middle-class communities. The only contact they had with Negroes was through their family servants. Could they identify in any way with what I was saying? I began again, forcing myself to sound resolute, optimistic.

"But now things are changing. Finally, Negro America is waking up. We are no longer content to let things go on as they have been. There is a new day in America now. Throughout the South, Negroes are rising up. In Mississippi, Alabama, Louisiana, and across the South we are saying 'no more.'"

But how many times do we have to say it, I thought, *and how loud?*

"The rebellion that is going on now in Mississippi will not last. Those whites who seek to keep James Meredith from enrolling in the University of Mississippi will not win." A cheer rang out in the crowded gymnasium.

"Today we call upon the federal government to use all of its full resources to put down this rebellion." Another cheer. The response seemed emotional and real. A cool New England breeze came in gusts through an open door. I waited for silence.

"All across the South now, young people, old people, Negroes from all walks of life are tired. And they are willing to risk their all, in many cases, to bring about a new day. You wonder what we are doing in the South? We are marching and singing in the South. Our protest is real. Today we are singing the words of that old Negro spiritual:

> Oh freedom.
> Oh freedom,
> Oh freedom over me,
> and before I be a slave
> I'll be buried in my grave.
> And go home to my Lord and be free.

How many of these kids, from their white northeastern homes, had ever heard a Negro spiritual, or knew what one was? I breathed again.

"Our friends in the North, we ask you to join us. We know there are problems here. We say that it is not enough to simply look south with righteous indignation at the evils there. You have a dual responsibility. The same problems of discrimination in jobs, education, and housing that Negroes face in the South also exist here. It will take your energies, faith, and sense of fairness to help resolve these problems."

One more breath and I would be finished. That had been the clincher: turning the tables, focusing on *them*. I had no idea how it would go over.

"This is a great gathering here today," I concluded, "and it can be the beginning of a new spirit, a spirit of change, brotherhood, and basic fairness finally coming to the fore. And it's been a long time coming."

A roar swept through the crowd. I had struck a responsive chord and, at least for one brief moment, I had gotten a sincere response. I had a glimpse of what it would be like if white people truly followed their better natures, if they truly wanted peace.

In the car on the way back to Clark, my head spinning with the day's events and the implausibility of my participating in them, I said to Jerry, "How in the hell did I end up here?"

"I don't know D'Army." He looked at me seriously. "But I'd say right about now there are several thousand other people wondering that same thing about you."

"A Negro kid from Memphis, thrown out of a Negro school in Louisiana for being—what have I heard people say?—about the most radical nigger ever to hit the state. And I end up in Massachusetts preaching to the white folks?" We both broke down laughing. "Nobody'd ever believe it, it's so absurd."

"Talking about spirits of change and brotherhood and fairness," gasped Jerry. "Right here in the heart of the fatherland!"

"The fatherland!" We howled.

"No, seriously," said Jerry when he had regained composure, "However it happened, I'm glad you came up here. Life's never dull anymore. Just watching people's faces when you walk into a room is entertainment enough for me."

"Yeah, me too," I said, realizing that, for the first time, I really was glad I had come.

We were silent for a few minutes, and then Jerry said in a deadpan monotone, "But I'd advise you to stay away from trees." I looked at him, puzzled. "Oh, you know, the L-word. That's been known to happen up here, and, well, you just never know."

I gave him a mock frown, and we laughed some more. But I knew that after that speech things would be different. I'd taken the first step toward reinvolvement. It wasn't enough just to walk around like a sociological case study answering questions about the South and posing questions about the North. I wanted more. And although I was almost positive that the L-word wouldn't come up, I wasn't sure what would.

~ 18 ~

Provocateur

When the object is to raise the permanent condition of a people, small means
do not merely produce small effects; they produce no effect at all.
—JOHN STUART MILL

THE NORTHERN STUDENT MOVEMENT (NSM) was led by
Peter Countryman, a quiet, determined, white Yale student who
earned respect from both whites and blacks. Along with his wife,
Joan—a black Philadelphian and niece of the black leader Reverend Leon
Sullivan—and another white Yale student, Tom Gilhool, they ran a smoothly
efficient operation organizing northern campuses to support the southern
movement. Using foundation grant money, they campaigned to educate
northern students on racial problems in the North and South, to help them
organize protests and boycotts in their own communities, and to recruit
volunteers to spend vacation periods in the South working with SNCC and
other southern-based groups.

I spent several weekends at Yale attending NSM-sponsored conferences
that fall of 1962. At the New Haven campus, a utopia away from the tough
and dangerous battlefields of southern protest, young and old veterans of the
civil rights movement shared information and strategies, fraternized, and
sang the movement songs "We Shall Overcome," "We Shall Not Be Moved,"
"Kum Bah Yah," and "Oh Freedom," which had by now become as comforting as a favorite blanket. Our gatherings often provided striking contrasts, as
dungaree- and denim-clad SNCC volunteers who had traveled up from the
South dialogued earnestly while casually draped across the carved oak chairs
and benches of Yale's medieval-style chapel. Fannie Lou Hamer electrified
the hall with her stirring songs and moving testimonials of struggle. John
Lewis, Jim Forman, Cordell Regan, and the SNCC Freedom Singers blended
easily with black strategists from the Northeast like Tim Jenkins and Bill

Strickland. The sense of spiritual communion and uplift I gained from these sessions was invaluable. They served to refocus my thoughts and recharge me with the excitement of moral purpose, of sharing a group vision or dream.

I started thinking that perhaps an affiliate student movement group on the Clark campus would help unity and morale there. At least it would help my morale, if no one else's. So I convinced about a dozen students to join with me and optimistically set about forming the Worcester Student Movement for Civil Rights, later to be known as WSM. Our goals were to support the programs of the NSM and to focus on civil rights problems in Worcester.

Before the Christmas holidays, we had drawn up a constitution articulating our purpose as being "to create a greater awareness and understanding of present social problems and to work toward the removal of social inequities." We laid out the duties of our officers and executive committee, and the rules governing our board of community advisors, our affiliations, membership, and programs. We pledged all monies and property, should WSM be discontinued, to the Student Nonviolent Coordinating Committee in Atlanta.

We began making plans to implement a high school tutorial program the following semester and perhaps to start a lecture series, bringing in key spokesmen for different movement factions. Civil rights had come home to Clark. I had become the executive director of my own civil rights organization. Suddenly Worcester was no longer a sleepy northeastern town, but a fertile testing ground for new ideas and new approaches to achieving racial justice. Somehow, while no one was looking, I had metamorphosed from a cute, exotic celebrity into the burr under everyone's saddle. I was back in my element and thrilled to be there.

Generally speaking, the faculty and administration were, at least in the beginning, supportive—that is to say, they did not stand in our way. I think they were sophisticated enough to be pleased to see a new and deeper dimension of student concern and activity emerging at Clark. Given the tenor of the times and the fact that America was coming of age in terms of its social consciousness on the racial front, WSM seemed perfectly timed to pull Clark into a new era. We were the forerunners of real student activism on the Clark campus just as similar offshoots of NSM were the forerunners of activism on other campuses. And throughout the Northeast, this activism was booming. I am sure that, at least at the beginning, the faculty and administration at Clark were pleased to see our concern and our passion. Moreover, they probably did some patting each other on the back for daring to bring me into the community in the first place. But once WSM was started and we were organizing support within the community, the situation really escalated out of their control. Oddly, it was out of my control as well, as I soon found out.

The least amount of racial friction occurs in places like Iowa where there are virtually no blacks, so prejudice is never stimulated. But that doesn't mean those feelings aren't there. In towns like Worcester with only a small black population, a basic, underlying antiblack feeling was not aroused until the civil rights protest challenged whites who had considered themselves above, and somehow immune from, racial conflict. When they were challenged—point-blank—and asked to change their subtle system of segregation, asked to back up their rhetoric with action, many of them balked and balked loudly. The attitude of the Clark students who questioned me in the cafeteria was the norm: "What are you doing, stirring up trouble? This is the North—we don't have racism here."

But they did. Obviously, no one appreciates being slapped in the face with the facts. Before I came to Worcester, there had been the NAACP, but its approach was quiet, conciliatory. WSM focused on confrontation—peaceful and nonviolent—but confrontation nevertheless. For this reason alone, many citizens of Worcester and students at Clark took umbrage at my gall in coming into their peaceful little community and accusing them of racial problems.

Yet, in 1963, that's exactly what I did.

"So are you going to come home with me or not?"

Maureen and I were sitting on the couch in my apartment, which had actually become our apartment—along with Bob's and Fred's—since Maureen was now living there, too. I was staring at the wall, trying, without much success, to imagine what it would be like at her house at Thanksgiving.

"My mother keeps saying she needs to know soon so she can plan everything and arrange a place for you to sleep and all that stuff."

"Of course I'm going. We've talked about this before. I'm going."

"Then how come every time you say that I have this feeling you're not?"

"I don't know."

"I haven't confirmed with my mother because I keep thinking you're going to back out."

"I'm not going to back out."

"You're sure?'

"Yes," I looked at her. She was not beautiful, but very striking in a healthy, robust, Scandinavian sort of way. She had blonde hair, sharp features, and intense, penetrating eyes that soaked up everything through large, wide glasses. Maureen was as strong-willed as I was. Together we had developed a kind of obliviousness to the stares and snickers, to the raised eyebrows and the mumbled words of warning. We simply didn't care. Eventually, the people around us didn't either. In contrast, this—I had a feeling—would be different.

"Just tell me what it's going to be like," I said.

Of course, it doesn't matter how many times you tell yourself it doesn't matter, or you tell yourself just to act naturally, or you tell yourself it's Thanksgiving and that will make everything okay. Well did I know that if I walked in the door with somebody's daughter who happens to be white, and if I just happen to be black, then I walk into someone else's nightmare. Instantly, she's beauty, and you're the beast.

The Robinsons picked us up at Clark and drove us to their home in a quaint Massachusetts village two hours away. They were rough-hewn people, with the same healthy robustness I saw in Maureen. They spoke with heavy, northeastern nasal accents and were impeccably polite. I'll never forget driving through that little snow-covered town, pulling up to the white gingerbread house, and feeling as if I'd somehow stepped into someone else's Christmas card. I wasn't uncomfortable with them; I was just extremely conscious of the fact that I wasn't supposed to feel uncomfortable. The Robinsons were obviously doing their best.

And the holiday was pleasant. We stayed around the house and read and cooked and chatted about any number of innocuous things. By that time, I had become accustomed to appropriate and genteel interaction with whites. Even though I was always aware I was the only Negro in a white household, I had trained myself to leave the tension and defensiveness of protest at the door. I wasn't there to prove anything; I was there to enjoy the Thanksgiving holiday with my girlfriend. And Mr. and Mrs. Robinson showed remarkable restraint and strength in treating me like a welcome guest. Maybe it had not sunk in that this was a serious dating relationship; maybe they just refused to acknowledge it or accept it. Whatever they were doing, they were very busy ignoring many levels of our relationship. They must have known ours was more than mere friendship. They could not have missed the signs that we loved each other. And they must have realized that we had slept together. Accordingly, the strain was sometimes evident in their faces, as if they had been caught off guard. There would be a fleeting pinched, detached expression, an awed horror that was quickly covered by a broad smile, a quick laugh, or an incongruous, "Well!" But they never said anything impolite or ungracious to me.

Given this studied refusal to acknowledge the obvious, it took Maureen's younger brother an entire year to confront us with how much the family was bothered by our relationship. Will was a good kid, and we'd never had any trouble before; he'd never seemed hostile or afraid. But by this time, the family had obviously done quite a bit of speculating about our relationship, and the gloves had come off. When Will arrived to visit us, he was overwrought with emotion.

"You have got to stop seeing him!" he nearly yelled at Maureen. "Don't you understand? He's a *Negro*."

"Oh, really? Thanks for pointing that out to me, Will. I hadn't noticed."

"Go ahead, joke, joke, joke. This is serious, Maureen."

"Okay, what's so serious all of a sudden? You've known about D'Army and me for a long time. What's the problem?"

"Well . . . we didn't think it would last this long. . . . I mean, Mom and Dad just thought it was a passing phase or something. . . . I mean, we're all really worried you're going to marry him or do something awful like that."

"Oh?" Maureen started laughing. "And why would that be so awful?"

"God, I don't believe you—are you really that stupid? Don't you know what will happen to you if you marry a Negro?"

"My skin won't turn black, if that's what you're worried about."

"Maureen! Stop joking. Do you want to ruin your life? Do you want to end up in a housing project? Do you want to live in a ghetto on welfare? Don't you realize what will happen to you?"

As the new semester began, I gave several speeches at local churches and civic groups, becoming increasingly blunt and outspoken at each engagement. In February, I appeared at a civil rights program sponsored by the National Federation of Catholic College Students (NFCCS) at St. Joseph's College in Standish, Massachusetts, where I delivered a speech peppered with statistics that traced the economic consequences of an intrinsically racist government: "One out of four nonwhites is functionally illiterate. Half of all nonwhites do not complete elementary school, and only one in five finishes high school. However, only one in twenty whites is functionally or officially designated as illiterate. Four out of every five whites finish elementary school, and half of them go through college. In 1959, a nonwhite worker could expect to average $2,844 annually and a nonwhite family, including a college-educated father, $5,654. A white worker could expect $4,487 annually while a white family including a college-educated father could expect $7,373. This approximate one-to-two pay ratio has remained about the same, except in World War II, for generations."

I continued the comparisons, noting that more than half of all nonwhites had laboring or service jobs, including one-fourth of those with college degrees. "Only one in twenty," I said, "worked in a professional or managerial capacity. But fewer than one in five of all whites was a laborer while one in four was in professional or managerial work. Within the 1960 labor force of 72 million, one out of every ten nonwhites was unemployed while only one out of every twenty whites was out of work."

Then I paraphrased from an SDS position statement based on the "Agenda for a Generation" section of the Port Huron Statement: "As man's own technology destroys old and creates new forces of social organization, man still tolerates meaningless work, idleness, instead of creative leisure, and educational institutions that in many cases fail to meet the challenge of our times. . . . With rockets we are emancipating man from terrestrial limitations, but from the Mississippi jails comes the prayer for emancipation of man on earth. No person is really free so long as there is a person somewhere in this world who is not." The *Worcester Telegram* ran a front-page photo of me standing with two white female members of NFCCS under the headline "Negro Student Says: Rockets Free Some, but Others Pray in Jail."

On March 18, WSM was in the news as we finalized arrangements for our South High tutorial program. Marcia Irwin, the chairman of the program and a nineteen-year-old Clark University sophomore, and I had spent weeks in conferences with the superintendent of schools, the school administrator, the director of guidance, and the principal of the high school. Finally, we had seventy students registered with individual tutors in every subject, from English and basic math to French and physics, and the go-ahead to expand our program to reach other Worcester high schools.

That Monday, the *Telegram* ran an editorial titled "Out of the Ivory Tower" commending "Clark students" for our descent from the "ivory tower" into the "cold, cruel world": "Should colleges be ivory towers where students learn about life but are protected from it? . . . [S]ome students at

Clark apparently have reached their own conclusion. . . . [T]hey want out, for at least a couple of hours a week. . . . From our viewpoint, at least, Worcester's college students are more than welcome to descend as often as possible from the ivory tower. Worcester has no shortage of activities for them to undertake."

It's not as if we were waiting for establishment approval, but for the next fourteen months, we members of WSM not only descended from the ivory tower, we rocked the tower's foundation.

~ 19 ~

The Original X Man

I am the man you think you are. . . . If you want to know what I'll do, figure out what you'll do. I'll do the same thing, only more of it. You get your freedom by letting your enemy know that you'll do anything to get your freedom: then you'll get it. It's the only way you'll get it.

—MALCOLM X

B Y THE SPRING OF 1963, Malcolm X, the leader of the Black Muslim organization, was attracting increasing attention in the national media for his harsh critique of the American system. I followed his progress with eagerness and curiosity. There was no one else like him, no one with as much uncompromising belief in the power of the Negro. I saw Malcolm as the intellectual guru of Negro activism, offering a welcome and fresh ideology on the racial conflict. Even though I came from a movement of philosophical nonviolence, I felt Malcolm added a new energy to our ideology and to the era itself.

From the beginning of the sit-in movement, we had been brutally assaulted, had felt such harsh resistance, and had witnessed the continual repudiation by our white adversaries of the concepts of love and nonviolence. Yet, we did not abandon these concepts because we saw within the repudiation, the rejection, and the violent response a validation of the efficacy of those nonviolent strategies. Most of us had grown up with the terror of the 1950s—the lynchings, the sudden brutal attacks of whites against one lone Negro. As we moved deeper into the 1960s, we began, through organizations like CORE and SNCC, to take control of the violence, to orchestrate it, and to turn it against the violent people through planned assaults on the *structure* that allowed the violence. Rather than allow these clandestine terror attacks, we intentionally made ourselves objects of white anger, bringing it out in the open, exposing it to public view. Only through the manipulation of white violence could we prove, by glaring contrast to our own nonviolent action, how utterly wrong it was.

Not only did Malcolm take us to an entirely new level of protest and challenge, not only did he offer shockingly honest verbal commentary on white presumption, superiority, violence, and tyranny, but he also offered an intellectual premise for the formation of a separate Negro state, the only method he saw for Negroes to achieve economic and political power and autonomy as a people. While I didn't feel I had to embrace the Muslim philosophy, and while at some level I feared its threat to the ultimate attainment of interracial harmony, I thought it was important that it was there. It was another weapon in our collective arsenal, and I did not feel it was incompatible with other approaches to achieving power and equality. The Muslims served as catalysts, encouraging other Negroes—Negroes who feared Muslim religious doctrine—to strike at the American social phenomenon that had created and nourished Muslim society: civil inequality. The Black Muslims showed us the disease in American society. I felt it was up to the student movement to center in on this disease and excise it.

I did not join the Muslims because their theology seemed too structured, too strict, too disciplined, too demanding of the surrender of the individual. I did not incline to surrendering my individual autonomy, whether to CORE, to SNCC, or to a religious movement. For his part, Malcolm seemed intelligent enough to appreciate the honesty and dedication of the young activists of CORE, SNCC, and even the NSM despite our different philosophical approaches to changing the racial climate in America. Ultimately, it was this intelligence, this ability to view one situation from many points of view, that made Malcolm such an effective leader. His multifaceted perspective was the source of his broad emotional appeal.

Born Malcolm Little, he had grown up in the ghettos of Detroit, learned the ways of street life, and ended up in prison. After periods as a pimp, a hustler, and a con man, Malcolm converted to the Black Muslim movement while in prison in 1947. By the early 1960s, he was chief lieutenant and heir apparent to Elijah Muhammad, the leader of the group. Malcolm served as program coordinator, chief spokesman for the Black Muslim movement, and manager of the movement's economic enterprises.

Over the Christmas holidays in 1962, I had realized that in order to make inroads in the thinking of students and members of the community, we had to have input from the cold, cruel, outside world—the world that extended beyond Worcester's boundaries. By February 1963, I knew the protective, self-satisfied shell that surrounded Worcester had to be cracked. And the best way to crack it, I decided, was to confront people by placing another viewpoint smack in the front of their eyes. If the viewpoint happened to come from the mouth of a famous person, all the better: perhaps their curiosity would keep them from running away.

Malcolm X was perfect. He was all over the newspapers and television. He was extremely controversial, irrepressibly opinionated, and very black. I called him in New York and was amazed when he picked up the phone. He was absolutely unpretentious, not the distant, cautious celebrity I had expected. When I described WSM and the Worcester community, he responded with understanding and interest. Yes, he said without delay, he would be very interested in coming to Clark to speak. I hung up the phone, dazed and happy. How could I just pick up the phone and call Malcolm X? How could it be so simple?

The WSM board of advisors was another matter. When I informed Reverend Handlan, the Episcopalian priest who was the chairman of our board, that I had arranged for Malcolm X to speak at Clark, he threatened to resign and to encourage the rest of the board to resign if I didn't cancel the speech. "Malcolm X preaches nothing but hatred of whites, and that kind of thinking doesn't do anyone any good," he said firmly. "This organization should not be involved in sponsoring such filth on this campus."

Unabashedly, I told him I couldn't cancel the speech, and we decided to call a meeting to discuss the matter further. During the meeting, some members agreed with him, others with me. Finally, after a heated conversation, Reverend Handlan offered a compromise: "Okay, how about this? Malcolm X can speak on campus, but only in a debate forum, and only if the second speaker represents a peaceful, nonviolent point of view."

"That sounds fine," I agreed, relieved that we had come to an understanding. "I'll see what I can do." I called Malcolm back and explained the problem.

"I would be glad to debate," he explained evenly, "but only if the person I am debating is Martin Luther King. King is going around the country spreading misinformation and misleading Negroes. It's time a few things were set straight. He knows I want to confront him, but he's been avoiding me." Malcolm's voice was strained, almost angry.

I assured him I would do my best to set it up.

"Don't worry. No matter what you do, it won't matter. King won't be on the same program with me. He's scared of me."

Nonetheless, for the sake of solidarity in WSM, I called the Southern Christian Leadership Conference in Atlanta. They told me Dr. King would not be available for such a debate and suggested I contact Bayard Rustin, an organizer with the Fellowship of Reconciliation in New York. Malcolm had been adamant that he would debate no one but King, so I called him again.

"Rustin is nothing but a flunky trailing after King's coattails," Malcolm said, his voice cold and hard. "He has nothing to say I want to hear. I don't need some flunky to debate me—I'll speak on my own."

At this point, I was becoming concerned that Malcolm might lose interest because of all the wishy-washiness, so I went ahead and confirmed April 11 as the date he would come to Clark. I then called Rustin, and he agreed to come on April 29 and deliver a "response" to Malcolm's position. If my board of advisors still didn't like it, I figured I would just keep on fighting about it until they gave in. I had made my best efforts to please everyone, and it hadn't worked. Nevertheless, I was determined one way or another to have Malcolm speak. Relations with Reverend Handlan were strained, but he did not resign. He stayed around, mumbling to himself and insisting that I, and all of Worcester, would come to regret my decision.

A month later, at seven o'clock on the morning of the speech, Malcolm called from a diner just outside Worcester. I gave him directions to my apartment. When he and his Muslim aide arrived, Maureen and I were dressed and ready.

"Do I look okay?" Maureen asked nervously.

"You look fine." I was nervous, too. I had been so looking forward to Malcolm's coming, but now that he was here, I had no idea what to expect. Would he refuse to ride in the car with Maureen? Would he be rude to her?

"I mean, do I look like a *nice* white person?" Her overemphasis of the "nice" made it sound like a bad word.

"I know you're a nice person. You're a wonderful person," I said, trying to sound reassuring. "That's all that matters."

"But will he know that?"

"I don't know. I hope so." I didn't know what to say. I had no idea what Malcolm would do.

"Oh, God, I hope so, too."

We both jumped when we heard the knock at the door. I squeezed Maureen's hand. "Okay?"

"Okay," she said firmly.

I answered the door.

"Hello, D'Army. It's so good to finally meet you." His voice was cordial and almost soft, his face relaxed. He extended his hand.

"We're honored you would take the time to come. Worcester may never be the same again."

Malcolm chuckled. "I should hope not." He and his aide stepped inside the apartment.

"Malcolm, this is Maureen Robinson. I've invited her to join us today."

"Ah, how nice to meet you, Maureen. And you're a student here also? His voice was serene. "Well, I hope you find the day's activities educational," he smiled.

"I'm sure I will," she said, sounding braver than I thought she would.

"Well, we've got to be at the radio station at eleven thirty. Let's go have breakfast and get you to your hotel," I suggested, feeling like a tour guide in a daydream preparing to introduce Rasputin to the czar's family. Even so, Malcolm seemed about as dangerous as a teddy bear.

When we arrived at WTAG, a crowd of people milled around us, trying to get a good look at Malcolm. The station was located in the same building with the city's two newspapers, which were owned by the conservative financier Robert Stoddard. The place was literally crawling with newspeople. We were big news in Worcester, an anxiously awaited event. Everyone wanted their piece of Malcolm X. Everyone wanted to prove him wrong.

Julie Chase Fuller, who was going to conduct the interview, came out to meet us in the lobby. She chatted briefly with us as we walked through the hallways toward the broadcast studio. "Today has been an exceptionally busy day," she told Malcolm. "There was a plane crash this morning, and more than a hundred people were killed. The phones have been ringing off the hook."

He smiled. "Well, that's just a few less white people we have to worry about," he said pleasantly. Julie stifled a gasp.

In the studio, the three of us sat around a central microphone. When a man in the control booth gave her a signal, Julie introduced Malcolm and me and explained how the Worcester Student Movement had arranged for Malcolm to come to town. Then she began her questions.

"Are you a racist?" she asked, still seemingly unnerved by his earlier comment.

"No, I am not a racist," he responded simply, his voice even and cool. "But I believe in the liberation of Negro people. I believe whites have done enough to destroy Negroes. Look around you. There is no room to make any more concessions to the white community, and I will not make any."

"What about your philosophy of separatism? Why is your Muslim organization advocating separate states for Negroes?"

"The history of America is a history of separatism," he said. "Muslim philosophy has grown out of a recognition that separation of the races is a reality built in by the white community. Negroes can no longer have any faith that whites will act honestly with them. To be safe and to grow without hindrance, Negroes need only to work among themselves in their own communities. If we could do that and could be allowed some small share of the wealth of the land, then we could prosper."

"Don't you consider yourself an American?"

"It would be foolish for me to sit at your table and watch you eat, with nothing on my plate, and call myself a diner," he said slowly. "Sitting at the table doesn't make me a diner any more than being here in America makes me an American."

As the interview progressed, more and more people left their desks and gathered at the plate glass window to look in on our studio. They were all whites, and all of them probably disagreed, on principle, with what Malcolm X stood for. Most probably feared him. And yet they were drawn to him, captivated by his wit and by some undeniable authoritative quality that drew them in and made them listen.

Julie then directed a question at me. "Isn't it true, D'Army, that many Negroes don't agree with Malcolm X?" I suddenly realized I was there only because she had hoped to set up a conflict between Malcolm and me. I hadn't expected this.

Basically, I thought, I don't have any disagreements with him. I was impressed by his intellectualism, by his all-or-nothing approach, and by his ability to shock people and shake up the assumed order of their lives. The only part of his analysis that I felt did not make sense was the idea of a separate black nation. I thought it ridiculous to assert that we could form a separate nation of wealth, growth, and prosperity within the next several generations. I thought true racial integration was the only hope for broad Negro advancement. However, it didn't make sense to engage him in a discussion about it because I was not going to convince him otherwise any more than he was going to convince me to stop dating Maureen. We would have to accept the territorial rights of the other, for the purpose of impact and for the purpose of progress.

"Yes," I answered, drawing a deep breath. "Some Negroes do disagree with Malcolm X. His philosophy is new. It represents a break from what many of us are familiar with and have been taught to believe. But because some Negroes may disagree with Malcolm does not detract from the significance of his message. There are many other Negroes, myself included, who share at least some measure of agreement with him."

"But don't you think he is actually stirring up more trouble for Negroes and making things harder?"

"No, I don't. Malcolm wants the best for all Negroes. He is just willing to fight harder than most people are to get it."

As we left the studio, we met the editors of the *Telegram* and the *Gazette* standing out in the hall. They wanted an interview with Malcolm. When he agreed, we filed into the long conference room. That morning, the *Telegram* had run a story on Malcolm under the headline "Extremist Leader Speaks Here." The article, carefully worded to avoid any overt commentary or editorial opinion on the man or the Black Muslims, stuck to more basic biographical information and history:

The Black Muslims are a group of Negro nationalists who claim Negro superiority and claim to follow the Islam religion. Their goals include: the formation of a united front of Black Men, racial separation, and economic self-sufficiency for American Negroes. They have adopted the Islam religion which has its roots in the East, and have repudiated Christianity as the White Man's religion, which keeps the Negro under the white man's yoke and retards his development. Its membership includes the young lower class Negro. Its regulations forbid intoxicating beverages, excessive eating, sexual immorality and laxity in morally binding temple regulation.

The article also included a policy statement I had issued to clarify WSM's position on Malcolm:

The constitution of the Worcester Student Movement mandates its members to work for the creation of a greater awareness and understanding of present social problems and to work towards the removal of social inequities. Our decision to present Malcolm X was in full realization of the duty imposed by our Constitution. . . . It should not be interpreted as an affirmation or a rejection of the Black Muslim Movement and/or its principles. To find that there are a number of students on this campus who are completely unaware of the existence of this Movement is alarming, to say the least. The actual membership of the Muslim Movement in this country numbers well over 200,000 with potential sympathizers running into the millions. That this organization poses a severe threat to the questionable peace and tranquility that exists between the black and white races of this country is a fact which cannot be denied. This group has made more inroads into the Northern Negro population than all other civil rights groups combined. The Black Muslim Movement cannot and must not be ignored.

As we filed into the long, narrow conference room, I couldn't wait to hear what these white men, these leaders of the community, really wanted to say. Would they be angry and defensive? Would they lash out? Would he?

"We are very interested in understanding your vision for Negro America," one of the men began.

"Well, it's not complicated," Malcolm explained. "I want no more and no less than what white Americans enjoy. I want a chance for my children to grow up, and to acquire wealth, and the good things in life. I want opportunities to be open to them. I don't want them to be hindered their whole lives by their race and background. Whites cannot fairly believe that some special effort shouldn't be required to aid Negroes. Certainly not if they recognize the strong history of denial and harsh discrimination which blacks have been subjected to in this land."

"Do you hate whites? You seem to preach hate."

"I do not hate any man. I hate the selfishness, the ego, the venom in the white man that keeps you from treating us fairly, that would have us remain second-class citizens in a white society."

"I do not understand the practicality of forming a separate Negro nation."

"There are 20 million Negroes in the United States. We are already a nation within a nation, but you do not recognize us. The Negro nation is a child struggling to be born. If the mother tries to prevent the child from being born, both the mother and the child will die."

Patiently, Malcolm answered their questions for over an hour. Ultimately, he tamed the white newspapermen. He made pussycats out of them because he gave them logical, direct answers. He was a careful, unemotional speaker, and he didn't shoot from the hip. He played their game better than they did, all the while smiling and listening and speaking his mind.

As the meeting was winding down, one of the editors asked Malcolm about the tie clasp he was wearing that was made in the shape of a fish.

"Well, I'm a fisherman," he said, as he smiled and fingered the clasp. "And when I go out fishing, and I want to catch something, I usually do." Malcolm chuckled a little, and the editors, clearly hooked at this point, chuckled right along with him.

At five o'clock that evening, I picked Malcolm up at the hotel and took him to a small French restaurant for a dinner with several members of WSM, local townspeople, and faculty members. Once again he was amiable and chatty with the group, most of whom were white. He never confronted anyone and never raised his voice, but he never appeared fake or contrived either. When the waiter came to take our order, Malcolm told him he was not eating, that he would just have coffee. He explained that it was a Muslim practice to eat only one meal a day because eating too much could dull the mind and senses. "I draw from the discipline it takes to maintain this eating pattern," he explained to the table of uncomprehending faces.

When someone asked him if he wanted cream and sugar, Malcolm asked for sugar but no cream. "I take my coffee black," he said smiling. "If you put cream in it, you weaken it." He said it so pleasantly that no one took offense.

As we were leaving the restaurant, the wife of our campus advisor, Mordecai Rubin, came up to me. "My, he's such a wonderful man," she said, her face glowing. "I'm so glad you asked him to come. He's just marvelous and, you know, I never dreamed he would be so attractive."

The speech was scheduled to begin at eight thirty. When we arrived at Atwood Hall at eight thirty-five or so, the auditorium was filled. I was pleased to see a healthy representation of Negroes, some of whom, I found out later, had come from as far away as New Haven and Boston. Several conservatively dressed Muslims stood at the entrance selling copies of the tabloid paper *Muhammad Speaks* for twenty cents a copy. Conspicuous and scattered throughout the auditorium were extra security and police guards we had hired for the occasion after receiving threats of some sort of violent demonstration against the Black Muslims. The feeling in the hall was undeniably tense, but as I scanned the crowd, I convinced myself that the threats had been unfounded.

As Malcolm and I headed down the aisle, he turned to me: "Now you tell people that it wasn't my fault that we're late. I was here on time. It's you all's fault that you didn't get me here to this program when you were supposed to."

I promised him I would take the blame in my introduction, and I did. Then Malcolm stepped to the podium. There is no sufficient way to describe his captivating energy, no way to describe how I felt, sitting just feet from him, as he spoke with his rare and riveting eloquence. I hoped, selfishly, that some part of that energy might bounce around the room and come back through me. I hoped I might suddenly discover what made him so strong.

Malcolm's speech was a cry for the liberation of Negro Americans. From the moment he opened his mouth, he was completely transformed. The cloak of reserve he wrapped around himself throughout the day vanished as he became fiery and unrelenting. His voice carried all the threat, the intimidation, and the anger that had given him, throughout white America, his nightmarish reputation. Yet, the largely white audience sat in their seats as if hypnotized while he spoke, in no uncertain terms, about the contradictions of American society, about the degradation and destruction Negroes had experienced, and about the cruel, exploitative traditions of white America. The crowd seemed not to move or even breathe, but to hang on his every word. I noticed members of the Black Muslims sitting and standing throughout the auditorium. The armed police and security guards nervously scanned the hall, their heads continually turning from side to side. It was a tense, highly theatrical scene, and it was such an about-face from the informal dinner of less than thirty minutes before that I actually began to wonder, idiotically, which Malcolm was more real. I wondered if he perceived himself as playing a role. Then, he went on to talk about his disgust with the preachers of nonviolence. He singled out Dr. King and others and accused them of misleading Negro America, of being leeches and twentieth-century Uncle Toms, charlatans who spoke only for a minority of Negroes and who sought to make their people permanent slaves to the white man's ego. I was shocked by the overt harshness of his attack, but his strong words captured my attention. As if the words themselves had picked me up by the scruff of the neck and shaken me, I was being forced to *listen*.

"I am not a theorist of nonviolence," he said. "I believe that there comes a point when you fight fire with fire, and we are at that point. The only way Negroes can survive with any dignity is if we stand prepared to fight back. We cannot wait for the white man to change. He has proven he will not change."

"I cannot condemn white men who refuse to hire Negroes because I believe Negroes should finance their own businesses and hire their own kind of people. The Negro is sleeping—socially, morally, and economically. We must be taught to wake up and see what time it is. Muslims are against welfare programs because they lead to laziness and dependency in Negroes. Our members are taught to stand on their own two feet."

He said that Negroes do not want integration; they want complete separation. "The only properties Negroes own in this country are their churches. We have failed to invest in job-producing industries and to participate in the economic life of the nation. I can promise you that our divorce will result in a property settlement. Moses led the Jewish slaves out of Egypt, but they carried with them a lot of Egyptian gold and silver." He said his group chose the Muslim faith because it is the only religion not based on race. Many in the audience booed when he said, "You have to be white to be a good Christian."

In his closing statements, he said: "The time is up for the oppressor. The end of time has come for whitism and colonialism. The white man is on the way out. Not us, but God Himself is against him. We want to separate ourselves from him and get on God's side. We are not anti-white, anti-integration, or anti-you, but we are pro-God. The motto of the Black Muslims is Wake Up, Clean Up, and Stand Up. We have reached the stage where we no longer think you are capable of treating us right. You do not have it in your hearts. We are turning to God."

Then he opened up the floor for questions.

"How can you support violence as a way to make progress?" one white student asked.

"I know violence is the only way to make change. And I know this because I know the history of America is a violent history. There is a tradition of Americans in war and peace to respond violently to anything they don't like. There are hundreds of times where white Americans have responded brutally when Negroes have been peaceful and nonviolent. And it continues this day. Fear and violence. That is what the white man understands." He went on to talk about the white man's response to Hitler and to Japan in World War II. He said that Kennedy did not threaten to stage a nonviolent protest when Soviet ships came into Cuba carrying missiles; he threatened to start a nuclear war.

The student who had raised the question stood in the center of the auditorium, uneasily shifting his weight. Then Malcolm began talking about the degradation of Negro women throughout American history, about the use and abuse of female slaves. "You all have trampled on our women too long," he said, pointing a sharp finger across the silent hall and glaring at the white questioner. "And we've been so nice and nonviolent. But let me tell you, brother, if you mess with our women, I'll cut your throat."

A female student stood and asked what contribution students could make to the Negro struggle for freedom.

"Whites who are sincere don't accomplish anything by joining Negro organizations and making them integrated," he said. "Whites who are sincere should organize among themselves and figure out some strategy to break down prejudice that exists in white communities. They can function more effectively and more intelligently in the white communities themselves. And this has never been done."

He declined to say how many Negroes were members of the Black Muslims, what section of the United States they wanted for their new nation, and how much land they wanted. One moment he was relaxed and smiling, and the next moment he was cold-blooded and deadly determined. Throughout the hour-long program, the audience was spellbound.

Later, at the reception in the lounge of a men's dorm, blacks and whites discussed and debated racial issues—sometimes heatedly, sometimes angrily, but with surprising sincerity and passion. Through all of this, Malcolm, with all his charm returned, answered questions with an eerie, smiling calm. That reception provided a forum for what was probably the most thoughtful, honest exchange that had occurred between blacks and whites in that area of the country in many years, if ever. And Malcolm X, the white man's consummate enemy, the same man who just minutes earlier had threatened to cut a white student's throat, stood at the center of it.

It was an eye-opening experience for me in more ways than one. Though I had agreed with many aspects of Malcolm's analysis before I met him, I had no idea of the complexity of his understanding of human nature and emotion or of his ability to manipulate it. You can hate white attitudes, I realized through watching Malcolm, and not be antiwhite. He unqualifiedly hated

what whites represented, but that did not mean he had to hate you personally just because you were white. He had a real hostility and venom not only
toward white arrogance but also toward white unfairness. He would stand
toe to toe with any white and bitterly contest that territory, especially if they
presumed it had nothing to do with them, wasn't their fault, and wasn't their
problem. On the other hand, Malcolm knew—as I know and as anyone who
is fair-minded knows—that color doesn't ultimately determine character. It
doesn't determine it for whites any more than it does for blacks. So, while
he could use a broad brush to attack white people, he understood there were
some whites who were just as much the victims of the society as black people
were. Just as he expected blacks to overcome their victimization, Malcolm
could have a great deal of respect for a white person who recognized and
attempted to overcome a situation weighted against him or her. Moreover,
that respect would stay with him, even though he might mount the podium
and give the most vitriolic, antiwhite-sounding speech.

This seemingly split-personality approach came, I think, from Malcolm's
realization that he was speaking to two audiences. First and foremost, he
spoke to blacks. Undoubtedly, he tried a form of shock treatment: to un-
flinchingly analyze racism, to tell it like it is, and then to embolden blacks
to overcome it. Obviously, he thought the most effective way to do that was
to give white people hell and to talk to them and about them in a manner
seldom if ever heard at that time in this country. Such blatant language and
such a raw display of power provided many blacks with a rare spiritual uplift
and a strong "right-on" attitude.

But Malcolm was intelligent enough to realize that white people weren't
going to disappear. When all the emotions calmed, there was still the tough
job of quiet diplomacy that had to go on between blacks and whites. For this
reason, he had become an excellent diplomat. He could talk to whites, listen to
them, even answer their questions. He could be polite, gentle. and solicitous.
And he could calmly make his position plain to them without yielding one inch.

The day he had started at seven in the morning wasn't over until after
midnight, when we finally left the reception and walked across the street to
my apartment. We chatted a little about the day, and Malcolm said he was
very pleased about the way things had gone. I told him I was amazed at how
his energy and patience never seemed to waver.

"Practice," he said, "is everything."

I wrote him a check for seventy-five dollars, which is what we had agreed
on to cover his expenses. He made a phone call, thanked me for inviting him,

and then went downstairs, where his aide was waiting to drive him back to New York.

On April 15, the *Worcester Telegram* ran an editorial titled "The Message of Malcolm X":

> Malcolm X, the fluent young Negro who brought the message of the Black Muslims to Clark University the other night, talked mostly pernicious nonsense. His dream of an independent Negro state, freed of all relationship to the white United States, is a chimera. His indictment of the collective white man for subjugating and demoralizing the collective Negro is a neurotic syndrome. His arrogant dismissal of Christianity as a "white man's religion," and his claims of superiority for his version of the Moslem faith are psychopathic rubbish.
>
> Nevertheless, Malcolm X has a message for all Americans, white and Negro. For the fact is that his mood of bitter alienation from American life is shared, at least in part, by unknown numbers of American Negroes disillusioned by their slow acceptance into the American mainstream.
>
> There is too much truth in Malcolm X's assertion that the American Negro does not have a fair shake in this county, and that the fault lies mostly with the white community. There is too much truth in his charge that many doors are closed to Negroes, even those well qualified. There is too much truth in his statement that the Negro who runs afoul of the law is treated differently than the white in a similar situation.
>
> The Black Muslim movement is a warning that Negro patience is not inexhaustible. The rights set forth in the Declaration of Independence and guaranteed by the Constitution cannot be denied to the Negro forever if he is expected to remain a loyal American Citizen.
>
> The Black Muslim Message of bitterness preached here by Malcolm X is a blueprint for disaster. Fortunately, most American Negroes so far are rejecting this counsel of extremism. But there is no guarantee that they will reject it permanently if their real grievances are not met without undue procrastination.

Malcolm's observations and analyses are as valid today as they were in

1963, with the exception of his strategies of racial separatism. But Malcolm himself, by the time of his death in 1965, had moved decisively away from the separatist philosophy upheld by the Muslims. By March 1964, he had officially broken with the Black Muslims in order to organize a new movement with an emphasis on black nationalism and the conversion of the Negro population from nonviolence to active self-defense against white supremacists in all parts of the country. He said then that he would cooperate with grassroots civil rights activities wherever Negroes asked for his help because he believed every campaign for specific objectives heightened the political identification against white racism and their commitment to overcome it.

In a March 9 *New York Times* article titled "Malcolm X Splits with Muhammad," he wrote:

There is no use deceiving ourselves, good education, housing and jobs are imperatives for the Negroes, and I shall support them in their fight to win these objectives, but I shall tell the Negroes that while these are necessary, they cannot solve the main Negro problem. I shall also tell them that what has been called the Negro Revolution in the United States is a deception practiced upon them because they have only to examine the failure of this so-called revolution to produce any positive results in the past year. I shall tell them what a real revolution means— the French Revolution, the American Revolution, Algeria, to name a few. There can be no revolution without bloodshed, and it is nonsense to describe the civil rights movement in America as a revolution.

Malcolm's developing black nationalist philosophies—philosophies of strong cultural identification, of determined group action, of political and economical realignment, and uncompromising force for self-protection— were sources of argument among black leadership for the rest of the decade. The "white man, move over" attitude threatened the old order of Negro leaders, the business and professional class and ministers, while at the same time seriously questioning the leadership of liberal whites in the struggle against discrimination. It helped destroy the old stereotypes of the shiftless Negro and the Uncle Tom and brought to the surface not only a fiery racial pride but a widespread hatred for white domination. Disciplined to almost puritanical excess by the tenets of the Muslims, articulate, shrewd, and dynamic, Malcolm, even to his detractors, was an undeniably positive symbol for the New Negro: he was the young, dynamic, self-motivated Negro who no longer felt innately inferior to the white man. He embodied an assertive, uncompromising spirit, a spirit he insisted he knew the black masses shared.

The philosophies central to the rising black nationalism of the late 1960s and to Malcolm X's agenda during the last year of his life are certainly valid for any attack on black political, social, and economic inequity today. Ironically, they are probably more out of place today than they were in 1963, a consequence of what I think of as our philosophical neutering; we have not grown to full equality. And when we fail to grow with changing times, our position actually regresses. I believe that we have actually lost focus, momentum, pride, and belief in ourselves. We have lost that aching anger and drive for equality that brought us to confrontation in the 1960s. We have done the unthinkable: we have compromised.

Although Malcolm's philosophy may appear more alien today than it did in 1963, his analyses are just as relevant in terms of the development, position, and condition of blacks vis-à-vis wealth and power in the United States. With a singular exception here or there, blacks are still sitting at the foot of the table getting the crumbs the white man drops. He still dominates the economy. He still largely dominates our government. Black people are still divided. We still have selfish and compromised leadership that thrives amidst our division. We still suffer from self-hatred and self-doubt. We still turn against ourselves with killings and muggings and shooting, acting like hoodlums and thugs—all the things Malcolm addressed. While poverty and the racial divide are still vast, Malcolm's clarion voice is gone. It should not be forgotten.

~ 20 ~

Brother Rat

Stand your ground. Don't fire unless fired upon. But if they mean to have a war, let it begin here.

—CAPTAIN JOHN PARKER AT THE BATTLE OF LEXINGTON, APRIL 19, 1775

THROUGHOUT THE SPRING OF 1963, Peter Countryman and several leaders of the Northern Student Movement (NSM) worked to gain foundation grants to run summer tutorial projects in Boston, Philadelphia, New York, Washington, D.C., and New Haven. Their goal was to open a headquarters staffed by six to eight full-time students in a target low-income neighborhood in each city. The students and as many volunteers as they could round up would go into the low-income junior high and high schools and recruit students for free tutoring services. The tutoring projects were visualized as a practical, grassroots means of approaching the civil rights problem, of keeping young blacks in school, and of making them aware of ways they themselves could combat the problems they faced.

Peter and the board of directors of NSM asked me to head their Washington, D.C., project. So, in late May, Maureen and I—armed with a five-thousand-dollar budget and a great deal of enthusiasm—packed a couple of bags and took the train to Washington. I had never been to Washington before and was struck by the sharp contrast between the inspired tranquility of the monuments, the Capitol, the Mall, and the blatant squalor of the teeming ghettos. On the one hand, there was a large black community struggling with crime, high school dropouts, low-level jobs, and seemingly inescapable poverty, and on the other, there was a cosmopolitan city filled with powerbrokers of many races and their families—a city of wealth, power, glamour, and constant change. A unique truce seemed to exist between the Washington powerbrokers and the city's poor blacks: beauty and hope existed side by side with urban decay and hopelessness, and neither community, it seemed to me at the age of twenty-one, considered that it should be or could be any different. We rented a three-story house on Meridian Place Northwest, just off Sixteenth Street in the heart of the black ghetto. I interviewed and hired a summer staff of five workers: Joe Simpson, a black graduate student in chemistry at Cornell; Mary Smith, a student at Howard; Betsy Wright, a student at Bryn Mawr and the granddaughter of the architect Frank Lloyd Wright; Steve Block, a motorcycle-riding student from Rutgers and a fiery believer in civil rights; and Allison Turaj, a young white woman who was not a student, but had been organizing tenants in the projects in Harlem before coming down to Washington to join us. Initially, we lived and worked out of the Meridian Place house, quickly making contact with the teachers and principals at nearby Cordova Junior High School and Shaw Junior High School. Our program was well recommended and endorsed by key political leaders in New York and Washington—including Attorney General Robert Kennedy—so the educators welcomed us into their schools. By the time classes were out for the summer, we were set up with two hundred seventh-, eighth-, and ninth-grade kids who needed help in basic reading, spelling, and math.

We called ourselves the District Action Project (DAP) and soon set up more traditional offices at 3418 Eleventh Street, a few blocks from Howard University in one direction and from a high-crime and prostitution area in the other direction. The need for tutoring services was so great that we began recruiting volunteers from among the college students in Washington. Soon we had 150 tutors holding day and night classes for junior high and high school kids. We held many classes at the Washington Presbyterian Church, which was just one street over from our house on Meridian Place. Reverend James Reeb and a second pastor who lived in the parsonage that backed up to our house believed in our efforts and offered the church for our use.

Everything progressed quite smoothly. The seven of us on the central staff became closer and closer as we learned more about each other and the people we were trying to help. We lived the experience around the clock; there was no going home at the end of a day's work and forgetting about it until tomorrow. If we weren't actually tutoring kids, we were taking them on trips to the zoo or the monuments, or we were dealing with our neighbors in the ghetto, or we were dealing with each other. Even going out for a few drinks or to dinner and a movie could turn into an ordeal. We were an integrated group, and so, besides challenging those around us, we constantly challenged each other. We attracted attention, aroused conflict.

It wasn't always easy. But I think human beings need that kind of immersion experience in order to break down any lingering psychic barriers to true friendship; and in doing so we forged lasting bonds, a kind of timeless camaraderie of struggle and growth. Together that summer we knew a rare freedom. We were free to look at the world analytically and to not only criticize it, but also to do something to change it—if only in very small way. The seven of us came to love each other, to accept each other for who and what we were. And even today, though I rarely see any of those people, I feel comfortable that those still living are, in their own way, still trying to do positive things, to bring human beings together, and to transcend the status quo.

Troublemaking or radicalism or whatever you choose to call it came to me by instinct or intuition rather than plan. I did not plan to become involved in civil rights activism at Clark any more than I had imagined myself leading marches and rallies as I rode the train to Southern my freshman year. Eventually, I became actively involved at both places because I felt compelled to, because the time was right.

In Washington that summer of 1963, the bells of protest rang once again, like an awakening alarm in my mind. By the time I began organizing the DAP, I had undergone a transformation of sorts from student leader to full-blooded, brash young activist. Soon I wasn't content to limit myself to the tutoring project. The experiences of the past two years—especially my recent meeting with Malcolm X and the writing and speaking I had been doing about integration and black activism in Worcester—weighed upon me, changing my perception. Just tutoring, serving as a role model, and offering these kids a few new experiences wasn't enough. It didn't strike at the root of any problem: it just served as temporary relief for a few symptoms.

This was especially troubling to me because I knew we were capable of striking at the root. Never mind the fact that I was a twenty-one-year-old college student: I knew I could set change in motion. I felt I understood how vulnerable people in power could be, no matter how unshakable they appeared. Moreover, I felt I understood the ways in which they could be challenged, be made to sit up and take notice, and eventually be made to alter their assumed course.

When I walked through the streets of Washington and entered the homes and schools of the young blacks we worked with, the poverty, the inequality, the discrimination, and the apathy I saw all around me burned like fire in the pit of my stomach. This was Washington, D.C., the capital city of America, the shining city on the hill itself, not some little Mississippi town, and yet somehow the by-products of racism were the same. It pissed me off; I couldn't stand it. I knew it was time to resume the fight.

One June night at our weekly house meeting, I brought the subject up. We usually used the time to share experiences and ideas, and this night Allison was talking at length about a family she was having a hard time dealing with.

"Okay, there are six kids in the family, one mother, no father," she began as she sat cross-legged on the floor. "Nothing new about that. The mother's been on and off of welfare. She works as a maid sometimes and does washing for people. Two of the kids are young, around seven or eight. One's twelve. One's seventeen or eighteen. The other two are twenty and twenty-one. The woman started having kids when she was sixteen."

"Are the kids in school?" asked Joe.

"Oh, well, that's just it," she said, her voice tense. "The two little ones just started at Madison Elementary. The twelve-year-old is a chronic class-skipper, the eighteen-year-old dropped out last year, and neither of the other two graduated."

"Al, there comes the point when people have to help themselves. I mean, what can we do?" asked Betsy. "We can't hold every kid's hand until he graduates."

"I know. I know," said Allison. "But these kids aren't dumb. I've talked to them."

"Where do they live?" asked Steve.

"Near Adams-Morgan in this tiny place. I mean, tiny."

"How did you meet them?"

"Leon is supposed to be going to Shaw, but he keeps skipping. The principal told me about it, so I went over there. He doesn't know how to help them, and neither do I." She picked at the carpet and then looked over at me. Allison always called me "Brother Rat," though she never told me why. Years later I realized that this was a reference to the intense solidarity that cadets at Virginia Military Institute build up during their Spartan training. Several films about this camaraderie were produced during the war years called *Brother Rat* and *Brother Rat and Baby* starring Priscilla Lane and Wayne Morris. Her constant use of the term seems to have been her nod to the kind of intense militant community we were developing in our rented house on Meridian Place.

"Brother Rat, what do you think? These are not stupid kids. They're dropping out of school because they don't see how it's getting them any-where. They see more of a future out on the street, where they can at least get what they want, or what they think they want—instant gratification. No waiting." She groaned. "It's so frustrating."

"I know it is. And it's frustrating for them, too." I said. "But I think it goes back to opportunity—it's got to. It's not just in the South where blacks are restricted from good jobs with decent wages and futures. It's here, too. It's all over the whole damn country."

"Most of these kids don't know people who have gotten out of the ghetto," said Joe. "They don't see opportunities outside of it, and nobody's telling them they ever will. So, why the hell should they bother to do anything?"

"How do you make people care about their own futures?" asked Betsy.

"I think you start by getting the system to care," I said slowly, working it out in my own mind. "Because if you grow up in the system and the system shits on you, you feel like shit. We see ourselves mirrored in the system. If we change the system, maybe the image these kids see of themselves will change."

"Yeah, Brother Rat," Allison squinted at me. "What are you getting at?"

"I think he's just mouthing off again." Maureen said quietly as she smiled at Al.

"Okay, okay."

"Yes?" They all knew I had something on my mind.

"I think we should launch some protests," I said, "and I think we should focus on job discrimination. What do you think, Al?"

"Hallelujah!" she hollered. "When do we start?"

"What did I tell you?" said Maureen sarcastically. "He's just not happy unless he's making somebody mad." We all laughed.

"Okay, so we need a name. What do we call ourselves?"

"And he's just got to have a name, right, Maureen?" said Allison, egging her on. "You know, Brother Rat, you might make a mighty fine bureaucrat after all."

We settled on DARE, District Action for Racial Equality. Since DAP was a tax-exempt, nonprofit service organization, its name could not be used in connection with any political protest activity. And so, though we worked out of the same headquarters as the tutoring project and just changed hats when we moved from working with teenagers to raising hell with the bureaucrats, DARE was officially a separate organization.

We immediately got busy writing letters and contacting local black leaders and educators, letting them know what we were doing and asking for support. We formed a committee to examine District hiring and employment practices and held several meetings with community members where people could air their complaints and make suggestions about issues warranting immediate attention. We began examining the city, searching for the object of our first attack.

~ 21 ~

DARE

THE SEARCHING SOCIAL questions posed in Bob Dylan's 1963 hit "Blowin' in the Wind" seemed to capture the spirit of that year. The summer of 1963 was one of brutality, of billy clubs and head wounds, of fire hoses and tear gas, of blood and death. There were protests in Birmingham, Alabama, and in Albany, Georgia. In Danville, Virginia, a group of sixty-five Negroes, led by Reverend H. G. McGhee, marched around the jail to protest the arrest of two ministers who had staged a sit-in at city hall, waiting to see the mayor. Reverend Lawrence Campbell and Reverend A. I. Dunlap were indicted for "inciting to riot," and bail was set at $5,500 each. As McGhee led the group of mostly women and teenagers around the jail singing hymns and praying, Police Chief E. G. McCain gave firemen the order to turn high-pressure hoses on the marchers, knocking them down and washing them into parked cars. As the marchers lay drenched in the streets, they were beaten bloody by police and deputized garbage collectors. Of sixty-five demonstrators, forty were hurt.

About the same time in Plaquemine, Louisiana, 236 people, including CORE leader James Farmer, were arrested for marching to city hall to protest segregated schools and accommodations. They were summarily jailed in improvised stockades for ten days. This was only the first of many protests that would send shock waves through Iberville Parish—where Registrar Ella Billings publicly vowed, "Niggers ain't gonna run this parish"—well into the fall.

As Independence Day 1963 drew near, a coalition of civil rights groups working throughout the Northeast under the leadership of CORE and including SNCC, NAACP, NSM, and forty other church, labor, political, and peace organizations met to develop plans to focus mass protest on the Baltimore area. One particular target was the Gwynn Oak Amusement Park, promoted as "Maryland's Favorite Family Playground." Blacks were not permitted even to set foot in the park. When we were contacted in Washington,

DARE was just getting off the ground. We had been closely following news of the events in the Deep South, and we were eager to get back in the action. Four of us drove up to Baltimore and met with 280 other demonstrators at Metropolitan Methodist church in West Baltimore. We were shuttled by bus the fifteen or so miles out to the sixty-eight-acre park in Towson, Maryland. Reverend Eugene Carson Blake, the CEO of the United Presbyterian Church, Bishop Daniel Corrigan, and other representatives of the Catholic, Protestant, and Jewish clergy, along with protestors from throughout the region, two-thirds of whom were white, filled the buses. It was the largest assemblage of clergy ever brought together to protest discrimination, and it marked a kind of philosophical/historical shift in how Americans would view the civil rights movement.

On the way to the park, we worked ourselves into the proper nonviolent onward-Christian-soldier mood by singing "Battle Hymn of the Republic," "Go Tell It on the Mountain," and "He's Got the Whole World in His Hands." Many protestors waved miniature American flags out the bus windows. Others of us finished making placards. The sky was blue; the air was thick and hot. I was excited. I felt alive. It had been too long since I'd been in a bona fide protest, since I'd tested myself, tested the rhetoric.

When we arrived at the park, the plan was to line up in rows across the fifteen-foot-wide concrete walk leading up to the booths where whites bought food and amusement tickets. We would move forward in ranks up the walkway where, if we were stopped or told to leave, we would sit down. We would be completely peaceful, but we would resist. We all knew we were likely to be arrested.

As our buses pulled up to the entrance, I immediately saw that the situation was worse than I had expected. A crowd of what must have been more than three hundred whites massed around the walk, and nearly a hundred park and county police, many in riot gear, ringed the whole area. I was truly shaken inside by the blatant hatred and anger on the faces of the jeering, taunting whites. This mass display of hatred by those in uniform and out was worse than anything I had ever seen or experienced in Baton Rouge the year before, and it was, frankly, overwhelming. Even so, I found myself standing up, leaving the bus, and walking toward the gate, propelled by the blind courage that comes from moral rightness, from the seemingly simple-minded assurance that good must overcome.

The police surrounded us, crowding us together. The whites screamed frantically: "Niggers and nigger lovers go home!" "This is our park!" As I scanned the crowd, I saw that many of the whites waved bottles, bricks, and sticks. "Come on! We've got something for you, white nigger!" The hate in the air was palpable. I felt dazed, but also strangely high, vibrating with adrenaline. As a line of clergy moved forward through the crowd, the rest of us fell in behind them. We locked arms and began to sing "We Shall Overcome."

Reverend Blake was met on the walkway by James Price, the co-owner and president of the park. It was ironic that as Price read the Maryland trespass law, we could all hear the happy shouts of white children riding the thrill rides and the jolly tune of a distant calliope. Dystopia seemed to have come to utopia, and the defenders of this white paradise were having none of it.

"You can leave now in obedience to the law, or you can be arrested," Price said.

We continued to sing.

Price nodded to County Police Chief Robert J. Lally, who announced through a bullhorn, "You have two minutes to disperse."

When Reverend Blake and the front line of clergy sat down, the rest of us followed. Moments later, a file of policemen waded into our seated throng. In precise movements, two policemen would detach themselves from the file and target one of us, often half-dragging, half-carrying us to the waiting yellow police buses. The angry crowd screamed vengeful instructions: "Drop 'im on his head! Throw 'em in the bus!" In order to maintain our resistance, it was important that we not stand up, even to help those who were being assaulted, though this was very hard to do. One woman was injured when a heckler threw a cherry bomb that exploded near her. The gleeful crowd laughed and cheered.

"I don't question whether the law is constitutional," Reverend Blake told a reporter as he was taken to Woodlawn Police Station, "I question whether the law is *right*."

The Baltimore county jail and courthouse are together in one big complex. Since there was not room enough in the jail or manpower available to rapidly process the crowd of protesters, about two hundred of us were locked in a courtroom from one in the afternoon until ten that night. Among those in this group was Mickey Schwerner, a young man from New York who was participating in his first civil rights protest. Within a year, Mickey and two other civil rights volunteers, Andrew Goodman and James Chaney, would be lynched in Mississippi and their bodies buried in an earthen dam.

As it was, we had nothing to eat, and our jailers provided us with no food.

The processing was unmercifully slow, but we passed the time making small talk, telling stories, singing, and complaining. As I looked at the people gathered in the cramped room, my eyes were drawn to one particularly intense white man with a full gray beard and long, dark, swept-back hair. He was circulating around the room, talking to almost everyone, and jotting notes in a small spiral notebook. He had the voice of an orator and the hard, bright eyes of a man with a mission. I admired his energy. When he came over to our group, he introduced himself as Mark Lane. He told us we would probably be sent to the state prison and would have to spend at least a day there while bail was set and posted. He said he didn't think the process would take long since so many prominent clergy were involved; the state was under a great deal of national pressure.

"It's kind of like God taking a stand on racism," he said, smiling. "That's a hell of a lot of clout. Whose word are they going to take?"

"And save face?" someone asked.

"What does a government have left, if it doesn't save face?"

It is no small irony that Mark Lane would later defend the Jonestown mass-suicide cult leader, Jim Jones, and Dr. King's assassin, James Earl Ray.

Finally, we were separated by sex and taken in groups of twelve or fifteen into the jail, where we had to wait another three hours to be transferred to the larger prison nearby. By this time, because we were mentally and physically exhausted, we stretched out on the green concrete floor, trying to relax. I took off my shoes and placed them one on top of the other under my head. In this mood of physical and emotional exhaustion, my mind raced.

I am actually behind bars, locked up, I kept telling myself. *My freedom to do almost anything: to walk around, to see the sun or the moon, to eat is really denied.* I began to know real fear.

Inevitably, the memories of being arrested as a kid bubbled to the surface. I thought of the time when I was with a friend who cursed a white woman, and they took us both down to juvenile court. Another time I was apprehended when I scraped someone's car and kept on going. But those were very short periods, and they didn't put juveniles behind bars. This was different, more serious. Everything about this place looked sinister. It had an odd odor of unwashed bodies and urine. I thought of my friends in Baton Rouge who had endured this kind of place for weeks on end. Then I had been the visitor, the outside man trying to free them. Now I was the one behind bars, and I felt very threatened.

At about one that morning, a guard came and opened the door. "You're being moved," he announced flatly and led us out to a bus. We rode for some thirty miles on a dark highway. It was terrifying not knowing where we were being taken, not being able to see; our whole existence was completely at the mercy of a white man's whim. When we finally arrived at the state prison, we were checked in and taken straight through the yard to the lock-ups. All twelve of us were put in one room. No one was abusive to us; all directions were brusque and efficient. Very little was said. We felt a little relieved when a guard brought us a loaf of bread and some bologna. Soon we all lay down on the floor and went to sleep.

When we awakened several hours later, our spirits were high, our minds refreshed. We knew that CORE and NAACP lawyers were working around the clock to bond us out. We knew that we had done the right thing by protesting. Moreover, we knew that photographs of our uncooperative selves being carried to the police buses were now appearing in newspapers through the Northeast. We knew that government officials throughout the state and in Washington were grappling with how to deal with this predominantly white and clerical attack on an exclusively white amusement park. Rationally, we knew all of this, and, by that standard, our effort had been a success: we had sown a few more seeds, perhaps even opened a few more minds. Even so, I couldn't shake the anxiety I had felt the night before. I paced back and forth, my mind clinging only to thoughts of how soon we would be released. I tried to imagine the prospects. Would we spend days, weeks in here? My mind would not accept such a thought.

At three o'clock on the afternoon of July 5, as I walked out into the humid Maryland afternoon, I felt like a reborn man. Of those arrested, 214 of us were charged with trespassing, while 69 of us were charged with trespassing and disorderly conduct. We were never brought to trial. As we headed back to Washington that afternoon, we read the newspapers, anxious to find out what the park ownership had to say. The *New York Times* quoted James Price: "The white man in this area simply does not accept the Negro on a social or recreational basis. I will lose substantial amounts of revenue if I allow Negroes to enter the park." When asked what he thought of the ministerial participation, he said: "It's very unfortunate. It's analogous to my shooting craps, and when the police come I begin to pray and then say I was arrested for praying."

Reverend Eugene Carson Blake said: "The churches in this country have for a long time been saying a great deal about discrimination. Almost all churches have made the right statements, but we can no longer let this burden of winning freedom for the Negro or any other oppressed people be the burden only of the oppressed people themselves."

On July 6, James Price made a more detailed statement concerning his opinions of the clergy's actions:

> Ordering arrest of the clergy was the most difficult thing I have ever had to do. . . . But after much soul-searching on the manner in which to protect the equally God-given right of our citizens to their private property, we felt we could not show less courage than the men of the cloth. Without attempting to debate the philosophic theories involved, we took the practical businessman's approach of meeting the conditions of the world as we find them to be, not perhaps, as we would like them to be. . . . Segregation is not being forced upon anyone; it is created and nurtured by both whites and Negroes themselves. Insofar as clergymen deliberately violated the law, we are compelled to note a time-tested truism that no matter how noble an objective may be, it cannot be obtained by ignoble means. If we accept yesterday's illegal act on the grounds of morals or conscience, on what tomorrow will we be asked to accept some other unlawful act to justify an ideal?

James Price's smug and illogical platitudes aside, the protest at "Maryland's Favorite Family Playground" was far from over. On July 7, a second wave of demonstrators butted up against the park's front gates. This time Allison was among them. As we gathered around the TV at the house on Meridian Place and watched the evening news, anxious to find out what had happened, we were shocked to see her being carried away from the scene bleeding from the head. As Allison and six other demonstrators had attempted to enter the park by wading across Gwynn's Falls, a stream that borders the area, she was struck above the right eye with a brick thrown by someone in the angry white crowd. The report also said that, as ten members of the white crowd were watching the arrests of ninety-five protestors, they spotted two Negro women entering a women's restroom just inside the entrance of the park, and with a whoop they broke from the rest of the onlookers, barged into the restroom, and began beating the women. Both were maids, employees of Gwynn Oaks.

In Washington, we paced around the house, vowing to round up as many people as we could and protest at the gates of the park for the rest of the summer, if that's what it took. We vowed to write letters to James Price, to

Governor Tawes, to President Kennedy. We were furious. Stunningly, things seemed not to have progressed one single inch since 1960; in fact, they seemed to be growing steadily worse. Maybe Malcolm X was right. Maybe nonviolent resistance was a joke, a myth, a parody of real human pride.

When she got back to the house late that evening, Allison's head was heavily bandaged. She had received ten stitches above her eyebrow. The white gauze had turned pinkish red, and her face had swollen. But Allison, always the trooper, still tried to smile as she walked in the door.

"Brother Rat," she said, "it looks like they got me this time."

Long after the others had gone to bed, she and I sat and talked. Finally, she looked at me and started to cry—something I had never seen her do before. "You *know* my commitment to fight against segregation and discrimination and all these terrible things we're doing to each other," she said brokenly. "I've been in this movement a long time. You know how much it means to me. There's nothing I care about so deeply, D'Army."

"I know. You don't have to tell me that."

"She breathed deeply and held her head. "Okay, so why the hell can't white people see it? Why can't they see what I'm doing? Why don't they understand that we have to change? If we don't change, this whole thing is going to destroy us. It's going to destroy everything."

We were sitting facing each other. I reached out and took her hands. There was anguish in the air. It was as if we were rushing headlong into chaos and were helpless to slow our descent. I shared her fear. At least if there were air raids, the howling of civil defense sirens, the threat of falling bombs, we could take action, find shelter, know the direction of the threat. But this was worse than fear of death. It was fear of an onrushing eternal hellishness, the fear of a perpetual hatred that wouldn't go away, hate that couldn't be overcome by any amount of love. I wondered if the Jews in Berlin had felt something like this before the rumors of death camps came to them like small fishhooks carried by the wind.

"God," Allison groaned, "you should have seen them go after those Negro women. Those women were wearing Gwynn Oak *uniforms* for chrissakes! But those people are so blinded by hate they don't even see who or what they are lashing out against. They believe they are so justified in their anger and their superiority, they don't need to look. They are above and beyond thinking or listening. They just kick, and beat, and burn, and destroy whoever stands in their way." She took another breath. "But, you know, these people are really killing themselves, aren't they? They're beating and stomping on themselves. They're destroying their own world, and one day it is all going to catch up with them. Right? It *is* gonna catch up with them?" She looked at me hard.

"You know damn well it's gonna catch up with them."

"Before it catches up with us?"

I understood what Allison was saying. I had felt that hatred that seems so invincible; I had felt it many times. As I looked at her, I saw the brutal reality of what hate could do. I saw the damage, the danger, and the irrationality of it. I, too, had wondered if I were that strong.

Two days later, area newspapers ran articles announcing that the Baltimore County Council had established a Human Relations Commission to "mediate between civil rights groups and the operators of Gwynn Oak Amusement Park." County executive Spiro T. Agnew said the commission was empowered to deal with "employment, housing, education, public accommodations, and any other field where intergroup relations may be in question."

Edward Chance, chairman of the Baltimore chapter of CORE, threatened continuing and larger demonstrations if measures were not taken to immediately integrate the park. The demonstrations did not continue, however, because for the next ten days the Human Relations Commission met with a team of civil rights representatives and the park owners, finally reaching an agreement at four o'clock in the morning on July 19. Gwynn Oaks would be opened to Negroes on August 28.

That same day, as picketers in Cambridge, Maryland, protested the convictions of two fifteen-year-old Negro demonstrators committed to indeterminate terms in state institutions for juvenile delinquents, 850 National Guardsmen were stationed in Cambridge for the weekend, and Maryland governor Millard Tawes delivered a strong statement urging an end to racial strife: "This nation is undergoing a social upheaval. We must move a decade in 12 months. Unless all the citizens of this state move quickly to satisfy the legitimate pleas of Negroes for equality, we will face not weeks nor months of racial strife, but years."

But the governor offered no hope for an early settlement of the racial disputes in Cambridge, where repeated outbreaks of violence during civil rights demonstrations had twice that July brought declarations of martial law enforced by the National Guard.

~ 22 ~

Encounters of the First Kind

The movement wanted to be both strategic and expressive, political and cultural: to change the world (end the war, win civil rights) while freeing life in the here and now. Sometimes these poles were compatible, sometimes not. The idea of the youth revolution was an exercise in finessing the difference.
—TODD GITLIN, *The Sixties: Years of Hope, Days of Rage*

ONE NIGHT THAT JULY, several of us were sitting around the kitchen of the house on Meridian Place when we heard a loud scraping and grinding noise and the unmistakable sound of muffled voices. Steve looked out the window toward the back parking lot.

"It's the group of kids who are always prowling around. Looks like they're pushing our Plymouth across the lot. C'mon."

I followed Steve outside. I knew the group he was talking about—black boys from about thirteen to sixteen, always hanging out on door stoops, sneering, watching, waiting for trouble. I'd often wondered what they thought about us—blacks and whites a little older than they were, obviously middle-class, moving into their neighborhood, living together. Did they resent us, or were they somehow afraid and trying to cover it up by acting cool and uncaring?

As we slowly approached the car, Steve hollered out, "Hey, what are you doing?" They all ran.

"They're probably going to that apartment building the next street over," I said as we walked up the drive. It seemed darker than usual outside, and there was no moon. I looked at Steve. "Let's go."

We ran though an alley that cut across the block and then walked slowly up to the building where we knew several of the boys lived. We couldn't see anything until we were right on top of them so suddenly that Steve and I both jumped.

"Hey, what's up?" I said, trying to sound nonchalant. About eight boys were sitting on the porch steps or standing nearby. None of them said a word. "I'm D'Army, and this is Steve. We live in that big house a block over. You know the one?" A couple of the kids nodded slowly. "Do you all know what we're doing here? Do you know why we're living in this neighborhood?"

"Naw. Why don't you go on back where you came from?"

"We don't need you around here, man."

"What do y'all think that we're just some kind of experiment for y'all? We ain't no guinea pigs, man."

Their voices were raw with hostility. Even so, I was determined not to let it phase me. I was going to talk to them like human beings.

"We're not treating you like guinea pigs. Most of us have been working in the civil rights movement all over the country. We know what's going on. We came here to work because the community needs help. We're in this together."

"No, we ain't. Y'all from someplace else. What y'all think you gonna do for us?"

"Look, we all want the same things, don't we? We want to be treated fairly. Isn't that right?" No one moved. "That's what we're doing over there in that house. We're a bunch of kids just like y'all trying to help all of us get the things we want in life."

"Like what?"

"Like good jobs and a future where you can choose what you want to do and go where you want to go."

"How do you do all that?"

"You a magician or something?" Several of them started laughing.

"No, we're just going into junior highs and high schools and tutoring kids so when they graduate they can get better jobs, make more money, and live better lives. And we're going around to different companies that aren't hiring blacks in good positions, and then we're protesting, marching, and getting them to change. We're standing up for our rights and your rights."

"Really?"

"Naw, man, no way."

"I sat down on the porch steps with them, and Steve leaned against the railing. I hadn't known whether or not this approach would go over, whether they would respond to reason or become aggressive. But the more I talked, the more they seemed to loosen up and lower their defenses. I realized with abrupt clarity that we were all too afraid of the rowdies and troublemakers in the streets. We see ourselves as too different from them, and so we tell ourselves we don't know how to communicate with them. That night, on instinct, I talked to them honestly and straightforwardly, not realizing until I was well into it that this confrontation was a crucial test. Would we, for the rest of the summer, stand for collaboration and conviction, aligned with the neighborhood, or would we resign ourselves to maintaining an uneasy distance and separateness?

That night presented the same kind of challenge I had faced when I sat in at a segregated lunch counter. I had had a faith that I would survive the encounter, though I didn't know this for sure. I had realized that if I didn't have the courage to sit at the counter, I'd better get into some other line of work. On this summer night, I was confident that these boys were more afraid of me than I was of them. They weren't afraid of what I could do to them physically, but rather, like the whites in a segregated restaurant, they were afraid that I would confront them with an appeal to their humanity, their better nature, thereby reminding them that they had one.

Eventually, I asked them if they would come back to the parking lot with me and help put the car back in its place. The leader of the group said they would, and they all followed us back to the lot. I went to bed that night with an almost smug feeling of having received high marks on a test I hadn't studied for. But, then, pop quizzes were becoming a way of life. We never knew, from one moment to the next, what problem we would have to deal with or what dilemma we would face. We were a civil rights organization tutoring kinds in the ghetto: anything could happen and usually did.

Early in July, in the midst of all the Gwynn Oak drama, Betsy had somehow managed to meet Joe Frank, an eighteen-year-old black kid. He was a loner, a quiet guy with an air of brooding volatility who seemed to have nowhere to go, no roots and no direction. Betsy, a Bryn Mawr student, in her open and naïve way, had struck up a conversation with him about our project and invited him to come by the house. Once he came over, she invited him to stay.

"He's a lonesome kid," she said. "He needs a lot of help. Where's he going to get it if not from us?" We reminded her that she was the one who had said we couldn't hold every kid in the District by the hand. She insisted Joe was different." He moved in, instantly becoming yet another side project. One of us was usually at the house most of the day, and we spent time talking with him. He helped with house chores, and when there was nothing to do, sat out on the front stoop and watched the world go by. For the first time in his life, it seemed Joe had a home, a place where he belonged. As the days passed, he opened up to us more and more and began, by all indications, to trust us. But his problems, we would soon find out, were bigger than any of us.

At the end of the month, Peter Countryman and his wife, Joan, came down from New Haven to check on our progress. One night we were all in the dining room having a big meal, joking and telling stories. Joe was sitting out on the front stoop. The talk turned to DARE and other protest activities that Peter and Joan knew were going on throughout the Northeast.

"Oh, I almost forgot. I've got to tell you this, D'Army, you'll love it." Peter said. We'd made it through several bottles of wine and were all talking and laughing together rather loudly. Peter tapped his fork against the side of his glass. "Listen up, Listen up!" We gradually stopped talking and turned toward him.

"A couple of weeks ago I was in New York meeting with the tutoring project people up there. Anyway, I was on the subway, talking with one of the staffers, a white guy, and I noticed this middle-aged white man standing next to us listening. He keeps turning his head. Finally, he can't stand it anymore. He turns completely around and pokes me on the arm and says in this real confidential kind of way: 'Why don't you kids leave that nigger organizing stuff to the niggers in the South? You and me both know we ain't got any problems up here.' So I say, 'Oh, really?' Like that's a big revelation. And he says: 'Sure.' So then I say, 'Well, sir, my name's Peter,' and hold out my hand. 'And this is Brian. And, oh, I'd just love you to meet my wife, Joan.' And Joan turns around and holds out her hand, and that guy almost swallows his upper plate!" We all cracked up and toasted to Sam Blerman's dentures.

What we didn't know was that while all this merrymaking was going on, Joe, who had listened to Peter's story and heard only the word "Nigger" and Peter's apparent agreement with it, had become enraged. He had left the front stoop and walked around to the back of the house and into the kitchen, where he began to call for Peter.

"Peter, I want to talk to you," he hollered in a strange, quivering voice. "I'm gonna settle with you. Come on back into this kitchen, Peter, so I can settle with you now."

We immediately quieted and looked at each other. Peter shook his head and shrugged. I motioned him back to his seat. None of us knew what was going on. We'd never heard Joe sound so strange. I walked into the kitchen, and he was standing there against the sink, shivering uncontrollably, holding a butcher knife.

When he saw me, he screamed: "Get that son of a bitch in here! I'm gonna kill him!"

"Joe, man, what's the matter?" I asked, trying to sound comforting. I stood against the kitchen door.

"You heard the way he talks. I'm sick of it!" he screamed, waving the knife.

"Joe!"

"I'm sick of it! You hear?"

"Joe, man, listen."

"If you don't get him back here, I'm going in there and get him myself. I'm gonna kill him! I'm gonna cut that white bastard's throat!"

He started shivering even more, and I knew he was serious. My mind reeled. What had we gotten ourselves into? Betsy started hollering from the other room: "What's going on? What's happening? Let us in!"

"No! Wait. Wait a minute," I yelled back. Then I tried to soften my voice. "Joe, you can't hold Peter responsible—I promise he didn't mean it the way you thought."

"Yes, he did. He's no good. Man, I know it. He's against us, man. He's against all of us, and I'm going to get him." He began walking awkwardly across the big kitchen, his eyes large and glassy.

I moved in front of him. "Joe, I can't let you do it. I'm your friend man, but you'll have to come through me first."

We stood there just a few feet apart, staring at each other. Then Joe started crying and dropped the knife. Betsy and Joe Simpson rushed in, and we sat on the floor with Joe and did our best to calm him down. From Joe's broken speech, we gathered that he was on the verge of a complete breakdown. He was confused, angry, helpless. Because Peter was a stranger, he was an easy target. He symbolized all that was alien and hostile to Joe; a white male world that was casually demeaning, casually destructive.

The next day, we had a house meeting and decided Joe would have to leave. He was too violent, too explosive, and had problems far beyond what we were equipped to handle. We were not set up to be a counseling center. Ultimately, we realized, with a great deal of regret, that if we continued to play mother and father to Joe, we might end up doing more harm than good to him and to ourselves. If we ended the relationship now, we rationalized, maybe we could all salvage some good from the experience.

Joe, we hoped, would always know someone somewhere had really loved him and treated him as an equal. Maybe that love would be a source of strength to him. Maybe it would help ease his pain. We didn't know if we had made a difference at all, but we wanted to think we had. We wanted to believe it was important and valuable to bend and try to help the simple souls, those people who are somehow separated from the forward flow of society, those who don't know the luxury of easy expression. We didn't understand how those people got lost, separated, disenfranchised. We didn't understand why they couldn't communicate their needs and their pain. How does one black teenager get lost in the shuffle? Why does he get lost? Whose fault is it? We wanted to lay blame so we could play the knights in shining armor. We wanted to feel rewarded for our good deed, to feel we had in some way made up for someone else's wrongdoing. We wanted to know we had done the right thing.

But we could never know. All we, with all our self-sacrificing (and self-serving) good intentions can do is remind ourselves that we always have an impact. And if we give someone love and attention, a warm bed, and caring conversation, that impact cannot be bad. We weren't able to experience the self-glorifying victory of watching Joe reach our goals for him, but that did not mean we had failed. We told ourselves that we hadn't backed out on Joe; we had given him what we could, and we had quit while we were ahead. Were we rationalizing? Perhaps. But we would be the first ones to admit we were not in any way experts on people. In the summer of 1963, there were many, many people we did not understand; and that was one important reason why we could not continue to care for Joe.

Telling Joe to leave was one of the hardest things I have ever had to do. The next morning, I went downstairs and found him sitting moodily on the bed in his little room. I sat down next to him. "Joe, I want to talk to you about something," I began.

He nodded without looking up,

"This is really hard for me to say, man, really hard, but I just don't think you fit in with our project any longer. We have so many things we're trying to accomplish here in the neighborhood, you know. We're working for fair hiring and fair treatment of blacks all over the district. We're trying to get the word out. You've seen what we're doing."

He nodded and then looked over at me. His eyes were red, his face expressionless.

"Joe, I just don't think we can spend the time with you that you need."

My voice started shaking. "We just can't give you what you need here, Joe. I'm really sorry, man. We're all your friends here, and we always will be. If you ever need help, you can call us. But I've decided for your own good and the good of the project you're going to have to leave."

We were both crying. I couldn't believe how hard it was. I was twisted in knots.

"I know, man. I understand," Joe said slowly. "I just don't know where to go. I don't got nowhere to go."

"What about your relatives in New York?"

"Yeah."

"Listen, I'll pay your bus fare to New York. Then maybe you can connect up with your family. Do you know where they live?"

"Yeah."

"Good, once you get with your family, I know you can make it from there, man. No problem. It'll be fine."

I tried to make my voice sound optimistic, although I wasn't really optimistic at all. The next day, I borrowed Joe Simpson's jeep and drove him to the bus station. I gave him a little cash to carry with him and wished him the best. Then I watched him get on the bus.

We never heard from Joe again.

~ 23 ~

DARE in Action

I still believe that the Albany Movement set back again and again by police power, has done a magnificent service to the Negroes of Albany—and ultimately to the whites who live in that morally cramped town. I still believe that the three hundred Negroes who waited in line near the county courthouse in Selma, Alabama from morning to evening in the shadow of clubs and guns to register to vote, without even entering the doors of that courthouse, accomplished something. But I no longer hold that simple repetition of such nonviolent demonstrative action, which effectively broke through barriers in other parts of the South, will bring victory. I am not convinced that the stone wall which blocks expectant Negroes in every town and village of the hard-core South, a wall stained with the blood of children, as well as others, and with an infinite capacity to absorb more victims, will have to be crumbled by hammer blows. This can be done in one of two ways. The first is a Negro revolt, armed and unswerving . . . which may be hard to avoid unless the second alternative comes to pass; the forceful intervention of the national government, to smash, with speed and efficiency, every attempt by local policemen and politicians to deprive Negroes (or others) of rights supposedly guaranteed by the Constitution.
—HOWARD ZINN, "THE LIMITS OF NONVIOLENCE"

I T WAS NOW AUGUST, and DARE had yet to launch an attack against any specific business or institution in the District. We had by this time gained the respect and confidence of many black civic leaders and had attended community meetings and sponsored meetings of our own. We were considering several different approaches against local department stores, industries, and banks, but as the summer of brutality continued, our attentions were continually distracted by events in the Deep South.

When Attorney General Robert Kennedy initiated prosecutions against nine civil rights leaders of the Albany Movement in the federal district court in Georgia, we couldn't ignore it. These nine leaders—eight blacks and one white, including Slater King, president of the movement, and Dr. William Anderson, a former president—were pioneers in protesting discrimination and segregation and among the most outspoken critics of Bobby Kennedy's failure to act to prevent the gross denials of constitutional rights to Negroes in the South that had characterized the past three years. Three of the leaders were being prosecuted on charges of obstructing justice for picketing the grocery store of a white juror who had voted against a Negro plaintiff in a damage suit. The Negro, Charles Ware, had filed suit against the white sheriff of Albany, charging that the sheriff had shot him after his arrest on July 4, 1961. Ware had sued Baker County sheriff L. Warren Johnson for $125,000, but the jury returned a verdict in favor of Johnson in April.

As a result of the Albany Movement's boycott and picketing, the white juror's store closed. The remaining six leaders were charged with perjury. Bond ranged from $2,500 to $5,000. Though there had been thousands of extreme violations of federal laws perpetrated against Negroes throughout the southern and border states—mass arrests, brutal and arbitrary violence, and total manipulation and violation of judicial process—in only an infinitesimal number of cases had whites been prosecuted.

We believed the nation was not being informed of the extent of police brutality and judicial abuse of Negroes in Albany and the rest of the South. We felt that the media were soft-pedaling the true story of white violence in the South, especially violence by police and government officials. And we felt that both Bobby and John Kennedy were seeking to gain popularity in the polls among moderate northern whites and racist southern whites by prosecuting the nine civil rights leaders. The southern Negroes were comparatively disenfranchised and hence voteless, while northern Negroes and white liberals everywhere were almost irrevocably committed to the Kennedy administration. With the voters and the press, it seemed the Kennedys could do no wrong. But in our opinion, they were doing plenty wrong. Consequently, we decided to picket the Justice Department on August 12.

On August 10, we advised the *Washington Afro-American* of our intentions and began recruiting people to participate in the picketing. We worked up a fact sheet listing our grievances against Bobby Kennedy for his handling of the Albany Movement and printed hundreds of copies to give out. The final point on the list read: "In large areas of the South, the Federal Government has been, up until the present prosecutions, the only hope of millions of Negroes dreaming of freedom, justice, and equality." We asked for a public appeal to Bobby Kennedy to drop the Albany case and to open the doors of justice to southern Negroes rather than continue to slam those doors in their face.

At eight thirty on the morning of August 12, we had twenty-five volunteers lined up in front of the Department of Justice Building at Tenth and Pennsylvania Avenue, NW, and Ninth and Pennsylvania Avenue, NW. We carried placards printed with the following slogans:

FBI—The Georgia Boot Licker
Albany FBI—Federal Bureau of Intimidation
United Front—FBI & KKK
In Albany Is Slavery More Constitutional Than Freedom?
Mr. Kennedy, If You Prosecute the Slaves, Why Not the Slaveholders?

We marched back and forth in the oppressive Washington humidity until after four o'clock that afternoon, giving out fact sheets, stopping people on the street, singing freedom songs. We were filled with a sense of power—however limited, however fleeting—because we knew we were being watched. We knew we were the hot topic up in Bobby Kennedy's and Assistant Attorney General Burke Marshall's offices. We knew we were bothering them. If only for a day, we were forcing our viewpoint into their consciousnesses.

Late that afternoon, John Doar, first assistant to Burke Marshall, issued a statement: "Anybody who breaks the law will be prosecuted," he said. "We cannot modify the law for certain individuals and not for others." He was asked about the arbitrary arrests of hundreds of protestors throughout the South, the charges of criminal anarchy for holding peaceful rallies, the use of water cannons, billy clubs, and cattle prods on peaceful, unarmed women and children. He was asked if these actions on the part of white police constituted violation of the law. He said he was not familiar enough with the incidents mentioned to make any comment.

We were outraged, taking his evasiveness as a blatant insult. We sent word to Marshall that his replies were not sufficient when the freedom of hundreds of thousands of American citizens was at stake. We demanded to see Bobby Kennedy. Ultimately, Kennedy did not meet with us. The next morning, the newspapers throughout the region ran pictures of us. The *New York Daily News* ran the headline "For Bobby, Picketing with a Personal Touch." We felt that we had won a certain kind of victory: we had made a public point. And that summer we were measuring progress in terms of inches, not miles.

Years later, I discovered that those eight hours were recorded in perhaps more lasting and indelible form than mere newsprint. The FBI, though I did not know it at the time, had begun keeping a file on me that included the protests at Southern in 1961. Our DARE protests and activities were thoroughly monitored and recorded in my file, which was at the time listed under the code SM-RADICAL MATTERS or SUBVERSIVE. My file was CLASSIFIED SECRET, and I was considered, according to the documents, potentially dangerous to the United States government. For the next ten years, the FBI would keep extensive records of my actions.

After the Justice Department protest, we were warmed up and ready to strike again. We wanted to milk our public impact for all it was worth, especially while DARE was, in the minds of the media, still novel and fresh.

On July 24, Howard University law professor Frank Reeves, D.C. Urban League director Sterling Tucker, Joe Simpson, and I met with the officers of American Security and Trust (AS&T), one of the city's major banks. At the meeting—which was attended by bank president William Baker, vice president Murray Preston, and assistant vice president in charge of personnel, Donald Mowbray—we presented a list of facts we had obtained from our extensive research of records of the May 29 testimony by AS&T to the House Committee on Education and Labor.

In the testimony, Mr. Mowbray had said, "It is a fact that we have got in the history books that the financial community has not employed Negro clerical help." Mr. Mowbray also testified that AS&T employed only 73 Negro employees out of 1,000 total employees and that only 11 of the Negroes were in jobs above the blue-collar level. The breakdown for the 73 positions was: 59 maintenance men, 2 messengers, 2 chauffeurs, 3 tellers, 7 bookkeepers, and 1 key-punch operator. Mr. Mowbray said that approximately 50 percent of the bank's job applicants over the previous two years had been Negroes. He also said the bank had an approximately 49 percent annual job turnover, and he estimated that 250 new positions, including 25 tellers and 120 bookkeepers and clerks, would be filled between June and January 1.

When we had met with the bank officials and presented their own facts to them, however, they vociferously denied that they could hire more Negroes. They said their hiring and promotions were based strictly on merit and ability and had nothing to do with race. We countered by observing that, statistically, it made no sense that only 11 Negroes would be employed in clerical positions, if in fact, 50 percent of the bank's applicants were Negro and the bank had a 49 percent turnover rate. The figures simply did not add up. We requested further investigation into the screening processes of the personnel department and into the backgrounds of the Negroes then employed by the company. The officers said they would take our request under consideration, and the meeting adjourned.

But in the intervening three weeks they steadfastly refused to meet with us again. After our protest at the Justice Department, we decided AS&T would be the ideal target, especially since the bank was just a few blocks away, at Fifteenth and Pennsylvania Avenue, across the street from the Treasury Department.

At eight o'clock Friday morning, August 16, we had fifty picketers parading back and forth on the sidewalk in front of the main entrance waving signs saying:

No Dignity/No Dollars
Inverst in American Security—Invest in American Discrimination
AS&T—Fair Hiring for Whites Only

Once again we handed out fact sheets reproducing the bank's testimony at the House Committee hearing and explaining our position. Our protest, we said, had been endorsed by the Howard University NAACP, the Non-Violent Action Group, the Students for a Democratic Society, the Interdenominational Ministerial Alliance of Washington, and the Washington chapter of Americans for Democratic Action. Our purpose, we said, was to substantially increase the number of Negro employees in positions of responsibility at the bank.

It was obvious to any interested observer that this wasn't a spur-of-the-moment protest. We weren't working from emotionalism but from a well-researched political and ethical premise. Inevitably, I couldn't help wondering whether the secretary of the treasury, J. Edgar Hoover, Marshall, Doar, or even the Kennedys themselves were watching us from their windows nearby. I was a Negro kid from the South, and here I was on Pennsylvania Avenue, right in the heart of American government. I was standing on an artery in the great body politic, and, for just a moment at least, I was disrupting the flow. This was the civil rights movement encapsulated: disruption and communication to pave a path to a specific moral goal.

We stayed there all day, marching around in circles and passing out our fact sheets. All day we tried to stop customers on their way to the bank and explain what we were doing. Some passersby acted shocked and frightened, waving us away like so many pestering flies as they ducked their heads and scurried around us. Some, when they realized that we would not ignore them and they could not ignore us, turned around and left. And others, openly curious, eagerly asked what was going on. Reporters from various newspapers talked to us and took pictures. Occasionally, we noticed a bank employee watching from the windows.

Toward the close of business hours, Philip Rosenfield, the attorney for the bank, came out to set up a meeting. "If the bank does not meet with us and come to some agreement this weekend, we will continue our picketing on Monday," I told him. "And if this branch doesn't make a real commitment to stop discriminatory hiring, we will move our pickets to the branch at the State Department."

Mr. Rosenfield went inside and, several minutes later, came back out. "Mr. Baker wants to resolve this before Monday morning, if possible. Will you agree to meet with him, Mr. Mowbray, Mr. Preston, and me here at the bank on Sunday?"

"That will be fine. What time?"

"Two o'clock."

On Monday morning, August 19, the *Washington Post* ran the following story under the headline "Bank Plans More Negro Employment":

Spokesmen for the American Security and Trust Company said yesterday the firm would initiate recruitment program for the purpose of increasing its number of Negro employees.

Representatives of the bank gave the assurance to leaders of the newly formed District Action for Racial Equality after meeting with them for six hours.

DARE, in turn, agreed to suspend demonstrations against the bank until after attorneys for both parties work out the details for the program. . . .

Philip Rosenfield, attorney for the bank, said "a complete understanding" was reached at the meeting and the new program "should result in substantially increased employment of Negroes . . . in all kinds of positions."

"Working out the details" took much longer than we had hoped, but AS&T did implement a minority hiring program over the next year, and, according to an agreed-upon schedule, blacks currently on the payroll were reevaluated and offered promotion. Our protest against AS&T publicly embarrassed a staid, conservative financial institution—a pillar of American capitalism and democracy—and forced it, if by nothing other than the pressure of expediency, to change its policies.

"Which side are you on, man?"

"Which side are you on?"

Reverend James Reeb, the Unitarian minister who had loaned us his church for classrooms, was a conservative and cautious man. After we formed DARE and began taking a more and more outspoken stance against racial inequity, jobs, housing, and education, he became increasingly alarmed and hurt. I was not listening to his suggestions of moderation, accommodation, and patience. And since his church was helping us, he felt I should heed his counsel. On the other hand, I felt that, since I was leading the project, he should go along with me. Somewhere deep inside, I even suspected that his difficulty with going along with our program came from *his* problem with taking orders form an assertive black kid. I thought he was far too accustomed to deference, and that when push came to shove, Reeb wasn't as liberal as he would have liked to appear.

"You have stabbed me in the back, D'Army, and twisted the knife," he told me late that August. I was surprised at the intensity of his feelings. "It is completely unfair that you won't take my guidance when I have opened my house to you."

"But we are trying to do something here. We don't have unlimited time, and we want to have an impact," I said. "That's the most important thing to us—making some kind of difference in the lives of these kids, giving them some kind of hope. Don't you understand? The more public and confrontational we are, the more we stir things up, the better. We're examples to these kids, the closest thing to role models they've ever had."

"There is always more than one way to handle a situation, D'Army. But you aren't interested in anyone's ideas but your own."

"What you don't seem to understand is that nothing, absolutely nothing, is going to happen by saying please."

I'm an easy person to get along with, Maureen often told me, if you do things my way. Later I would realize she was very right.

Reverend Reeb was just cutting his teeth on the movement, just grappling with the idea of taking risks and pushing for progress. And I had very little patience with him. He was undoubtedly a good man with good intentions, but he had limited exposure to social activism. I interpreted his hesitancy and his problems with me as indicative of some deep-seated racist hangups for which I had absolutely no sympathy. But, as I was later to learn, my assumptions were very wrong.

In March 1965, this same James Reeb was drawn, in peace, to Selma, Alabama. He and two other ministers were walking back to their lodging after having dinner at a Negro restaurant when they were attacked by a group of young whites. They were there to join thousands of others from across the country to take part in the second march from Selma to Montgomery. The first had ended with brutal beating of marchers on what came to be known as "Bloody Sunday." Reeb was beaten unconscious with a bat and died from his injuries.

At an outdoor memorial rally for Reverend Reeb organized by WSM on the Clark campus on March 15, 1965, Father Gilgun, a longtime WSM supporter, in an impassioned, almost mythical speech, said that there were only two sides in America: the one represented by Alabama governor George Wallace and the one represented by Martin Luther King. Quoting the words of Christ, Father Gilgun said, "He who is not with me is against me."

"I believe Northerners should go to Selma," Father Gilgun continued. "If men like the Reverend Mr. Reeb didn't go there, Negroes could demonstrate until hell froze over and not obtain their rights."

Reverend Richard Norsworthy, who had just returned from Selma, told the mostly white crowd of 1,500 that it was like "returning from a foreign country." "The white citizens of Selma," Norsworthy said, " believe not in rights, but in whites."

Fellow WSM leader Hank Chaiklin voiced concern that the death of James Lee Jackson, a Negro shot by an Alabama state policeman in February, was not given the same attention as Reeb's: "We must protest that the clergy and politicians were not equally outraged by the shotgun murder of Jackson," he said. "It is ironic that the Reverend Mr. Reeb's death has evoked the essence of prejudice—that we don't feel the same concern for James Lee Jackson's death."

"Jim Reeb and I were called 'white nigger' by racists in Alabama," said Father Norsworthy, "but Jim still believed that racism could only be overcome by love. Reverend Reeb and James Lee Jackson have brought Selma, Alabama to us. We are part of their struggle."

Travelling from law school in Boston to speak at the rally, I said I believed that Reverend Reeb's death had finally stirred the conscience of white America. Perhaps now, I said, white America would come to see the senseless, frenzied brutality and violence that racism engendered: "I think we must look not only at Selma, we must look at Boston, we must look at Harlem, for the problem doesn't end at the Mason-Dixon Line. It is national in scope. Unless we act in time, and in time means *now*, there will be another Reverend Reeb next week, next month, and next year."

That evening, we recited the Lord's Prayer and sang "We Shall Overcome" as we walked to our homes and cars.

"Reverend Reeb believed racism could only be overcome by love," Hank said, as we walked slowly across campus to his apartment.

"Do you believe that?"

"I don't know. I think I did—once."

"But how do you act love? That's what I don't understand. How do you combat with love? If Reeb had had time to hug those bastards in Selma and tell them he loved them anyway, do you think they would have stopped beating him?" I asked. I remembered the arguments between me and Reeb two years earlier in D.C.—how impatient I had been, how demanding. I hadn't had time for love.

"Of course not. They would have called him a 'nigger lover' even louder and beat him harder."

We walked for a while in silence through the cool March night. "He didn't know what he was getting into down there, did he, D'Army?"

"No, Hank, he didn't. Reverend Reeb was what I think you'd call an innocent man."

~ 24 ~

The March on Washington

When the architects of our republic wrote the magnificent words of the Constitution and the Declaration of Independence, they were signing a promissory note to which every American was to fall heir. This note was a promise that all men, yes, black men as well as white men, would be guaranteed the "unalienable Rights" of "Life, Liberty and the pursuit of Happiness." . . . America has given the Negro people a bad check, a check which has come back marked "insufficient funds."

. . . And so, we've come to cash this check, a check that will give us upon demand the riches of freedom and the security of justice.

We have also come to this hallowed spot to remind America of the fierce urgency of NOW. This is no time to engage in the luxury of cooling off or to take the tranquilizing drug of gradualism.

—MARTIN LUTHER KING JR., FROM HIS SPEECH AT THE MARCH ON WASHINGTON, AUGUST 28, 1963

IN RESPONSE TO THE continued stiffening of white resistance to desegregation, SNCC, CORE, and other young, militant civil rights organizations threatened more massive and more uncompromising protest demonstrations. In the spring of 1963, as we were beginning our District Action Project, several of these organizations had made the daring announcement that they were going to bring thousands of people to Washington during the summer and march to the White House. They pledged to stay there until they got some concrete answers to their demands for greater and more decisive federal action in halting the state government–endorsed reign of terror that plagued the South and until the federal government promised swift legislation to overrule the segregation and discrimination endorsed by state laws. The organizers threatened to close down the streets, to block Pennsylvania Avenue, and even to block the runways at the airport in order to effectively close the city down if they had to. This was the original idea: no more compromises, no more waiting.

Needless to say, this plan sent shivers down the spines of John and Bobby Kennedy; established civil rights leaders Roy Wilkins, Whitney Young, and Martin Luther King; and the white directors of the New York–based foundations. They were all alarmed, first and foremost because they were not a part of the march and therefore had no control over what would take place. For King, it threatened his commitment to nonviolence. For Roy Wilkins and Whitney Young, it threatened the compromising, peaceable, get along–go along relationship they had with whites. For the white foundation leaders who supported the NAACP, the Urban League, and Dr. King's SCLC, the proposed march represented a deviation from the orderly, slow and steady racial progress they had been funding. SNCC especially was still viewed by these older groups as an outlaw organization, more counterproductive than progressive.

So Dr. King, Wilkins, and Young joined with A. Phillip Randolph, Bayard Rustin, and Walter Reuther of the United Auto Workers (all leaders who worked closely with organized labor) and planned a meeting with John Lewis of SNCC and James Farmer of CORE. During this time, the Kennedy administration was in continual communication with these "establishment" organizations, including the labor unions and the foundations, encouraging them to work together to stop the march.

Obviously, by this time President Kennedy was no great hero of mine. I didn't feel that the issues of black America were a high personal priority to him. He was responding to crises as they presented themselves, but he was too willing to compromise on civil rights issues to protect himself and his administration politically. I didn't feel that he was motivated by any strong principle or that he had any great moral plan to right the wrongs of race in America; he seemed motivated to act only when it was expedient. Still, he was an appropriate symbol for the times, a youthful leader who had a sense for dramatic staging and a flare for mouthing the right rhetoric at the right time. Negroes were supposed to show sufficient appreciation for Kennedy so that other white people wouldn't be discouraged—so they wouldn't think that we weren't duly thankful.

But I knew that there were many things Kennedy was not addressing. So when I had to pass judgment on Kennedy's real performance on civil rights rather than the Kennedy who was a good president and a "Friend of Black

People," honesty forced me to be more critical. Kennedy was a full-blooded eastern liberal, with a gilded, mythical quality about him. He symbolized the popular moral and political positions of liberal America: youth, freedom, equality, justice, opportunity. But Kennedy was not a populist. He was not a down-to-earth, "Let's put our shoulders to the wheel, dig in, and solve this problem" kind of leader. He was, in my opinion, far too concerned about how his political supporters perceived him—and therefore far too quick to compromise.

The March on Washington became a key symbol of the first part of the decade. It was, on the one hand, a celebration of youth and unity and the cathartic power of thousands of people joining together to express a common belief in freedom, and, on the other hand, a study in careful compromise. The leaders of the various organizations met at the Carlyle, a fancy Fifth Avenue hotel in New York City. As discussion began, Lewis and Farmer were adamant that the march would continue. And so the assembled establishment leaders, faced with the fact that they couldn't head off the dreaded demonstrations and that they were under a presidential directive to do so, vowed to become involved.

In the end, then, after days of heated discussion, the March on Washington was not ended: it was co-opted. It was transformed from a mass protest aimed at bringing Washington to a halt and demanding that the government recognize its people, to a demonstration organized in collaboration with the government, with planned march routes and time schedules and everything controlled by the book. It was taken out of the hands of the radicals who conceived it and turned into a media propaganda festival with all the civil rights leaders, politicians, labor leaders, and even movie stars marching together in racial harmony and contentment, as if everything were rosy. The anger that had sparked the original idea for the march was so dissipated that the final gathering seemed more like a picnic than a protest.

It's not that there wasn't a good deal of spirited rhetoric on jobs and freedom for all men: there was. Dr. King gave his famous "I have a dream" speech. Rabbi Joachim Prinz of the American Jewish Congress spoke of his experiences under the Hitler regime, memorably asserting that the most urgent problems facing America were not bigotry and hatred, but rather silence in the face of bigotry and hatred. Floyd McKissick spoke for James Farmer, who was in jail in Plaquemine, Louisiana. Joan Baez and Mahalia Jackson sang, along with Peter, Paul and Mary, Bob Dylan, Marian Anderson, and

Odetta. In short, leaders from all the organizations had their turn at the podium.

Malcolm X offers a searing portrayal of the dynamics that transformed the march in his speech "Message to the Grass Roots," given November 10, 1963, in Detroit. The speech ranks among *American Rhetoric*'s top one hundred:

It was the grass roots out there in the street. [It] scared the white man to death, scared the white power structure in Washington, D.C. to death; I was there. When they found out that this black steamroller was going to come down on the capital, they called in Wilkins; they called in Randolph; they called in these national Negro leaders that you respect and told them, "Call it off." Kennedy said, "Look, you all letting this thing go too far." And Old Tom said, "Boss, I can't stop it, because I didn't start it." I'm telling you what they said. They said, "I'm not even in it, much less at the head of it." They said, "These Negroes are doing things on their own. They're running ahead of us." And that old shrewd fox, he said, "Well, if you all aren't in it, I'll put you in it. I'll put you at the head of it. I'll endorse it. I'll welcome it. I'll help it. I'll join it."

A matter of hours went by. They had a meeting at the Carlyle Hotel in New York City. The Carlyle Hotel is owned by the Kennedy family; that's the hotel Kennedy spent the night at, two nights ago; [it] belongs to his family. A philanthropic society headed by a white man named Stephen Currier called all the top civil-rights leaders together at the Carlyle Hotel. And he told them that, "By you all fighting each other, you are destroying the civil-rights movement. And since you're fighting over money from white liberals, let us set up what is known as the Council for United Civil Rights Leadership. Let's form this council, and all the civil-rights organizations will belong to it, and we'll use it for fund-raising purposes." Let me show you how tricky the white man is. And as soon as they got it formed, they elected Whitney Young as the chairman, and who [do] you think became the co-chariman? Stephen Currier, the white man, a millionaire. [Adam Clayton] Powell was talking about it down at the Cobo [Hall] today. This is what he was talking about. Powell knows it happened. Randolph knows it happened. Wilkins knows it happened. King knows it happened. Every one of that so-called Big Six--they know what happened.

Once they formed it, with the white man over it, he promised them and gave them $800,000 to split up between the Big Six; and told them that after the march was over they'd give them $700,000 more. . . .

No, it was a sellout. It was a takeover. When James Baldwin came in from Paris, they wouldn't let him talk, 'cause they couldn't make him go by the script. Burt Lancaster read the speech that Baldwin was supposed to make; they wouldn't let Baldwin get up there 'cause they know Baldwin's liable to say anything. They controlled it so tight-- they told those Negroes what time to hit town, how to come, where to stop, what signs to carry, what song to sing, what speech they could make, and what speech they couldn't make; and then told them to get out of town by sundown. And every one of those Toms was out of town by sundown. Now I know you don't like my saying this. But I can back it up. It was a circus, a performance that beat anything Hollywood could ever do, the performance of the year. Reuther and those other three devils should get an Academy Award for the best actors 'cause they acted like they really loved Negroes and fooled a whole lot of Negroes. And the six Negro leaders should get an award too, for the best supporting cast.

Still, I am not at all sorry I was part of the march. A group of us camped out near the Washington Monument the night before. We drank wine, sang, and talked. We watched the stars and felt our excitement build. The next morning, we saw thousands of people arrive, spilling out of buses and cars and covering the grassy field. Despite the corralled, controlled, overplanned nature of the march, I felt a palpable sense of power just from being a part of a gathering of so many other people who, if nothing else, at least believed in freedom and justice for all and saw it as a goal.

But was the March on Washington symbolic of *the* movement to me? Did it represent some sort of climax or emotional peak? No. It didn't because the movement that forced the real change in society was, to me, stronger than that march: the movement was a lonely, personal, one-on-one battle of wills, exemplified by an individual risking everything with nothing to fall back on. And in that kind of confrontation, there is no compromise.

~ 25 ~

A Bona Fide Negro

Three years ago, in a wave of sympathy for civil rights agitators in the South, the student body voted to raise funds for a scholarship for some Negro thrown out of a university for participating in sit-ins. . . . We got much more than we bargained for. The student selected was a bona fide Negro, alright.
—"HERE WE GO AGAIN," EDITORIAL, *Clark Scarlet,* NOVEMBER 5, 1964

I GUESS IT WAS JUST my fundamental inclination for agitation that pulled me into organizing a group and pushing it into action—agitation or the limelight, or both. A full-page photo of me appeared in the Clark yearbook my first year over the caption: "Injustice Rankles Me into Leadership, Though Ego Plays Its Part." So when I returned for my last year at ·Clark and started our Worcester Student Movement up again, I wasn't content with a single agenda of tutoring. After a summer of directly confronting the powers that be in the nation's capital, tutoring no longer provided enough agitation for me.

Ultimately, inspiration came early that fall in the person of Norman Thomas. Six times he had been the Socialist Party's candidate for president, and each time he had lost. Even so, this was no Harold Stassen of the left-wing fringe. The steadfast firmness of his demand for morality and decency had left a mark and made him a legend, even among those who disagreed with him. When we brought him to speak at Clark, he was near eighty and showing it. Hosting Thomas in Worcester gave me a sense of personally interacting with history and of being graced to be in the shadow of one of the century's great heroes. I helped him in and out of the car, up the steps to the off-campus guest house where he was staying, and, later, to the podium where he spoke. Although he trembled as he talked and was nearly blind, he had a volcanic spirit. Oddly, his physical decline accentuated the strength of his spirit and his commitment to his beliefs. Even though he knew by then that he would go to his grave without seeing the ascension of his ideology, nothing in America was going to change Norman Thomas.

As he was a generalist, he spoke across the whole spectrum of the day's issues—the arms race, full employment, and the still obscure disaster unfolding in Vietnam. His solution to the civil rights issue was disarmingly simple, yet revealing of the depth of his perception of the American condition. If we were to treat everyone as if they were "white," he said, "then we could try to have all the white people treated right." His brand of socialism was steeped in a love for his fellow man above all. His challenge was a summons of good men and women to action. Following his visit to Clark, I soon took as my own his summons to action.

But Worcester was a world apart from Baton Rouge, Louisiana. In the South, whites had simply pushed us beyond the limits of what we could accept, even with our ingrained mind-set of acquiescence. The southern white segregationists were narrow-minded, irreligious, and undemocratic. Inevitably, as black people grew in awareness of the American experience because we traveled more, went to college, and read books, we became uncomfortable with acceptance and began to demand change. And, just as inevitably, the segregationists were offended that blacks would have the temerity to insist upon change. They got their backs against the wall and tried to withstand the challenge, while the country, after a century of tolerating this segregationist rule, finally had to make white segregationists aware that the Civil War had indeed been lost. The conservative philosopher Edmund Burke wrote that a society without the means of change is without the means of its own self-preservation. If Burke was right, the civil rights struggle seemed a certain victory because the South appeared to have lost the ability to change.

In Massachusetts, while the bigotry was not so open, the racist behavior was just as dehumanizing for blacks. I observed a sophisticated eastern reserve that was used to ignore the racial contradictions that northerners didn't care to confront. The contradictions are not ignored in the hope that they will disappear but to affirm that they are beneath concern, insignificant. Clark was viewed as a bit left-wing, and it had its share of eccentrics on the faculty. But students come and go, and the faculty didn't want to put their careers and well-ordered lives on the line to stand behind students.

While there certainly were liberals in Massachusetts, they were for the most part uninvolved liberals. Every fall seemed to bring a new crisis from the South as another round of schools was desegregated. In 1962, it had been Meredith at Ole Miss; in 1963, Birmingham erupted—quite literally—when four little black girls were murdered by a bomb while they listened to a Sunday School lesson entitled "The Love That Forgives." Each of these crises gave smug, comfortable New England plenty of cause for righteous indignation, but Birmingham represented only the most violent and hysterical reaction to the challenge to the segregationist's power. Its awesome violence obscured the simplicity and commonness of the protest movement. Every professor was a major player. Every battle scene was a major battle scene. Everyone involved was taking a risk and making a sacrifice. The appearance of concern among many in the North was largely polite posturing. Instead of the liberal people, intolerant of bigotry, I found people in clapboard houses with their doors locked, unconcerned with the injustice in their country and in their midst.

The black community in Worcester was small—only 3,000 out of a population of 175,000—and largely compacted into a single neighborhood called Belmont Hill, which was about a twenty-minute walk from campus on the other side of downtown. These blacks felt relatively confident that they would not be subjected to the open discrimination and indignities of the South. But they were stuck in the same low-status service jobs. It was clear that there were battles here to be fought. The absence of formal racial barriers in public accommodations and voting was not having a discernable impact on black poverty. Ordinarily, I would have finished my education and gone on to other things. If I had stopped to worry about our weaknesses, that would have been the end of it. But I began to sense that the inherent weaknesses of the political scene could be turned into strengths.

If apathy were the prevailing attitude on campus, then there was a vacuum of political activity waiting to be filled. Because the Worcester NAACP was passive to the point of being moribund, younger, more militant blacks were all the more surprised and pleased to see some signs of concern when our student organization began to take action. If the activist community in Worcester was small, it was that much easier to bring it together.

Some of the white students at Clark admired the courage of the young black activists who were confronting southern segregation. They respected and were willing to follow black leadership, which they had seen in action on the battlegrounds of the South and compared it to the lack of constructive leadership among whites, whether it was Ross Barnett's intransigent hatred or the platitudes mouthed by the Kennedy administration that were paraded as action. The Worcester youth were coming of age, and the civil rights cause was just the thing to give true-to-life meaning to their philosophical perceptions of what was right and what was wrong. All they needed was an opportunity to become stage players in this great moral drama.

Even if the core of our group never came to more than about twenty students, they were hardworking and dedicated. We began by surveying the black neighborhoods about discrimination in housing and jobs, looking for a target upon which to focus our action. Partly through a little press, partly through the NAACP—which, though essentially beholden to the status quo of Worcester, was still the only game in town—we became the fulcrum around which the radical elements of Worcester were drawn.

From the campus, we drew people like Dave Raboy and his wife, Lila. Dave—whose father had created the Flash Gordon cartoon series—was a Marxist from the school of New York radical Jewish activists, ready for a cause and more than ready to make things uncomfortable for the establishment. Then there was Hank Chaiklin, another young Jewish student from Hartford, Connecticut. His background was not terribly radical—his father was in the insurance business—but Hank was different, restless and intolerant of rationalizations about things as they are. He started as a critic of mine, challenging me for being too autocratic and big-headed. I thought his aggressiveness would bring helpful energy to the organization. Since he was a year behind me, I thought whatever leadership he could assume as a result of his challenge to me was fine. Someone was going to have to pick up the baton when I left, and Hank ultimately did just that.

Eventually, off-campus Worcester activists found us. Father Bernard Gilgun, for instance, was an angry priest of about forty who had built up an explosive rejection of the status quo. The Worcester Student Movement provided a vehicle that changed everything. He and another priest, John Goyna, were two of WSM's strongest supporters.

Abbie Hoffman and his wife, Sheila, were two others who gravitated to us early. Abbie, with a head of thick, slightly longish hair and a prominent nose, always had a somewhat mischievous smile on his face even when he was serious, which sometimes made it difficult to know the difference. The couple had been floating around Worcester, Abbie's home, where he was working as a pharmaceutical salesman. He wanted to belong, to be part of a movement, and we provided one for him to come and be fed by. He also had energy to burn and began putting out a mimeographed newsletter, the *Drum,* which reported on our activities even though it was foremost Abbie's forum for tweaking the noses of the Worcester establishment. Abbie was not a stickler for accuracy. At times he exaggerated the number of people at a meeting or demonstration. Not that this ever bothered me—this was Abbie's thing, and I just accepted it as his own style—but it did concern some of the more sober members of our group. When I'd ask Abbie about it, he'd say, "Well, it's as close to the truth as I could find out, and sometimes you have to make up a little bit, you know." Then he'd just laugh.

Well, how does one accommodate an unpredictable, superenergetic, happy-go-lucky Jewish guy? Ultimately I came to see that there wasn't a mold for Abbie in the normal order of things; he was unique. In a few years his irreverence and damn-the-decorum attitude would make him a household name, but at this point, he hadn't yet found his stage. He was a Yippie about to be born. I really wasn't surprised when he carried his rather kooky approach to politics to the full extreme; the only thing that surprised me about Abbie's ultimate fame was that craziness could become so marketable.

So we were small, but we never stopped to worry about our weaknesses. Instead, we focused on our strength, which was simply that we were there to ask the questions. When you ask questions, your power is multiplied because you are the alternative, representing the other side—all of the other side— whether they're members of the group or not. We represented what was different from what was—that was our power. And we were ready for a fight.

Denholm & McKay had been a Worcester institution for ninety-one years; it was the city's largest department store, right in the middle of downtown. So it wasn't surprising when someone threw out their name as a target for investigation, and it didn't take much of a look to figure out that they were vulnerable. There was no disguising Denholm & McKay's pattern of excluding blacks from responsible jobs. They were so brazen about it that they hadn't even attempted to disguise their practices with tokenism. Among the more than five hundred employees, Denholm & McKay had included sixteen blacks—eight elevator operators, six maids (including a woman with a master's degree), no sales clerks, and no white-collar workers of any kind.

Despite their record, it wasn't difficult to get an audience with some of their top officials. There had never been any racial trouble in Worcester. Safely ensconced in the heart of a New England industrial town with only a minute number of blacks, Denholm & McKay had no reason to expect a challenge now. Our group presented what we thought were fairly modest demands for a company that had consistently relegated blacks to the fringes of their work force. The most important demand was a commitment to hire twenty to twenty-five blacks in white-collar jobs. Years later, a company probably would have been smart enough to quietly come to an agreement. But their response, stated in a position paper, was full of platitudes that promised no action. The store would neither hire nor even seek more black employees. "An individual employer cannot, acting alone, accomplish very much in improving the employment status of Negroes," the paper said. "We regard that problem, insofar as it concerns Denholm's directly, as essentially the lack of qualified Negro job applicants."

Their basic attitude seemed to be: "It's not our fault. Why are you bothering us? Don't you have anything better to do at Clark?" So the lines were drawn. We had our fight. We went back to campus, called a meeting, prepared some mimeographed fact sheets, designed some picket signs, and called the press. The next morning, Saturday, about twenty of us were picketing in front of their store.

We held our picket throughout the day. We didn't have the numbers to wage an ongoing campaign, but the importance was the picketing itself. It was an embarrassment to Denholm's to have these picketers in front of their store with signs accusing them of racism. Our purpose was to show them in public for what they were and then let them worry about how they would explain it away. I knew that once Denholm & McKay was in the public limelight, even for a day, they would never again exhibit their former brazen self-assurance. We achieved that goal. Because a civil rights protest in Worcester was a first, we got press coverage around the state.

The local press, however, gave more attention to a break within our ranks. The Reverend John Stringfield, a black minister who had been part of our delegation to the Denholm's management, and Reverend Toussaint Davis, president of the NAACP, were quoted expressing opposition to our demonstration. Stringfield called our demands "unethical, unfounded, and beyond reasoning." We were not surprised to learn later that Denholm's contributed significantly to his church. Apparently, his peace money was threatened.

Stringfield's was a challenge we could no more let pass than we let Denholm's promises of good faith pacify us. When a black man who has been playing patsy with the white establishment publicly challenges your movement to a fight, you have to knock him out of the way so that the white who is discriminating can't keep hiding behind him and will be forced to come out in the open to do battle. That had been the situation with Felton Clark at Southern, and that was true of Stringfield and Davis now.

Of course, rank-and-file blacks in the community knew Denholm's sorry employment record very well. "Anyone who says Denholm's doesn't discriminate is a fool," one Belmont Hill resident told the school's newspaper, the *Clark Scarlet*. When the NAACP met the following Tuesday, it may have been the largest meeting in its history. There were more than one hundred people, mostly our members and younger blacks happy to have a new voice in the WSM, which was not a prisoner of the status quo. As a result of that meeting, the organization endorsed our protest, and Davis blathered on about being misquoted. Ultimately, he was forced to back away from his opposition. His complicity was exposed, and now he was clearly distrusted. Now that the black opposition had been silenced, we knew what to expect when we got around to our next protest. We began recruiting other students and local activists to join local activist allies as members for the NAACP, just to make sure the organization was going to be on our side.

Meanwhile, we contemplated further action against Denholm & McKay. We hoped that since it was November, with the Christmas season approaching, their self-righteous denials of discrimination might prove unprofitable. Surprisingly, they suddenly managed to find three "qualified" black women to work as sales clerks.

We didn't have much time to revel in our small victory over Denholm & McKay. Within a week, on November 22, President John F. Kennedy was assassinated. Everyone who was alive then can remember where they were when they heard the news. I was in the midst of the most mundane of activities, walking to downtown Worcester to get a haircut. I noticed that a couple of cars had pulled to the side of the road, and I saw the people inside listening intently to the radio. I asked someone what had happened, and he reported that the president had been shot in Dallas. When I arrived at the barbershop, the radio was on. Somehow this small barber shop seemed this day even smaller. I felt tightly packed, almost as if drawn in embrace with the barbers and other customers as our ears connected in unison to the radio news. Even before I was out of the chair, the voice of an announcer came on the radio with the news that Kennedy was dead. Now, I was in Massachusetts—Kennedy country—so inevitably the bullet that took his life seemed to strike personally at everyone. In this overwhelming gloom, I found that even an ordinary game of ping-pong in the student union within earshot of the television was treated by those glued to the set as an unpardonable distraction.

By coincidence, I was going to Washington the coming Thanksgiving weekend for a SNCC conference at Howard University. I remember driving late one afternoon into a city that was literally darkened by the gloom of winter, as if nature were adding its own commentary to the tragedy. Lyndon Johnson had ascended to the office of president, but the capital was still in mourning, traumatized.

Yet strangely, I can remember almost no outward reaction from the movement activists who were gathered that weekend. I can remember Fannie Lou Hamer making an eloquent speech about being beaten in a Mississippi jail for trying to register to vote. James Baldwin spoke, fresh off the success of *The Fire Next Time,* expressing the anger and brashness we all felt. Baldwin was a bold, important voice of the 1960s who described the black condition with poetic strength and searing commentary. In the sober and dark mood of a capital in mourning, Baldwin's voice pierced and hung in the night air. But in spite of the tone in Washington, and in spite of our own horror, the conference did not mourn.

I had picketed Bobby Kennedy's office the summer before, and though those of us in the civil rights movement felt the tragedy of the assassination, we weren't great fans of the administration. We believed that the president should give moral direction to the nation, and yet we perceived in Kennedy's actions a certain unresponsiveness or disinterestedness, a certain compromising of the duties of his office. From our point of view, Kennedy had failed to grab the reins of leadership and clearly guide the administration down the path of freedom and justice.

But more than that, our emotions were spent on the suffering and threats in the South. We didn't focus emotionally on the mystery of the president's murder. Perhaps we had been conditioned by the assassination of Medgar Evers in Jackson the previous summer. Perhaps the SNCC activists had been hardened on the battlefields of Mississippi and Alabama and Georgia, where everyone was risking what little security they had, as well as their lives. The weekend that we were meeting in Washington, Malcolm X observed in New York that "the chickens came home to roost"—an all-too-biting response to the assassination that was typical of the rather emotionless reaction of many in the movement. Ultimately, it was largely business as usual in the movement; we just continued pursuing our own agenda.

Even so, the assassination's impact on white America would have tremendous repercussions for us. The violence and hatred of the decade were no longer just a danger to black people; it had become tragically obvious that it could destroy the dreams of whites as well. The struggle for civil rights was no longer the isolated agitation of black people, to be viewed with a detached notion of sympathy. It had become part of a broader sense of insecurity and change, less deflected and deflated as whites experienced it closer to home.

Under the determined leadership of the new president following the tragedy, the great civil rights bills would be passed by Congress. But these were more the signal of the end than of the beginning. America's sense of self-assurance, comfort, and insularity had been torn down, and they couldn't be rebuilt while the embarrassing shadows of Ross Barnett, George Wallace, and "Bull" Connor loomed large. There was too much uncertainty to attend to discrimination conflicts as well. So the new civil rights bills, viewed as great progress at the time, were more accurately the washing of hands.

I never thought it was good to glamorize any one individual in the movement because that distorts the movement's commonness and utter simplicity. Every player was a major player taking the same risks and making the same sacrifices. Still, James Meredith's experience was singular. At least in Little Rock there were nine students who were tasked with challenging the segregated school system. When the universities of Alabama and Georgia were integrated, Meredith had already gone before at Ole Miss. But when Meredith went to Oxford, Mississippi, in the fall of 1962, he was the first and he was alone. His life was threatened because of the role he was playing on a national stage. He became the object of the most violent segregationist hatred, and at the same time he was the personification of an entire people's hope. Because of all this, in February 1964, the Worcester Student Movement brought Meredith to Clark to speak.

He and I met at the airport and spent most of the day together. He was likeable in a way because, although his role in the events at Ole Miss had made him internationally famous, he was not a bit pretentious. He relaxed comfortably in an armchair in my modest apartment as I talked about the Worcester community and the things we were trying to achieve. Even so, he had a view of the world and a thought process that somehow seemed just a bit out of sync. I expected him to share some war stories or some insight on his experience, but instead he would throw out some almost Republican theories about where things ought to be going. I was familiar with no ideology that fit Meredith's unpredictable views, which seemed skewed, zig-zagging right, left, and then down the center.

I don't remember much of his speech except that it didn't hold together, and that I wasn't sure until he finished whether or not he was going to embarrass all of us. I almost feared he was going to come out more in agreement with the segregationists than with us. He repudiated the movement line and fashioned his own, which was neither liberal, nor conservative, nor radical, and which apparently was not terribly encumbered by reality.

Reluctantly, I had to conclude that Meredith made a strange symbol for the civil rights movement. I had expected a person who had endured the kind of storm he had to have achieved an inner peace, but Meredith seemed to still have an internal controversy going on. It was like Ole Miss was a stage play, and offstage you couldn't be sure if you were meeting the character in the play or the person who played him. Maybe he felt inadequate for the moment of history that had fallen to him. I believe that Meredith was a victim of Ole Miss: like some of the soldiers who went to Vietnam, he was suffering from combat stress. His experience there just blew his mind. By the end of the day, I had little respect for his vision. He was truly more of a symbol than a man of substance, courage, and presence.

In the days that followed Meredith's visit, WSM began to consider its next move. If there were a more inviting civil rights target in Worcester than Denholm & McKay, it was the Wyman-Gordon Company. The company operated a huge heavy-manufacturing plant with large defense contracts of such consequence that the company was reportedly on a Soviet Union strike list in the event of a nuclear attack on the United States. The company president was a powerful archconservative whose company had a history of not hiring blacks as anything other than broom pushers. Thirty-two of their thirty-three black workers were janitors, and the other was the janitorial supervisor. Of course, it had not always been so. Because of its government contracts, Wyman-Gordon did have to meet some equal-employment provisions. When federal inspectors came, some of the black workers found themselves promoted, even transferred to other plants in the company as window dressing for the inspection, only to be returned to their former roles as janitors after the inspections were completed.

Robert Stoddard was the president of Wyman-Gordon, but that wasn't his only claim to fame. He also owned the local newspaper and a TV and radio station. At the same time he was the national secretary of the John Birch Society, a platform he used to attack as unconstitutional the pending federal Civil Rights Act of 1964 outlawing discrimination in public facilities and employment. What better way to answer the John Birch creed than for a group of activists to be sitting in the company's conference room with its president, taking him to task for his racist employment practices?

Our delegation—Father Gilgun, Dave Raboy, Hank Chaiklin, Reverend

Davis from the NAACP, and me—obtained a meeting with Stoddard in early May. He was a dapper man in his mid-fifties with silvery hair and highly polished Wellington half boots with shiny buckles across the instep. He was self-assured and spoke with an air of authority; he had the manner of a man who had never been challenged. Still, he was a bit wary and respectful since he wasn't sure who we were or what powers we may have had. But he knew that he was Bob Stoddard, and that he had no intention of changing his ways, certainly not at the demand of some college students who were quietly but determinedly telling him how to run his business. At the end of the meeting, he would only promise a "review" of the company's record, which was another way of telling us not to bother coming to see him again. He refused to let us take part in the review, let alone to see the records. As Stoddard later told a reporter, his "colored employees were completely satisfied." He found it arrogant, insulting, and unacceptable that we were not similarly satisfied.

We had known when we went in there that if he told us "no," we had to back it up with a fight, and that meant picketing his company. As soon as we hit the sidewalk outside his office, we started laying our plans for the siege. But I didn't want to be caught unawares like we were with Denholm's when Davis and Stringfield attacked us publicly. On the sidewalk, I turned to Davis and said, "We're going to picket, and I want you to be on the picket line." He said something about being out of town, so I pressed further, saying we would ask for the NAACP's endorsement in advance. We had been adding memberships and gaining strength in the organization all spring, and some of our clashes with Davis had become heated. I felt sure the white activists would support us. When the meeting came that Thursday, Davis wasn't there: he had just sent a telegram saying he was resigning as NAACP president effective immediately. At the end of the meeting, the membership unanimously endorsed the picket, to be held the next day. That, in turn, caused a case of cold feet among three of the janitors who had helped initiate our action against Wyman-Gordon. They had never imagined that a complaint to the NAACP would get past the point of a wordy resolution. Instead, they realized they had set in motion a process of confrontation, and they were worried. They came to us wanting to withdraw their complaints and thus call off the demonstration, but we told them we had already gone too far for that. They were informed that if they wanted to take their names off the complaints, that was their business, but we were going to picket anyway.

Dr. Jefferson, the president of Clark, also felt Stoddard's pull. He called me into his office the next morning. I wasn't sure why. He hadn't spoken to me about our activities before. But Stoddard was on his board of trustees and was a major financial contributor. Dr. Jefferson also wanted us to back off. I told him we did not intend to harm the university, but we felt we had responsibilities beyond just being college students. It soon became clear there was no possibility of convincing him of the correctness of our actions. He was thinking about the money. So I strung out the conversation until I figured our pickets were at the plant. Then, knowing it was too late, I said, "Let me go talk to my people."

Ironically, Stoddard's stature cut both ways. No one with his brazenness and his kind of power could avoid having a lot of enemies in the community. Labor people, in particular, were angry because Wyman-Gordon was a non-union plant. The American Civil Liberties Union also joined us in calling for a state investigation of Wyman-Gordon's hiring practices. When I arrived at the plant after meeting with Jefferson, we had more than fifty picketers set up in two lines—one at the front offices and one at the truck entry gate. I was dismayed that, in front of the office, perhaps a dozen conservative Clark students were protesting the protesters. I had to wonder whose idea that was—Stoddard's or some university authority. Around back, Wyman-Gordon workers began to line up on the loading dock to jeer us.

We hoped to discourage as many 18-wheeler trucks as we could from crossing our line, but would let the driver of the truck decide whether he was going to go in or stay out. All day long, no union trucks would cross. When a company truck would come through the gate, the workers on the loading dock would give out a cheer. Ultimately, it became kind of a verbal tug of war between the conservative protesters and the Wyman-Gordon employees on the one side and the WSM picketers on the other. Then, unbeknownst to me, our side decided to raise the ante.

I was on the front picket line when it happened. A police sergeant rushed up to me and told me to follow him around back. There was a problem, he said. On the spur of the moment, our pickets had decided to stop opening their line for the company trucks to pass through and had formed a tight circle around one that had tried to back through the gate. The sergeant said they'd have to disperse or be arrested.

"I don't like the son-of-a-bitch any more than you do," he said. "He's no good for the working man. But I got a job to do." My initial thought was: "Good. Let's carry this thing to another dimension. Let's all go to jail." So I joined the circle around the truck, while the sergeant sent for the paddy wagon. There was just one problem. The reporters had already gotten their stories and left for the day, and if we were going to be arrested, we needed the publicity. I looked for Abbie Hoffman, our press officer, to get the newspeople back to the plant. He was standing off to the side, hanging back, hesitating. I was surprised and wondered, was Abbie afraid of going to jail? Perhaps it was that this was the first time the game had real stakes. He had to put his cards on the table, and instead he drew his hand back. Here's how Abbie describes the Wyman-Gordon standoff in his book *Major Motion Picture:*

> The protesters decide to crawl under a diesel truck to prevent it from entering the factory. The oversize tires tower over us and grease smudges our shirts. On the street you can hear paddy wagons arriving and some workmen screaming: "Jungle bunnies, Commie bastards! Go home to Russia!"
>
> Through the din comes the voice of the plant's personnel manager. He's leaning under the truck shouting, "Abbie, your father's here and wants to have a word with you. Could you come out for a second?"
>
> "Don't go," D'Army insists, grabbing my arm.
>
> "I gotta, D'Army, I just gotta. My pa's got a bum heart. They're his best customers. I don't know what to do. Save me a place, I'll be right back." I duck out and sneak past the hecklers.

Ultimately, though, we didn't go to jail. Father Gilgun made a plea for us to relent and let the trucks through, and, as practical matter, I agreed. If you're going to jail, you should make that decision before you hit the streets. You have to know who's going to bond you out, who's going to represent you, who will lead the organization while you're locked up. So we backed off for the moment and let the truck through, but we didn't stop the movement. The next day was a Saturday, and the plant was closed. So we made a huge banner and marched through downtown and picketed Stoddard's newspaper.

We couldn't have asked for more from our protest. The conscience of Worcester was pricked, and the issue was being debated weeks later. When the Worcester Area Council of Churches invited Stoddard to speak in June but wouldn't allow any of our representatives to present the other side, we picketed their meeting in a driving rain. We weren't going to let self-assured Worcester ignore us into obscurity while it papered over discrimination. Our show of support strengthened the resolve of the janitors, who filed three formal complaints with the Massachusetts Commission Against Discrimination (MCAD). We also sent our complaints to the U.S. Air Force chief of staff, Curtis Lemay. Anyone taking a cursory look at their operation could see that they were lacking in fair opportunities for blacks. In July, Stoddard's newspaper ran a story on the MCAD dismissal of our complaints headlined "No Probable Cause Found Against Plant." Buried in the story was the real meat: "The findings followed an agreement with Wyman-Gordon that the company would change its hiring and promotion practices."

By now the school year—and, with it, my undergraduate career—was ending. I felt proud of what I had done at Clark. I had stirred some people to think and to challenge, and I had left an imprint and an organization, probably two-thirds of which was white. Yet, I didn't find these white students greatly different from the black kids at Southern. They were all decent people, and they were fighters. If you had taken the white kids at Clark and put them in Baton Rouge, they would have been in the front lines, perhaps not as ready for the vehemence of the southern reaction, but with the same spirit. We all were one in having within us a deep anger at injustice. After all, when we left the Southern campus to sit in at Woolworth's and Kresge's, we really didn't care that much about eating at those lunch counters. Most of us usually went to the little joint just off campus and ate po' boys. In a way, we were just as much carpetbaggers in downtown Baton Rouge as the kid in Massachusetts was at Denholm's and Wyman-Gordon. We were outsiders dedicated to fairness, showing that simple decent streak that is truly America's greatness. There's a rich vein of that compassion in this country, however much it's feared, misunderstood, and beaten down. Sometimes you have to wait through nine days of remission to see one day of that richness. But we had our day at Clark. I had done the initiating, and that was more than Clark had expected when I got there.

The following fall, when the WSM discussed raising money for another scholarship for a southern black student, the *Clark Scarlet* student newspaper responded with an editorial entitled "Here We Go Again":

Three years ago, in a wave of sympathy for civil rights agitators in the South, the student body voted to raise funds for a scholarship for some Negro thrown out of a university for participating in sit-ins. We got much more than we bargained for. The student selected was a bona fide Negro, alright. He seemed at times to go out of his way to be discriminated against. . . . WSM has calmed down a bit since Mr.

Bailey, the Negro recipient of that particular scholarship, departed for
Boston University's law school. . . . And now someone wants to start
the whole foolish cycle again. . . .

Campus advocates of civil rights can do enough in Worcester with
personnel now on the scene. They need not bring in outside problems
at considerable expense. One hopes that the membership of this now
worthy group will forget about any more imports.

—Michael Sandman, editor, *Clark Scarlet*

Student voices protesting the editorial were quick and strong, spreading to
three pages of the next *Scarlet*.

First, The Scarlet editor reveals his bigoted tendencies towards stereo-
typing the Negro race because of his distasteful experience with one
member of that race. This prejudice is reinforced in Mr. Sandman's
reference to this one Negro student as a "bona fide" Negro—implying
that all real Negroes go out of their way to become victims of discrimination. I would suppose that Mr. Sandman prefers the "white
Negroes" which Clark so adroitly attracts annually. . . .

I would suggest it was the strength with which Mr. Bailey upheld
his ideals of equal opportunity for all Americans that Mr. Sandman
found unpleasant and that this prevented him from a rational assessment of the work Mr. Bailey accomplished.

—Henry Chaiklin, executive director, Worcester Student Movement

I read your article entitled "Here We Go Again." You are right—"we
got more than we bargained for" when we brought Mr. Bailey to
Clark. The nerve of him, why, he had the audacity to act like a man
and not an Uncle Tom. His challenging the "power structure" of both
races in the Wyman-Gordon Affair was really taboo.

His letter to a local newspaper concerning the life of a Negro student at a white northern university showed that he would not sit back
and pretend that the *problem* did not exist.

What a character Bailey was! He even had the nerve to awaken
"some" of the complacent Worcester Negroes, by illuminating the
"normal" Ecological Processes that produced the Clayton-Laurel
"ghetto." But that's not all—Bailey committed the unpardonable sin.
He worked to prevent the glory- and status-seeking, pseudo liberals

and bigots from gaining power and fame at the expense of the civil rights movement.

—Jesse Pendleton, geography graduate student

The editorial and letters seemed to summarize the conflicts and questions inherent in an atmosphere of protected white liberalism. The campus was still confronting those questions, and it wasn't just a passing thing. I wasn't one to dwell much on what happened yesterday or the month before, but I knew that, in the time I had spent at Clark, I had not let myself down nor those who believed in me.

The time had come to look to the future, which for me meant the study of law. Since my days as a youth in Memphis volunteering with black leaders, I had seen that many of these leaders active in trying to organize the black community were lawyers. When I went to Louisiana and became involved in the sit-ins, black lawyers gave us their guidance, helped us to develop strategies, and represented us when we were in jail. They demonstrated an ability to analyze and strategize, to survive by learning the rules and turning them to their advantage.

Not least important, the law was also a way to make a living. I wouldn't have to go and stand in somebody's employment line, application in hand, to get a job and then have to dance to their music. I have never envisioned a life without activism. The law was a tool that would help me survive and grow as an activist, equipping me for yet more battles to come.

Index